TALES OF THEIR LIVES

Daphne Field

One Printers Way
Altona, MB R0G 0B0
Canada

www.friesenpress.com

Copyright © 2023 by Daphne Field
First Edition — 2023

All rights reserved.

No part of this publication may be reproduced in any form, or by any means, electronic or mechanical, including photocopying, recording, or any information browsing, storage, or retrieval system, without permission in writing from FriesenPress.

ISBN
978-1-03-912988-7 (Hardcover)
978-1-03-912987-0 (Paperback)
978-1-03-912989-4 (eBook)

1. BIOGRAPHY & AUTOBIOGRAPHY, PERSONAL MEMOIRS

Distributed to the trade by The Ingram Book Company

For Darien, Lesley & Stuart

TABLE OF CONTENTS

Preface	vii
Acknowledgements	xiii
Outline	xv
Geographical Context: Where they all lived	1
Stathern: History and my memories	3
1. A look at village life	3
2. The First Beckwiths	21
3. The Adventures of John (1797-1877) and Lucy (1798-1877) Beckwith	27
4. Edward (1836-1889) and son John Beckwith (1863-1938)	37
5. Great Grandma Lucy Heathcote's Story	47
6. The Warburtons	59
7. The Warburtons of the 19th Century	71
8. The Heathcote Story: Cath marries Joe	79
9. John Heathcoat: Could we be related?	87
10. The Hubbards of Saxelby and Wyfordby	93
11. The Hubbards in Eaton - John Stayed Behind	99
12. The Hubbard brothers: Thomas, William, Henry & Jonathan	105
13. Grandad Hubbard's Story	111
14. The Story of Louisa Rippin Smith	129
15. Andrew Smith's Story	137
16. The Browns	143
17. Elisha Brown and the Elliotts	149
18. Grannie Brown and William	153
19. The Slaters	167
20. James Slater, the Entrepreneur and his legacy	171
21. Auntie Beat Tells her Story	173
22. Conversations with my Father	181
23. Conversations with my Mother	207
24. More Conversations with my mother	229
Epilogue	255

THE HEATHCOTE FAMILY: A HISTORY
Preface

I am the storyteller in our family.

I have been called by my ancestors to put flesh on their bones and make them come alive again. In doing so, I tell my family story: I will know who lived and died before me. I will breathe life into the facts of their lives: dates, names, and places.

I was never particularly concerned with history but recently I have become intrigued with my personal history. What am I made of? Where did I come from? Whose genes do I carry?

I have written the stories of my ancestors: How they lived; how they struggled, surrounded in their social history and geography and finally, how they died. I am motivated by interest. If you wish, it is my legacy to you: Stuart, Lesley, and Darien.

My main source of information was Ancestry.Co.UK. I am grateful to those who populated Ancestry providing me with a foundation from which to build. I am grateful to those who documented the census and transcribed it even though errors were made in the process. On certain documents, my relatives placed an X because they were illiterate. The first census providing primary credible information was taken in England in April of 1841. It was written by a local scribe. A census was subsequently taken every ten years in the UK.

In 1911, for the first-time, individuals prepared their own census document which requested names, ages, birth places, addresses, numbers of children born, and which had died, as well as occupations of residents. So, in these stories, while names, dates of birth or baptism, dates of marriages, dates, and places of death are as accurate as they can be, the scenarios woven around these facts are created from my knowledge, research and imagination.

I acknowledge this text will never be complete: There will always be more. The internet provided significant context for the biographies: population statistics, the industrial revolution, pictures, maps, and the facts of everyday life in each Century in England. I must also acknowledge Wikipedia, a useful source of background information.

To Stuart, Lesley, and Darien: Starting with your earliest ancestors, I describe their lives, families, progenies, occupations, residences, struggles, and heartbreaks. But I do not know for sure. I explore how they were different than or similar to one another and to the norms of their day. I ask: Who was supporting the family? How did they make decisions? What alternatives did they have? We will never be certain, but we can wonder and hope. Some of our ancestors died prematurely, some lived long lives, some died in workhouses, and some died in the Great War, far away from home. Relatives bravely emigrated to the USA. Almost all of our ancestors were illiterate until schooling became mandatory in the mid-19th century because an educated workforce was required to support the industrial revolution. There was a movement from teaching what was "useful," that is, domestic science for girls, towards reading, writing, and mechanics. Even the classics were tolerated! Our family failed to take advantage of education at a secondary level for whatever reason. They seemed to limit themselves as your Nana did. I (Daphne) was the first to attend the English Grammar school. Your father/uncle (Geoff) was the first to attend University.

While the siblings of our direct ancestors are not our ancestors per se, I have included stories with ours because their experiences illustrate the social environment in which the families lived. To omit these family members would suggest our ancestors lived in isolation, unsupported and alone.

We witnessed the movement from service and farming to railways and to a never-ending possibility of occupations.

I could not write the stories without giving credence to the historical context of the era. I attempted to answer the question of what was happening around these people who were your ancestors. For instance, our story starts in the 17th Century (I could not reliably trace further back), during which our ancestors witnessed the execution of a king, endured civil war, plague, crop failures, fires, extremely cold weather, religious unrest and finally the return of a Monarch.

This extraordinary century was indeed the start of the renaissance. We see unexpected beginnings and disasters. Shakespeare was writing his plays until his death in 1616: Rembrandt was painting his art, Bunyan wrote Pilgrim's Progress (a book I studied at school), Galileo worked on his compass, Harvey discovered the circulation of the blood, human temperature was measured for the first time, the first water toilet appeared, Newton invented Calculus, the London Stock Exchange commenced operations and Barbados was colonized in 1625. A review of this timeline is not to be missed.

https://www.britishempire.co.uk/timeline/17century.htm

In 1600, the population of England and Wales was approximately 4 million. By 1700 it had grown to about 5.5 million. During this century, the status of merchants improved; however, wealthy landowners held the power and influence. Our ancestors, in the bottom 10% in terms of influence and wealth, would see little improvement in their lives over the century. 17th century towns and villages were dirty and unsanitary. People threw filthy water and their rubbish into the narrow streets. At night, streets were dark and dangerous. Towards the end of the 17th century, however, towns grew much larger despite periodic outbreaks of plague. Fleas living on rats transmitted bubonic plague. Humans bitten by fleas were likely to fall victims. Unfortunately, at the time no one knew either what caused the disease or how to treat it.[1]

The average life span was 35 years, but many children died in infancy: between one third and one half died before their teenage years. However, if they survived to their mid-teens, they would probably live to their 50s, 60s and sometimes beyond.[2] What will be of significance is how well our ancestors beat the statistics, or didn't.

In these times, the church was the focal point in the community. We know that Henry VIII broke away from the Catholic church in the 16th Century and proclaimed himself Head of the Church of England which became the dominant faith. So, our ancestors adopted the Church of England faith. They would have donned their Sunday best to attend church services every Sunday. All marriages took place in the church: the Minister had the status to witness the union and keep the records.

Babies were welcomed into the church congregation with a ceremony called baptism or christening very shortly after birth. The baby was named at that time. With death all around, a safety net was essential. Each child would have had three Godparents, bestowed at the time of baptism. Indeed, that was also the norm in my day. A son would have had two male friends or family as Godfathers. I am Godmother to Heather's son, John. I was able to locate more information from baptismal records than from birth records because church records are more accurate and available. I do not believe that you three have been baptized: hence you have no Godparents.

Funerals were also conducted by the Minister within the church and were intended to ease the departed's journeying back to his or her maker. The church minister held an influential position within the community. Since he was perhaps the only person who was able to write in those early days, he likely maintained the records. These records would have been transcribed, errors made and errors corrected, and hence became the source of important population records.

The Parish church was a focal point in each community. The Parish church was administered by the local parish council, comprising prominent members of the community. The church would have been built by serfs under the power of local nobleman, constructed from local materials. I will frequently make reference not only to the Parish Church but also to the Parish Council. The Parish Council took responsibility for the unfortunate who were unable to take care of themselves, sometimes referring to them as paupers or imbeciles. Occasionally these individuals were referred to the local workhouse where they would be housed to their shame and with great discomfort. We have such individuals in our history.

In the early 17th century people began eating with forks for the first time. During the century new foods were introduced into England (for the rich) such as bananas and pineapples. New drinks were introduced, chocolate, tea, and coffee as examples. In the late 17th century, there were many coffee houses in the towns. Merchants and professionals met there to read newspapers and talk shop. Our ancestors would have been aware of these luxuries beyond their reach. Ale at the local pub would have been a lifestyle to which they aspired and enjoyed.

Wealthy women enjoyed reading and playing musical instruments. They also danced and attended the theatre. Puppet shows like Punch and Judy were popular. In the late 18th century, the circus became a well-liked

---

1 local histories.org
2 local histories.org

form of entertainment. Girls played with wooden or rag dolls. Travelling entertainers would have visited the villages. Toys would have been handmade with wood, straw or fabrics. While I hope our ancestors sang, danced, and had fun, I think when they had time, they would have made their entertainment in their own way.

The affluent lived an extravagant lifestyle, supported by the lower classes, whereas the poor subsisted without creature comforts and good food. They lived in a couple of rooms on food such as bread, cheese, and onions. Ordinary people also ate pottage each day which was made by boiling grain in water to make a kind of porridge. Vegetables were added and possibly pieces of meat or fish as well as whatever they could catch or forage.

In the 17th century most households in the countryside, where our family lived, were largely self-sufficient. A housewife (assisted by her servants if she had any) baked her family's bread and brewed their beer (water was unsafe to drink). She was also responsible for curing bacon, salting meat, and making pickles, jellies, and preserves (all of which were essential in an age before fridges and freezers). I remember these tasks as a child. Very often in the countryside the housewife also made the family's candles and soap. A housewife perhaps also spun wool and linen and sewed the family's clothes.[3] I recall hooking rugs and constructing something new out of something old, which was a school project for me!

Living in the country offered additional bounties: hedgerows with berries, apple and pear trees, and the space for a country garden to grow fruits, vegetables, and herbs. In the countryside, the women would keep chickens and pigs which would not only provide much needed protein for the family but may have been a source of income.

While most of our ancestors worked the land and were in service, some did enter the realms of the middle class. One key indicator: they had a servant themselves!

The following timeline outlines the historical features of the 18th Century. I note that the first pianos appeared in the year 1700.[4]

https://www.britishempire.co.uk/timeline/18century.htm

To set the scene of the 18th Century, at its beginning, as many as half the population of England, then approximately 5.5 million people, lived at subsistence or bare survival level. Of note is that between 1700 and 1760, London was involved in a passionate but staggeringly destructive love affair with gin, popularly known as "the mother's ruin." The city was positively drowning in the stuff. It was cheap, and was sold everywhere, by purveyors without a license. Many people ruined their health. Yet for many poor people drinking gin was their only comfort. The situation improved after 1751 when a tax was imposed on gin.[5] How involved our ancestors were in this activity we will never know!

Moving forward, the population of Britain boomed during the 19th century. In 1801, the population was about 9 million whereas by 1901 it had risen to about 41 million. This was despite many people emigrating to North America and Australia to escape poverty. About 15 million people left Britain between 1815 and 1914. There were, however, also many immigrants. In the 1840s Irish immigrants moved from Ireland, fleeing a terrible potato famine. In the 1880s, the Tsar began persecuting Russian Jews. Some fled to Britain and settled in the East End of London.

---

3   local histories.org
4   https://www.britishempire.co.uk/timeline/18century.htm
5   https://munchies.vice.com/en_us/article/53jj7z/how-a-gin-craze-nearly-destroyed-18th-century-london

So, we have a glimpse of how our ancestors might have lived, endured, and died in the lowest strata of the social and economic structure. Fortunately for them, our family members were country folk.

Once I started accumulating the data, I wondered how I would present this material. By listening to others and by reading family histories, the structure evolved and became workable. The historic detail has been presented as narrative, peppered with creative non-fiction. Whereas names, dates, and places are known, the stories surrounding these names and dates emanate from my imagination. Sometimes, I have allowed our ancestors to speak for themselves. Imagined of course. I have avoided too much detail to keep your interest. You may read the ENDNOTES which provide supplementary information.

Structure

The structure emerged when I worked on each branch of the family tree. I arbitrarily started with our great-grandmother Lucy and her family, the Beckwiths. When I moved to the Heathcotes, I found the maternal side of that branch of our family tree, the Warburtons, which presented me with abundant information that I felt compelled to pursue and document. Having gained huge insights into the historical context of the times, I moved to your Nana's side of the family: the Hubbards, Smiths, Browns, and Slaters. Finally, I have included conversations I might have had with your Nana and the Grandad you never knew and would have loved.

There is an annotated Outline as a guide so you may start anywhere in the text and know exactly where the story fits into the whole.

This work has taken many years due to a false start. At first, I found the subject matter overwhelming. When I decided on its structure, I knew the work would be finished and would be sad when it was finally at an end. I know too that more information will become available so whereas the text will be finished, it will never be complete.

Inevitably, I must think about what I learned. Some amazing people went before us. Lucy Beckwith emerges as one of those: without formal education, she became a school headmistress. Others had amazing courage. The illiterate Hubbard brothers emigrated alone to Indiana, USA. I was delighted to be in communication with one of the current Hubbards. Our ancestors followed the times, making the most of the opportunities offered to them. The wealthy side of the Heathcote family may not even have known how their distant cousins suffered. But I am proud of them all for surviving and giving us the tools to succeed. In our background, we have farmers, brewers, blacksmiths, framework knitters, bus drivers, bookkeepers, carpenters, a midwife, and only one schoolmaster and mistress. Not until my generation, did we have scholars when Geoff and I graduated from university.

The reason I wrote this text was out of my personal interest: I wanted to know who our ancestors were. I needed to honour their lives and remember them. Then you all began to take notice and spurred me onwards. Your Nana, on the other hand, was not encouraging. When I asked questions of her, she said I was more interested in dead people than those who were alive. For instance, I could never ascertain what happened to her mother; that is, until I obtained her death certificate.

Historical societies in Coleorton and Countesthorpe have shown an interest and have assisted with stories from their records. The extraordinary photograph of Lucy Beckwith was included in the book Memories of Coleorton and is provided by Coleorton Heritage Group. She did not have any teeth!

This is the oldest photograph we have, one of Lucy Beckwith. Read about her soon.

(Photographer: Unknown)

Having explained my approach and set the scene, I hope you three and many others enjoy the read.

ACKNOWLEDGEMENTS

Friend Heather Hopper has been a wonderful source of information and a great critic of the work. Geoff has developed a curiosity and has added his memories. I am grateful to Pat Corson and Julie Luckevich who agreed to edit the document. Ancestry provided me with invaluable basic information. Our relatives also working on ancestry provided stories of their own. Robert Warburton contacted me as a result of my research. We share a common great, great, great grandfather: Robert Warburton dating back to 1799. I was supported by my book club and writing group members. Thank you also to friend, Catherine Farley who designed the lovely book cover. I am grateful to you all.

REG AND KATHY

REGINALD LESLIE HEATHCOTE:

Parents:	Lucy Caroline Beckwith m Albert George Heathcote
Grandparents:	John Beckwith m Elizabeth Woolley
	Joseph Heathcote m Catherine Warburton
Great grandparents:	Edward Beckwith m Rose Caroline Daniels
	Robert Warburton m Jane Root
	David Heathcote m Elizabeth (Betsy) Herbert.

KATHLEEN ELIZABETH HUBBARD:

Parents:	Wilfred Alec Hubbard m Ethel Rose Brown
Grandparents:	Arthur (Bradley) Hubbard m Sarah Ann Smith
	William Brown m Caroline Slater
Great grandparents:	John Hubbard m Mary Tyler
	Louisa Smith m Andrew Smith
	Elisha Brown m Sarah Elliott
	George Slater m Elizabeth Gilding.

OUTLINE

I am providing an outline to help you navigate through these stories of lives lived, including three background chapters: A Preface, a Geographical context, and a story of Stathern: A history and my Memories.

The First Beckwiths.

1. Your paternal great grandmother's family, the Beckwiths, is where we start the story in Essex, in South East England in the year 1759. The story imagines the lives of Edward and Sarah in Castle Hedingham in Essex. An educated family.
2. The Adventures of John and Lucy Beckwith, the story of the youngsters who, as newlyweds, left home in Essex to venture to Coleorton in Leicestershire to pursue an assignment offering an amazing opportunity.
3. John and Lucy's children and grandchildren. These are the sad stories of those ancestors of the next two generations.
4. Great Grandma Lucy (Beckwith) Heathcote's Story. Your great-grandma will tell her story, of her parent's lives, of her tragedies, and memories of her sisters. I so wish I had asked her more questions and become closer to her. But I didn't know how.

The Warburtons

5. These were the descendants of William the Conqueror who invaded England in 1066. The story begins in the 17th Century in Leicestershire. The Warburtons were the female line of the Heathcotes. They were framework knitters. I gained a wealth of information about framework knitting, an occupation unknown to me.
6. The Warburtons of the 19th Century. We trace these families to daughter Catherine who married Joe Heathcote. This story is set in Countesthorpe.

The Heathcotes

7. I was able to glean very little knowledge about the early Heathcotes other than knowing they endured an occupation similar to the Warburtons. Cath Warburton married Joe Heathcote. We look at the lives they may have lived ending with the arrival of your great-grandfather, Albert. Cath and Joe look back over their lives. But who really knows?

8. John Heathcoat: Could we be related? One cousin, John, became wealthy. I am including his story here although I have been unable to establish how closely he was related to us. At least we know the possibilities….

The Hubbards

9. The Hubbards of Saxelby and Wyfordby
   We move to your Nana's side of the family. I outline the lives of the first Hubbards in the area of Melton Mowbray and describe this central market town.
10. The Hubbards in Eaton - John Stayed Behind
    The Hubbards moved to the Eastwell/Eaton at around 1800. The Iron Ore industry provided employment opportunities other than working on the land.
11. The Hubbard brothers: Thomas, William, Henry & Jonathan.
    I could not resist telling this story of courage and bravery: A side story of adventure I felt I must include. These four illiterate Hubbard brothers emigrated to the USA.
12. Grandad Hubbard's Story. My grandad Hubbard tells his story with the help of the photographs I found. I remember him so fondly. He will tell us about his folks arriving in Stathern.

The Smiths

13. The Story of Louisa Rippin Smith, who was your Nana's grandmother on her father's side. So now we will look at your Smith ancestors.
14. Andrew Smith's Story. Andrew was Louisa's second husband. He tells us his story.

The Browns

15. The Browns are the maternal side of your Nana's ancestors. The first is the story of the earliest Browns I could find and the location where they lived, in the Vale of Belvoir in the County of Nottinghamshire.
16. Elisha Brown and the Elliotts. Our Brown story continues.
17. Grannie Slater Brown and Will. Grannie Brown tells her story of her family and life with William Brown.

The Slaters

18. The Slaters. The back story to the prior story of your Nana's maternal grandmother.
19. James Slater, the Entrepreneur and his legacy. This is a side story I could not resist telling you.
20. Auntie Beat Tells her Story. This story is told by your Nana's Auntie Beat, her mother's elder sister.
21. Conversations with my Father. You never met your grandfather. I have told his story in his own words. You would have loved him.
22. Conversations with my Mother. This is the story of your Nana's life before you knew her and before she became a widow.
23. More Conversations with my mother. These conversations took place after your Nana became a widow and after you were born. You will recognize the photographs. She lived to be a ripe old age.

Enjoy the read with my love and best wishes………………………

Geographical Context: Where they all lived

Before we start the historical journey, we should see where our ancestors lived. Here is a sketch of England and Wales showing the location of Leicestershire with Derbyshire and Nottinghamshire to the north. Rutland and Lincolnshire to the east.

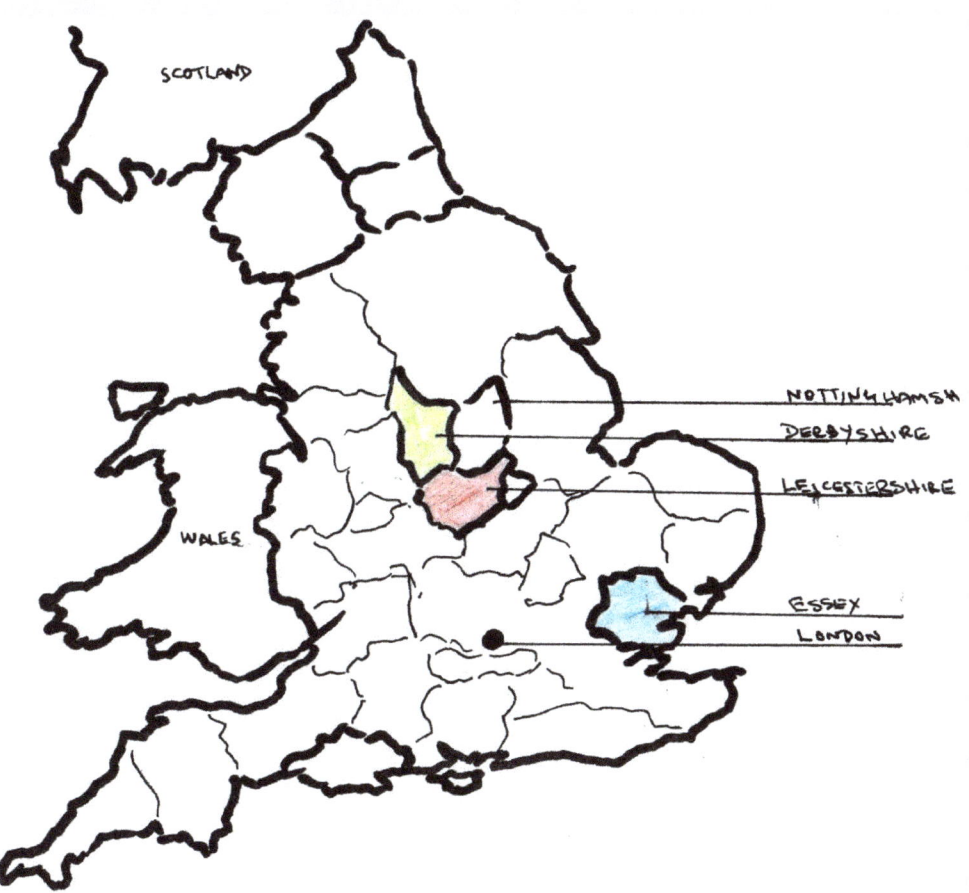

Our ancestors lived in the "shires" in the heart of England as did I. This map helps us locate Leicestershire relative to other Counties. Parishes are clustered into Counties with hap hazard boundaries as shown on the map of England. Each village has a council and a Parish Church. Villages and towns grew around their parish church.

Right in the middle, known as the heartland of England, you will find Leicestershire, where the majority of the stories of our ancestors are focussed.

You will see Essex in the southeast where the Beckwith family started their lives. In order to travel North from London, the only road available was the one the Romans built: The Great North Road. No doubt they travelled partway on this road.

This is a sketch of the County of Leicestershire (and Rutland) where our stories are focussed.

Stathern is located between Melton Mowbray and Bottesford in the northern part of the county. Coleorton is located close to Coalville in the western part of the county.

Yes, we have a local castle! Belvoir Castle, The home of the Dukes of Rutland. Sometimes I refer to the Vale of Belvoir, pronounced by the locals as Beaver! The Vale includes approximately 50 villages that surround Belvoir Castle in all directions an irregular circular boundary identifying the land originally the property of the Duke of Rutland including sections of the counties of Leicestershire, Nottinghamshire and Lincolnshire. Stathern is on the southern tip. Eaton and Eastwell are close by, just outside the Vale. Stathern Woods are part of a much larger wood system that reaches Belvoir Castle, the home of the Dukes of Rutland. You will be hearing about the Castle, located in the centre of the Vale, in some of our stories.

Stathern is located in a valley. Driving to the village from the airport, a pause at the top of Stathern Hill is a must. The view is breathtaking. I would always stop after an overnight flight, to take in Heathrow view and know I was home.

Stathern: History and my memories
A look at village life.......

Many of our ancestors on the Hubbard and Brown side of the family were born, lived, and died in Stathern, Leicestershire including your Nana, who spent almost all her life there. I find there is an attraction for the village where my roots lie. I am happy my roots are there. I look at old and new photographs and remember.

I came across this old whimsical postcard showing Stathern and St Guthlac's church, with a series of historical cartoons around the margins.[6]

---

6   I am grateful to Mike Saunders, who owns the original postcard, and Bottesford Community Heritage Project for allowing me to include the image in this publication.

Village life was good as a child: the freedom, the outdoors, the fresh air. As I grew, however, there was insufficient activity in the village to keep me interested and challenged. Nevertheless, I will always be attracted to Stathern for sentimental reasons even though the village has changed substantially since I lived there. I delivered the Saturday papers when I was 12 and knew everyone.

Now on Google Earth, I see there is construction in the fields next to our house!

(Photographer: D. Field) This huge plaque, erected after I left, is in front of the house where your Nana lived from aged 3 to 18. Behind the large hedge was a garden allotment tended by your great-grandfather. He was a keen gardener, encouraged by his father. Note there was only a small garden attached to this house.

The UK City and County Directories of the mid-1800s describe Stathern as follows:

> Stathern, a village and a parish, in the Hundred of Framland, a fertile and highly picturesque district, belonged in the Union of Melton, in 1841 there were 549 inhabitants on 2,043 acres, mainly pasture. The church dedicated to St. Guthlac is an old building, consisting of a nave, aisles, and a square embattled tower crowned with pinnacles and with four bells. A National school was built in 1845 at the sole expense of the rector. The Wesleyan Methodists have a chapel here. The Nottingham and Grantham canal passes on the north side of the parish. Lacemaking, matting, and brick making are carried out here.

I note a Henry Barke operated The Red Lion, public house and there were carpenters, beer retailers, boot and shoemakers, a blacksmith, a grocer and baker, a butcher, a maltster, a ferrier, a miller, and many farmers in the village at the time, mid-1800s.

The village nestles at the foot of the Leicestershire Wolds, where, not so long ago, cattle were rested and watered on the way to market in Melton Mowbray, 16 kilometres away. Tuesday was and still is market day.

The image of Stathern church is from my personal records. We know the Parish Church is the focal point of all villages. Indeed, without one, there would be no village. The 11th Century St. Guthlac's Anglican Church in Stathern has a rather unusual dedication to a Saxon saint of the 7-8th century who lived in the East Midlands. St. Guthlac, as a young nobleman, was a tearaway. Later he changed his ways and began a monastic life. St. Guthlac's is constructed of local ironstone with limestone dressings and a lead roof. Below is how the church looks nowadays. Beside the church was the rectory. I do not recall ever entering the rectory but your Nana mentioned that when she was young, there were activities for her there.

(Photographer: Kate Jewell). All marriages were solemnized, baptisms witnessed and funerals held uniting the sorrow within the church: the church representing a community that hosted and documented memorable occasions. Church records are an excellent source of information. [7]

---

7   https://www.geograph.org.uk/snippet/15930

Houses were first built around the Church in medieval times and are still there. I recall when I was a child there was a dwelling literally built into the hillside near the church.

Your Nana particularly liked the Harvest Festival service in the church.

All our ancestors who lived in Stathern were baptized there, heralding their membership to the congregation. A child was named during this ceremony. The organist would have played the ancient organ while the congregation sang. The church bells would ring and still do. Stathern has witnessed many of our family's weddings but not Geoff's and mine. We had both left the village before we married.

The village expanded northwards and eastwards towards the flatter part of the Vale. Stathern currently has a population of 670, with a good cross-section of ages, living in some 320 households. There are two village pubs – The Red Lion and The Plough Inn and a busy garage, a local butcher, a well-stocked village store, a post office in The Plough Inn open 3 mornings a week, and a mobile library calling weekly.

Stathern has a flourishing 'excellent' primary school (78 children). [8]

While the village would have been smaller 150 years earlier, there would have been vibrancy, especially as market day approached in Melton Mowbray.

I will not forget the dawn chorus before 5 am. The birds sing no longer because their numbers are severely diminished as a result of pesticide use in the fields. Unbelievably sad. I remember the melodic din they made when I wanted to sleep. Now I delight in the songs of birds when I hear them.

(Photographer: Kate Jewell) Alternatively, marriages were solemnized in the Wesleyan Chapel in Stathern I attended as a child. The Chapel is seen here at the bottom of the lane. The building is no longer in use as a chapel.

(Photographer: D. Field) A reminder of how close we lived with the farm animals of the village!

(Photographer: D. Field) My earliest recollection of the village green near to where we lived. The village green had a central well in the 1940s which was everyone's water source. Your great-grandfather fetched the water from this well. The little lane on the upper right led to the school. The church can be seen in the background.

---

8   https://en.wikipedia.org/ https://en.wikipedia.org/wiki/Stathern,_Leicestershire

I recall the blacksmith's shop in the village. I would peek into the hot, dark room to watch the blacksmith hard at work hammering a red-hot piece of metal into the form according to a plan. The heat source was red hot coals: Hot and dirty work. the red-hot iron. All his tools were hanging on the wall

(Photographer: D. Field) Every village seems to have a village hall; in our case, built as a War Memorial. Ours was used for all communal events: the photographic society, Women's Institute, Community gatherings, and regular Saturday dances. According to an undated report in the Melton Times, by Jack Smith, ours was built by public subscription and fundraising events. People could buy a brick for 2 shillings and 6 pence to help the building fund.

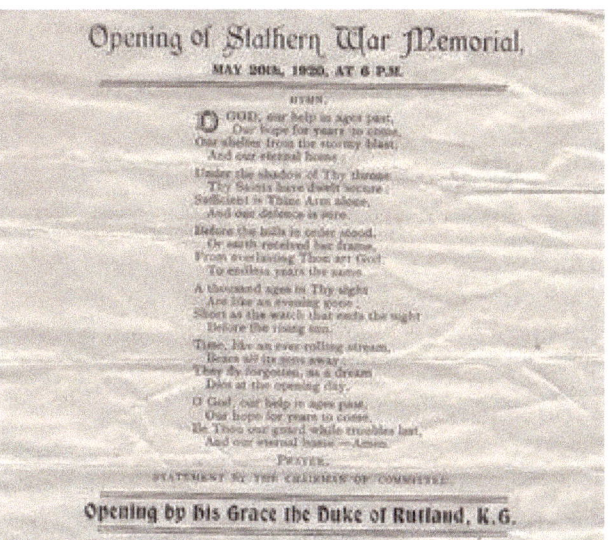

(Photographer: D. Field) The Hall was officially opened on May 20, 1920 by the Duke of Rutland to honour the war dead of WW1. Over one hundred years ago!

(Photographer: unknown) Here is a photograph of your Nana, on the left, participating in a fundraising activity near the Institute on Main Street. Emily Jopling is on the right. (you will read more about her). Cousin May is standing in the centre of the group.

(Photographer: D. Field) Stathern has one Main Street. This is a view from the north end. Your Nana grew up in the first house, with the red door. Many generations of Hubbards, Smiths, and Browns lived in the houses on the left side of the road.

(Photographer: R. Heathcote) This photograph is of Main Street in winter, looking north, dated January 7, 1979. On the Main Street right next to the red telephone booth, there is a bus stop. In my day there was a bus service to Nottingham and to Melton. On the right side was the dairy, later the butcher's shop. The butcher shop sold amazing ham from the bone. In her later years, your Nana would buy a fruit cake from there every week. The butcher's wife was quite the chef as I remember!

(Photographer: D. Field) In this photograph, Stu and your Nana look the homes of great, great Grandad and Grannie Hubbard on Main Street. The Hubbards and Browns raised their children here. You will soon read about them all.

(Photographer: Unknown.) The Red Lion had been an operating public house for a few centuries. It now supports outstanding cuisine which attracts patrons from all over the county. Here is Geoff enjoying a pint. I recall one May, while I was visiting, I was treated to a display of Morris dancing in the car park of the Red Lion. Local performers!

(Photographer: D. Field)

(Photographer: D. Field)

(Photographer: R. Heathcote)

(Photographer: K. Jewell)
The Plough Inn is the other public house in the village. On the prior page is how it looks today.

Here is an old photo showing the garage and Village Hall on the left and Stathern Woods in the background. The Plough boasted a skittle alley. There was a lovely garden at the rear for parties.

Loyalty was everything! Patrons of one pub would not patronize the other! But the Red Lion was my favourite. Win and I would gravitate there for a shandy (beer and lemonade) and a packet of Smiths crisps.

The village primary school in Water Lane dates back at least to 1868 and in some form to 1845, originally built by the church rector [9]

I have fond memories of the school which I attended until aged 9. I am told that smells linger in one's memory. I shall not forget the smell of the sand in the sandbox on my first day at the school: indescribable and distinctive. Now there are more children around the village. The school has been refurbished and is more vibrant than in the 1940s when I was there.[10]

(Photographer: D. Field) I recall the two-roomed schoolhouse with outside toilets and no running water. Students were served milk, one-third of a pint in small bottles, in the morning: school lunches were cooked on the premises by a Mrs. Belt.

The school's Log Records have been maintained by the headteacher and staff at the school for nearly 140 years. The following is an excerpt are from the School Log

---

9   https://en.wikipedia.org/wiki/Stathern,_Leicestershire
10 The Public Elementary School (National School) was built in 1845 and enlarged in 1894 to hold 183 children.

Records, of April 6, 1868: *Admitted 35 children into the school. Appointed two monitors, Hannah Greensmith and Elizabeth Alice Clarke. Examined children in reading and arithmetic.*[11]

Every year at the same time in May, there would be the Stathern Fair, operated by Ashleys. The travelling entertainers with their merry-go-round and stalls where one threw a bean bag at an object to win a prize. I remember the excitement, the loud music. The Fair and the entertainers stayed for a few days before moving on to the next village. Now no Fair is celebrated. I am sure they have other festivities!

The village changed quickly after the second world war ended. I recall a hosiery factory flourished in my early memory. Now this land supports new houses. The corrugated steel Nissan huts that once housed the war refugees have gone too: more new houses.

Apparently, our splendid Norman Church of St Guthlac was the first in the Leicester diocese to be lit by electricity. The three public houses, shops, and businesses were connected to the supply, followed by the houses in the village.

The cost was 30 shillings to have one light installed and 25 shillings for any others. Eventually, over 100 homes were connected. Mr. Green's daughter, Emily, recalled at 13 years of age how she went around the houses to read the meters every quarter, prepare bills, and collect the money.

Emily Jopling was a particular friend and neighbour of your Nana. They visited one another often. I would visit too when I was in the village. She did tell me this story but it didn't register with me at the time. The penny dropped when I reread an undated account by Jack Smith in the Melton Times. His headline is "Stathern, a pretty village nestling in the Vale of Belvoir, was the first in the area to have electricity and became the envy of its neighbours." So now we know!

(Photographer: R. Heathcote)

(Photographer: Kate Jewell) The disused factory in this photo is a relic of Vale engineering works and still stands in Stathern. I discovered the building had another use! An enterprising toolmaker and engineer, Mr. Ernest Green, persuaded the villagers in 1926 to lay aside their oil lamps and take new-fangled light from a wire! He came to Stathern to manufacture engineering components in the former lace factory. He installed a large National Gas Company engine run on crude oil to generate electricity, built a battery storage house, and a network of poles and lines.

---

11   https://www.stathern.leics.sch.uk/website/school_history/148775

(Photographer: D. Field) This house on Main Street belonged to the Steward family. The house included a dairy and a beautiful apple and pear orchard. The Steward children grew up with us: your Nana and I were particularly fond of Susan and Alison. In their 80s, your Nana and Jean Steward would share tea each afternoon for as long as Jean's health made it possible.

(Photographer : D. Field)

(Photographer : D. Field)

On the left of the driveway of the Steward House, in a patio area, was a row of three small houses. Your Nana was born in one of these and lived there until the age of 3. By 1919, the Hubbard family had left the tiny cottage and moved to the house with the red door on Main Street. The Stewards removed the three houses when they became derelict. I snapped this photo of your Nana peeking out of the tiny cottage window, before they were demolished.

Then they moved to a new house which had two rooms and a kitchen downstairs and three bedrooms upstairs. One of the downstairs rooms, known as the "Front Room," kept closed and orderly, was used exclusively for special occasions and visitors. The house was rented for 10 shillings a month. The square, unimposing semi-detached house, newly constructed from

(Photographer: D. Field) In the 1930s, the Hubbards moved to a house newly built by Mr. Rowbottom, a local builder. The house, Wood View, Stathern, later 27 The Green, had land for a garden and numerous outbuildings. Here she is next to a huge lavatera bush.

(Photographer: R. Heathcote) This is an early picture of the side of the house in the 1940s. You can just see the laundry hanging on lines down the garden path. The apple trees were severely pruned. I had quite forgotten the small hedge that defined the small garden by the side of the house. I had a swing in the tree in the centre. I would swing too high and would be told off!

local sandstone and red brick, had no running water, a large garden, and apple trees.

The kitchen had a "copper" in one corner which was used to wash and boil sheets. There was a place for coals underneath. Monday was wash day. Laundry was washed in a dolly tub, a large tin barrel that was filled with hot water. A dolly peg (three-pronged wooden stick) was used to agitate the laundry.

The gardens provided room for clotheslines as drying had to occur on Mondays ready for ironing on Tuesdays using a flat iron that was heated on the fireplace in the living room.

The living room contained a fireplace that had a water boiler and an oven attached. The fireplace had to be "blackened" with a substance that resembled shoe polish. Friday nights were bath nights in front of the fire as each family member took turns having a bath in the same water.

I was born in this house. We went to bed with candles as there was no electricity and no heat upstairs. We had hot water bottles. But it was cold.

The outside toilet was attached to the back of the house; a smelly, cold place where one never lingered. The toilets were manually emptied as part of the municipal service. Your great-granddad would fetch water from a tap in the centre of the village using a yoke and buckets. No water would be wasted. Rain water was also collected.

(Photographer: D. Field)

(Photographer: D. Field)

(Photographer: D. Field)
This is the vegetable garden, your great-granddad's garden, overgrown now and neglected. He would be horrified. Once there were carrots, potatoes, peas, runner beans, broccoli, rhubarb, herbs, and black currant bushes. But no one grows their own produce these days!

Your Nana loved her garden and pottered around there late into her life. She seemed to have green fingers. She would snip off cuttings wherever she was and by a miracle, they would root and thrive.

Stathern is situated in a valley surrounded by woodland and hills. I could not resist taking pictures

(Photographer: D. Field) Lovely terrain around the village: Leicestershire's rolling hills.

(Photographer: D. Field) I took Stu to a place where I played. We girls would climb a tree to talk. The tree is no longer there.

On summer Sunday evenings, our family would walk through Stathern woods. I loved that walk. We would hear the birds and animals we did not see; see the wood keeper's hut which reminded me of the hut in Lady Chatterley's Lover; admire the huge rhododendron bushes and smell a unique aroma for that part of the world, as well as hear the call of the cuckoo. Each time I take an evening walk, I remember those times and that vista.

(Photographer: D. Field) I would drive from London Airport or Heather's house in Solihull to visit your Nana and would see this magnificent view from the top of Stathern Hill, looking down into the village entering the Vale of Belvoir. The view would literately take my breath away and I could not resist a photograph. While there are no fields of cowslips now, there is a sense of permanency knowing that our family lived here for centuries. Some left their bones here: even though we left, the beautiful countryside remains.

ENDNOTES

Parish Council Minutes of meetings are now available on the internet. This is the first time I have ever read them!! Your Nana had no interest in governance matters and did not care to inform us about the Council. As such, we lived in ignorance. Until now!! https://www.stathernparish.co.uk/minutes-2021

Laundry

As I ironed today, my thoughts wandered into the past. I thought about washing clothes and ironing in my early days. Rain or shine, wash days were always Mondays in working-class 1940s England and were always a chore of major significance.

They didn't wash outer clothing nearly as often as we do nowadays: perhaps undergarments too. Your Nana always wore an overall. We were encouraged to change into our grubbies for lounging around the house and playing outside. We possessed few clothes: we had one set of Best Clothes.

The following is a portrayal of a typical wash day:

The Monday would start with your Nana lighting a fire under the "copper." Water to fill the copper from the rain barrel. Sheets, towels, and nappies were boiled in the copper in which the water was heated.

A dolly tub was a galvanized metal ribbed tub that stood about four feet high. Laundry was sorted into whites, which went into the copper to be boiled. The cleanest items were washed first as water was reused. The washing in the dolly tub would be manually agitated using a dolly peg. Much like the central agitator type top-loading washing machines. This exhausting activity built upper body strength!

The clothing fabric could be unforgiving. Make a mistake at either the washing or the ironing stages, and we would be stuck with the results. Clothing made from wool was a particular case in point. Wash woollen clothing in too hot water and you would be left with a matted miniature of your original! Some interesting colours might arise too if a red piece of clothing was included by mistake!

The Mangle

After the washing came the arduous task of rinsing out the soap. First, your Nana would wring as much of the soapy water out of the washing by hand as she could, thus building wrist strength: this water was returned into the dolly tub to be used for the next load. Then the washing would be put through a mangle to squeeze out as much water as possible. Our mangle was a made of wrought iron with huge wooden rollers that efficiently removed water from the washing.

Then the washing would be rinsed in cold water in the scullery sink until the water ran clear and there seemed to be no soap left in the clothes. The laundry would be mangled again until all the water was squeezed out.

Often the whites, especially if bars of washing soap had been used, would tend to turn a little yellow. The blue bag countered this and restored the appearance of the whites. So, the final rinse of the whites was in blue water from a bluebag which was a small muslin cloth tied round a small cube of blue substance kept in a bowl of water.

Ensuring the bag never leaked was important because otherwise little particles of blue would leak and leave small blue dots on the washing. (The blue bag was also used to dab on insect bites and stings to ease the pain.)

Tablecloths were starched. Starch was purchased in granules, looking rather like dry stem ginger: it was mixed for use every time. First mixed with a little cold water, and then boiling water was quickly poured onto it. If the water was not hot enough, the starch would not thicken, and if the stirring wasn't rapid enough, the starch would go lumpy. The process was rather like making custard or sauce.

After rinsing, more mangling, to remove as much water as possible before the clothes dried because there were no efficient drying methods. The washing had to be dried either outside in fine weather or indoors in bad rainy weather. Indoor drying resulted in a damp, musty room.

This was incredibly hard work: washday was a weekly event, no matter what the weather. Women needed to be strong to lift sheets and tablecloths in and out of the various baths because wet washing was much heavier than a dry load. Often, we would hear that the village women "Took in washing" for extra cash and were paid a pittance. With no rubber gloves and no labour-saving devices, can you imagine what women's hands must have been like with all this washing!? Smooth hands were a status symbol, indicating a woman had servants. Working-class women always tried to hide their red and rough hands from public view. This was probably the reason many wore elegant gloves. When it was cold outside your Nana's fingers would become so cold and chapped. I remember her hands.

The washing was then pegged onto clotheslines that were simply lengths of rope, slung between trees or hooks in the garden. Sometimes the lines broke. The clothes pegs were what were known as 'gypsy clothes pegs' because gypsies made them and came round knocking at front doors selling them. Each peg was made from a piece of wood, split lengthways, and held together with a nailed-on strip of tin can.

Each item of the wash had to be pegged in such a way the wind would blow through it to blow out the creases. This was to make Tuesday's ironing easier. The collars of shirts would be bent taut over the line and pegged where the collar met the rest of the shirt, and pillowcases would be pegged at the open end loosely and on one side only so they would billow out as the wind blew through them. Sheets were folded double and pegged at each end, with one side pegged taut along its whole length and the other side sagging slightly. Your Nana was very specific when she showed me this. Thankfully I don't have to use this knowledge.

Sometimes all didn't go to plan. Your Nana would groan if the clothes fell off the line, the line broke or the rain started. Everything would then be brought inside and hung on wooden racks. I use racks too. How far we have come?

Your Nana would put her whites on the line in the frost because, she said, it helped to keep them white. I used to help her shake them vigorously before bringing them in to get rid of the frozen water so that they would dry more quickly.

The clothes were ironed on Tuesdays. I did ask your Nana about the Monday, Tuesday routine. She couldn't remember its origin. I asked her whether there was a routine for the remainder of the week. There was not. I am surprised Tuesday was ironing day as Tuesday was market day in the nearby town of Melton Mowbray.

My earliest recollection of ironing day was your Nana heating up a flat iron on the fireplace being careful to keep the iron clean of coal. She had two of course: one for ironing and one for heating up so as not to waste time.

Clothes being dried indoors resulted in a damp house which was most uncomfortable. I noticed the dampness in your Nana's house when I visited.

Another specific activity was to air the clothing. I was never sure about this process but realize now that in the damp English environment, laundry was not truly dry even after ironing. So, the laundry was draped over the wooden racks and placed in front of the fire. There was a lot of competition for a place in front of the fire.

Eventually though life became easier for your Nana: the copper was removed, an electric washing machine purchased. She also had a boiler for hot water and an airing cupboard for storing sheets and towels. Yes, she also had an electric iron!

I have just finished washing my sheets, drying, and replacing them on my bed. The whole process took no effort. No ironing because my lovely Miele dryer does not leave sheets wrinkled. Either that or I don't care.

I have hung my 'no iron' blouses on hangers, straightened out the collars, and given them a shake. My hands are smooth: they were never wet, hands so unlike your Nana's. Her washing days are forever imprinted in my memory.

1.

THE FIRST BECKWITHS

Our story begins with the Beckwiths who married into the Heathcote family. This story tells of the lives of the first Beckwiths, Edward and Sarah, I can trace: your Great Grandma's family. This is the first of four Beckwith biographies in which we acknowledge their lives, remember them, and imagine how they lived.

Firstly, a look at the name Beckwith. The surname is an ancient Yorkshire locational surname, which derives from the village of Beckwith, in the Nidd Valley, near Harrogate in Yorkshire.[12] Did our Beckwiths originate in Yorkshire? We cannot be sure.

In the sketch of England in the Preface, we see England's counties. The sketch provides a frame of reference for our story, a story which begins in the mid-1700s in the village of Castle Hedingham in northeast Essex, on the ancient road from Colchester to Cambridge, sitting on the River Colne, north of Baintree, near Halstead.

The village developed around the Norman Hedingham Castle and boasts many well-preserved medieval buildings. The 900-year-old Norman keep of Hedingham Castle stands in 160 acres of spectacularly beautiful landscaped gardens and woodland where the Lindsay family, descendants of the original owners, the De Veres, still live. Note how close Essex is to London.

Today, advertisements describe Hedingham Castle as not just a place: romantic, beautiful, ancient, historic and wild, but somewhere to set your imagination free. Privately owned, its character is unique: its history, the heritage of us all. Images of the Castle as it is today possibly resembling that of the 18th Century.[13] Visit the

---

12 http://www.surnamedb.com/Surname/Beckwith#ixzz5CK4tlEAp
13 https://www.hedinghamcastle.co.uk/castle-and-gardens/

castle and the village on YouTube.[14] Or take a virtual drive through the village as it is today and imagine how it was 200 years ago!

England in 1700 was a land of hamlets and villages: its towns, such as it had, were located on the coast, none more than 50,000 souls. The population of England then was about five and a half million, which increased to approximately six and a half million by mid-century. This began a period of steady migration from the country to the towns. By 1801, the population of England had reached 9 million.[15]

We cannot be certain how well or poorly this first family of Beckwiths, Edward and Sarah, lived but we can guess. Undoubtedly, they lived meagrely on food that they grew, raised, foraged, or caught. Their dwelling would have been small, damp and dark, of brick or stone construction. They would have had few possessions. Their clothes would have been handmade and passed down from family and friends. The women would have done their own quilting, rug making, knitting, tatting, and cooking. There would have been a garden supplying the family with fruits, vegetables, and herbs. They might have made their own cheese, beer, and even candles. They might have kept chickens and a pig. Without either electricity or running water, life would have been difficult in the cold, damp English climate.

Wood or coal fires would have heated their homes, if they could afford it. The whole family would live and rest in the kitchen/dining/living room near the fire. There would have been a local pub but no store. The family would have interacted with few people outside of the village. But then villagers talked to one another and delighted in knowing everyone's business. Perhaps they sang and danced. They would have been unhealthy: their knowledge of hygiene would have been negligible. Children would have constant colds and runny noses. We know infant mortality was high. About one child in four died before its fifth birthday. Most married women had several children without expecting all would survive: pregnancy was difficult, childbirth hazardous. They lived and died without anaesthetics and medicines. Women quite often died in childbirth. Generally, life expectancy would have been short, unpredictable. Remember, there were no antibiotics. These then were the expectations and typical living conditions. But how did our family fare?

Women worked in and around the home, and housework was very time-consuming. There were no convenience foods and no labour-saving devices. Most married women did not work outside the home because they did not have time. Child-rearing would have just happened without thought or skill. Even middle-class women were kept busy organizing their servants. Life could also be tough for spinsters who worked as spinners, tailors, milliners, midwives, milkmaids and washerwomen. Many were domestic servants.

Women wore long dresses for warmth. In the 18th century, they did not wear knickers. Whereas fashion was very important for the rich, poor people would have owned two sets of clothing: their "Sunday Best," and a set for every day without regard for fashion. The Beckwiths fit well into this category.

The first census in 1801, where my research starts, simply divided residents into those employed in agriculture and those in the trades or manufacturing. Forty years later the census gathered detailed occupational data but imposed no real order. The first occupational classification, introduced in 1851, was concerned with social status as well as with occupations, as it began with the Queen, followed by government officials and then by 'the learned professions'. The Beckwiths were none of these. In their social strata, the men would have been labourers, usually working the land.

---

14 https://www.youtube.com/watch?v=uf6GCvbjZGQ
15 http://www.localhistories.org/life.html

Within this social context, we look at the first Beckwiths I could identify.

Edward (1759-1836) and Sarah Dobnam Beckwith (1761-1844)

Our earliest ancestors on this side of the family were your great Grandma's great, great Grandparents, Edward and Sarah Dobnam Beckwith. Edward was born in 1759 in the village of Castle Hedingham in Essex. At the age of 28, he married Sarah who was two years younger. Edward lived all his life in the village and was most likely a labourer. Sarah gave birth to six children who lived to adulthood: Edward, Samuel Dobnam, William, Sarah Ann, John, Hannah, and Mary Ann. We have no way of knowing the number of children she bore who did not survive.

This family appeared to have a benefactor. Their children were given an opportunity not often granted to village children. Not surprisingly, their sons' vision for their lives extended beyond the village. Their daughters? Not so much.

There were no records to identify who was first to leave the home. I suspect that firstborn Edward, born in February, 1788, and second son, Samuel Dobnam, named after his mother's family, born in August 1789 most likely left together, aged barely twenty. We can imagine Edward and Sarah watching with sadness and resignation as the wagon left in its journey to London. The time would have been before 1810. The date is imprecise but we know Sam married in November that year in Bloomsbury, London. There he became a woodturner and then a tanner: a craftsman. An opportunity offered to a country lad was taken.

Son Edward appeared to join the elite. He was placed on the electoral register because of his house ownership at 39 Keaton Street, St George, Bloomsbury in London. I have been unable to find more information about this wealthier family member who died at aged 57 on October 28, 1845.

On January 17, 1871, Lucy Sandford, daughter of James and Sarah Sandford of Belchamp Walter, approximately 8 kms north of Castle Hedingham, was welcomed into the family. Lucy may or may not have been educated but was no shrinking violet. Perhaps Edward and Sarah wondered whether she was a good match for their mild-mannered, clever son John. There being no church in Belchamp Walter, Lucy and John, both 19 years of age, married in the parish church of St Nicholas in Castle Hedingham. The church bells would have rung their joyful carillon on that day.

Shortly after their wedding, Lucy and John embarked on their adventure to the Heartland of England. Edward and Sarah would never see their grandchildren.

William, their third child, born on August 12, 1792, decided to become a servant/labourer in All Saints Parish in the centre of Northampton, as recorded in 1838.

Interesting side story: their daughter Hannah stayed home and initially married Henry Lovack in 1836 when she was 38. Sadly, he died two years later. Hannah had a son, William, born in 1833: father unknown. Hannah was charged with Larceny in August 1838 but was found not guilty. Happily, her circumstances were to change. She married John Harrington in 1839 in the village: John adopted William.

Sarah and Edward's last child, Mary Ann, was born on November 8, 1807 in Castle Hedingham to her 46-year-old mother. Mary Ann married Joseph South at the age of 22 in 1825. He was a roof thatcher, a skill he passed to two of their sons. The following is an example of his work. A thatched cottage.[16]

---

16 http://www.thatchco.com/thatchpg/faq.htm

(Photographer: R. Heathcote)

For fun see the little thatched house a man built. https://www.youtube.com/watch?v=kC-7ZGe5cwA

I recall that your Nana told me that our next-door neighbours, Uncle Phil and Auntie Liz (Brown), used to live in a mud house in Stathern: Possibly similar to the house in the picture. I didn't believe her. Now I know what she meant. Apparently, a piece of it fell on Auntie Liz one day so they moved!!

Geoff added: *I remember the mud houses. They were on a lane opposite The Red Lion. I am sure it was called Mud Row. Cannot recall who lived there but I do remember them being pulled down to build the council houses that are there now. They were pretty handy to the village tap!*

Returning to our Beckwith story…. The patriarch, Edward, died at the age of 77 and was buried in the village on July 2, 1836. Sarah then moved from the tranquillity of Essex to the hustle and bustle of London residing with son, Samuel and daughter-in-law Elizabeth at 10, Hartford Street, St. Pancras in the heart of London until her death in 1844 at the age of 83.

The early Beckwiths were mobile and appeared to have connections to London. Those that wished had the opportunity to move and did. Some become educated and wealthy. Others were skilled in a trade or were entrepreneurs. Nevertheless, I found no wills or legacies left by this section of the family in the 1800s.

The next chapter continues with the story of John and Lucy, your direct ancestors.

Chart 1. Family Group Sheet for Edward Beckwith

Husband:	**Edward Beckwith**
Birth:	1759 in Castle Hedingham, Essex,
Marriage:	1787 in , Essex,
Death:	1836 in Castle Hedingham, Essex,
Burial:	02 Jul 1836 in Castle-Hedingham, Essex
Father:	Beckwith

Wife:	**Sarah (Dobnam) Beckwith**
Birth:	1761 in Castle Hedingham, Essex,
Death:	18 Dec 1844 in Pancras, London
Burial:	22 Dec 1844 in Middlesex,
Father:	Samuel Debnam

Children:		**Sarah (Dobnam) Beckwith**
1 M	Name:	Edward Beckwith
	Birth:	08 Feb 1788 in Castle Hedingham, Essex,
	Death:	28 Oct 1845 in Holborn, London
2 M	Name:	Samuel Dobnam Beckwith
	Birth:	16 Aug 1789 in Castle Hedingham, Essex,
	Marriage:	25 Nov 1810 in St George, Bloomsbury,
	Death:	Jan 1857 in Pancras, London
	Spouse:	Elizabeth (Sharrenton) Beckwith
3 M	Name:	William Beckwith
	Birth:	12 Aug 1792 in Castle Hedingham, Essex,
	Marriage:	17 Nov 1823 in Harlestone, Northamptonshire,
	Death:	26 Aug 1868 in Kettering, Northampton
	Spouse:	Charlotte (Fleckney) Beckwith
4 F	Name:	Sarah Ann Beckwith
	Birth:	09 Mar 1794 in Essex, England, Gosfield
	Death:	Sep 1848 in Baintree, Essex
	Burial:	24 Sep 1848 in Braintree, Essex,
5 M	Name:	**John Beckwith**
	Birth:	21 May 1797 in Castle Hedingham, Essex,
	Marriage:	17 Jan 1817 in Essex, England
	Death:	01 Apr 1877 in Ashby de la Zouch, Leics
	Spouse:	**Lucy (Sandford) Beckwith**

6 F		Name:	Hannah (Beckwith) (Lovack) Harrington
		Birth:	12 May 1799 in Castle Hedingham, Essex,
		Marriage:	22 Jan 1836 in Castle-Hedingham, Essex to Henry Lovack
		Death:	1879 in Castle Hedingham, St Nicholas, Essex,
7 F		Name:	Mary Ann (Beckwith) South
		Birth:	08 Nov 1807 in Castle Hedingham, Essex,
		Marriage:	15 Jul 1825 in Little Braxted, Essex,
		Death:	Abt 1840
		Burial:	17 Feb 1840 in Little Braxted, Essex,
		Spouse:	Joseph South

2.

THE ADVENTURES OF JOHN (1797-1877) AND LUCY (1798-1877) BECKWITH

One morning in early 1817, a carter delivered a package containing a letter that would change the lives of the Beckwith family. John would have eagerly but carefully opened the package and read the offer he had received to his parents and excited wife. We cannot know whether this offer was expected but it must have been a surprise. John was just 20 years of age but mature for his age. He was offered the post as Master of an hospital and endowment school in faraway Leicestershire. His excited bride, Lucy, might have had mixed feelings.

Undaunted, John accepted the challenge. That the pair moved away from their parents at such a young age is unimaginable. Their parents must have been devastated to watch them prepare for their journey. But leave they did, away from the comfort of their surroundings in Essex, their parents and siblings to a new locale. We can imagine the pair dressed in their Sunday best, perhaps their wedding outfits, carrying their meagre belongings and the package of food and water handed to them by their weeping parents. After handshakes, hugs, good wishes and tears, the couple would have climbed into a cart which would take them to the stagecoach, possibly for the first time in their lives, and commenced their long journey. Lucy must have wondered how she would manage without her mother and what life would be like so far away. But she was tough and would become the driving force in their relationship.

I am grateful for the background details provided to me by Terry Ward from the Coleorton Historical Society and the agreement with the school[17] offered to John and Lucy.[18]

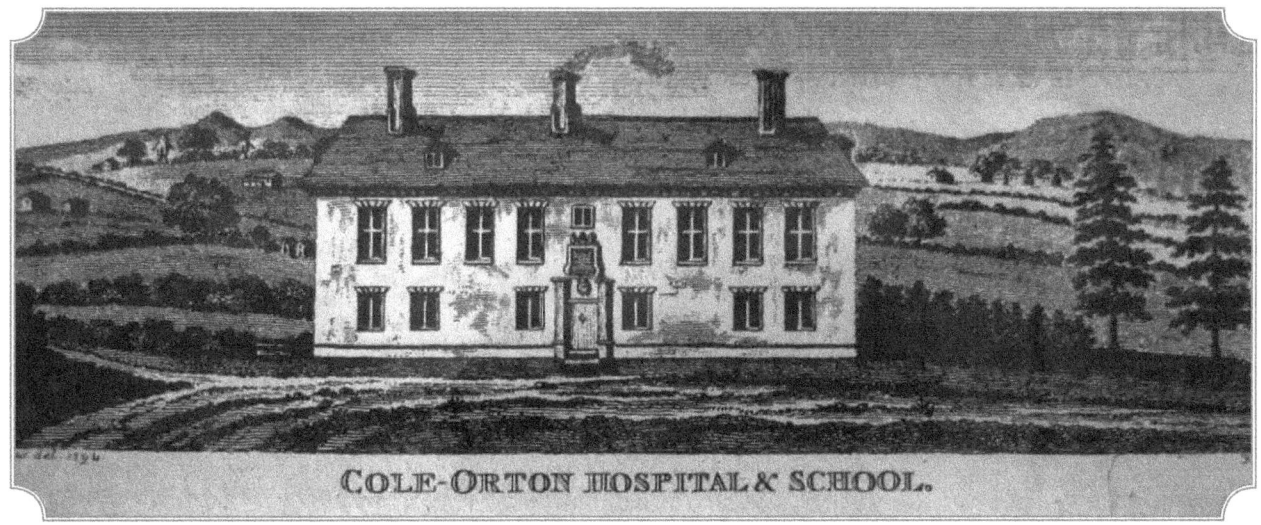

This engraving of John and Lucy's new home was provided by Coleorton Heritage Group and was made by S Shaw in 1794: The Cole Orton Hospital and School. "Hospital" was a term for alms houses where elderly widows were given accommodation and not a medical hospital, the term we use today.

John and Lucy were to teach poor village children to read and write, at no charge to their parents. In addition, the elderly widows who resided in the property were also in his care. Imagine being responsible for six widows of his grandparents' vintage as his tender age?

As the coach rolled along, John might have listened to the sound of the horses' hooves on the packed earth and wondered himself whether he had made the correct decision to move from home. He would have mused whether he would succeed in his duties as a school administrator in Coleorton, Leicestershire and whether he could make a successful life there.

Perhaps they travelled to London first to visit John's brothers, Edward and Samuel, who both lived in Bloomsbury, before embarking on the journey north, most likely on the Great North Road, the one the Romans built. The roads north would have been uneven, perhaps rocky with numerous pot holes. As the pair looked out

---

17　Terry Ward <terryjward@aol.com
18　*(from an article published in the Coalville Time by 'Lavengro' on 21.05.1965)*
　　Founded in 1702 by Lord Viscount Beaumont, a hospital and school became a prominent feature at Coleorton: his Lordship's purpose being the accommodation of six poor widows and the education of poor children. The building which was liberally endowed, contained ten rooms on the ground floor, six of which were occupied by the widows and the remaining four by the schoolmaster.
　　Over the schoolmaster's rooms there was accommodation for 60 boys and 60 girls. A yearly income of £120 was produced by the tithes, and out of this the schoolmaster and his wife were paid a joint salary of £80.
　　A weekly stipend of 4s. 6d. was paid to each of the six almswomen, and coals to the amount of £20 were provided annually for the hospital and school. A further benefit to each widow was the provision of a stuff gown, every other year. In addition to this amenity Coleorton was one of the three parishes entitled to send Almswomen to Ravenstone Hospital.

the of the windows of their carriage, they would have seen fields and hedgerows similar to but different than those in their home county of Essex.

They would have welcomed the stops along the way to water or change the horses and to stretch their legs. Perhaps the constant sound of the horses allowed Lucy to snooze as the carriage swayed to and fro. After a couple of day's ride north they would have reached the old town of Stamford in Lincolnshire, where they would have taken a night's rest in an Inn, approximately 160 kms north of London. The next part of the journey would have involved many changes as they travelled across land in a westerly direction, first to Oakham, through Melton Mowbray and on to Coleorton, not in a coach with four horses but in a pony and trap perhaps. The 90-some kilometres cross country would have taken a few days as they waited for rides from carters who would pick them up and drop them off.

Undoubtedly, both John and Lucy wondered about their new village Coleorton. He might have known coal mining, quarrying, textile and engineering industries were prevalent in the vicinity at that time. One can imagine, however, the dirt and dust floating in the air. Coleorton was then a scattered settlement in the north-west Leicestershire coalfield area, about 7 kms east of Ashby de la Zouch and 16 kms west of Loughborough.[19]

But there is a conflicting image of Coleorton. Some two hundred years earlier, prior to the mining activity, the area had been a centre of arts and literature thanks to the patronage of a local baron, Sir George Beaumont. As well as being an accomplished artist himself, Sir George sought out leading artists and writers of the time such as Wordsworth, Constable, Coleridge and Reynolds and made a point of assisting up-and-coming artists and bringing their talents together. The Beaumont family had a considerable impact on the community in terms of education and support.[20]

Nowadays Coleorton is said to be one of the most beautiful villages in Leicestershire. Sadly, I never visited the area.[21]

Upon arrival, the exhausted pair would have been welcomed with cheers and smiles by the inhabitants of Coleorton, particularly the six widows with whom they would reside, potentially six expectant grandmothers willing to participate in the lives of the young master and his family. Would they have been surprised to see the youngsters, stiff and weary from their journey? John no doubt stood upright attempting to appear beyond his years.

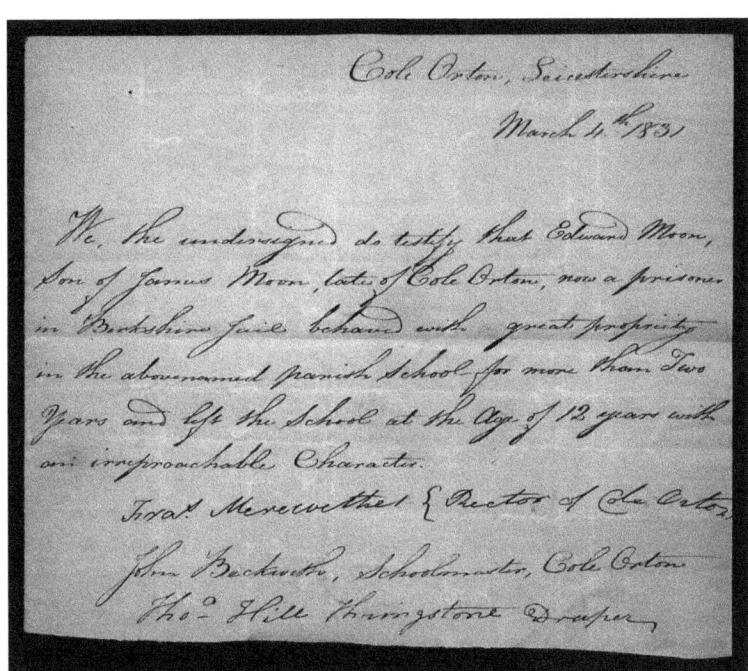

This letter written by John provides a character reference to one of his prior pupils, Edward Moon. It provides an insight to the depth of compassion John felt towards his former charges.

---

19 https://en.wikipedia.org/wiki/Coleorton
20 www.coleorton.org.uk/coleorton.html
21 http://www.viscountbeaumonts.leics.sch.uk/history.html

First impressions aside, they would have been shown their school and their new home. Nevertheless, for Lucy and John, this environment must have felt very different than their serene Essex home, although Coleorton does border Charnwood Forest providing a beautiful aspect to the location.

No doubt to the delight of the poor widows, by 1826, John and Lucy had started their family: Ann Amelia was born in 1822 and Emma Lucy was a new-born.

By 1839 John and Lucy had a large family: John named after his father arrived in1827, followed by James Edward a year later and named after Lucy's father. Charles Frederick was born in 1831 followed by Frances Hannah in 1834. Edward, named after John's father, was born in 1836. Mary Ann, named after Lucy's sister was born in 1838.

In 1839, there were 50 boys and 40 girls registered in the school, although the average was said to be 60 boys and 50 girls. The master was allowed to take paying pupils as well, if there was room – the number of these rarely exceeded 6. The children attended school only when they could be spared from their duties: farm labourers, laundry assistants, servants and the like. Many families were dependent upon their children's earnings.

The girls were taught by Lucy whose services were paid from within her husband's salary. But Lucy and John had eight children at the time. How could Lucy possibly fulfil her commitments to the school? A comment was made: 'There are no educational wants in this parish'.

As indicated below, on the day of the census, June 12th, 1841, John and all his family resided in the Endowed School and Hospital in the Parish of Coleorton. John and Lucy's occupations are shown as School Master and Mistress. John was the Enumerator of the facility: his penmanship excellent.

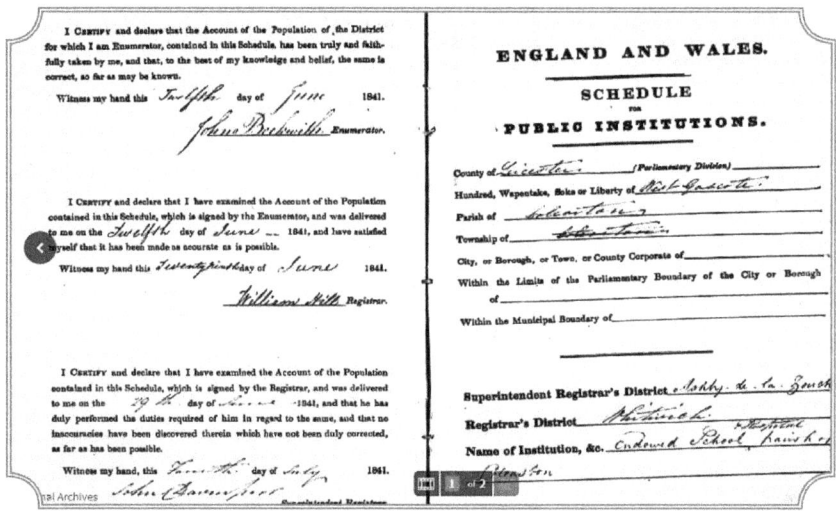

Two more children had been born: Elizabeth in 1840 and a year later, when Lucy was 44 years old, she gave birth to George. Unbelievably this educated pair had 10 living children: Lucy was fertile well into her 40s. We have no way of knowing whether any children died as infants.

Six widows are also shown to be in residence in the 1841 census. Their ages ranged from 57 to 80. I note that these widows had a room each whereas John and his family were allocated only four rooms! I am comforted to know that John and Lucy lived amid a nest of mothers and grandmothers who no doubt assisted in household duties as well as child-rearing and educating the girls in the school. I wonder how John and Lucy found time to raise all their children as well as educate others; and how they lived in such confined quarters. That the family and the widows lived as a community is likely. As such, the children would then have been nurtured by no one and everyone.

Lucy emerged as a driving force within the school, described as a formidable woman. She was most certainly the School Mistress in charge!

At the time of the 1841 census, only Ann had left home. Ann's occupation is listed simply as FS, a female servant. She was in residence close by in Coleorton Hall, a 19th-century country mansion, formerly the seat of the Beaumont baronets of Stoughton range. Currently, The Hall is a Grade II listed building converted into residential apartments.

By 1851, John into his 50s, was the National School Master. He, Lucy, and their six youngest children lived in the Church Town School House in much expanded quarters compared with their prior abode. All of the children living at home were scholars: even 16-year-old Frances. John was likely musical. I noticed in one census that he was a volunteer church organist, most probably in the 13th-century church that was located nearby.

John would have retired from teaching at aged 60 in 1857. He no doubt watched a new endowment school being built by Canon Beaumont in 1867. Since then, it has been extended and modernised but many of the original attractive features remain. Today the school, still known as Beaumont's School, is a co-education Primary Day School where students still honour and respect the Beaumont family.

By 1861, John and Lucy had become farmers of 26 acres while operating a farm shop in Coleorton and living on a street called The Moor. Also residing with their parents in 1861 were eldest daughter Ann and younger daughter Mary Ann who both helped with the farm and farm shop while 19-year-old George kept the books. More importantly though, the family had a servant: 16-year-old George Burley who likely helped on the farm. Having a servant meant they were officially part of the middle class!

Ten years later, John had reduced his acreage to 6. He, Lucy, and Mary Ann, a dressmaker, lived together on The Moor. Ann had moved out to live on her own.

(Photographer: unknown) This priceless picture of Lucy from the book: Memories of Coleorton, Reminiscences of the Residents, recommended by Terry Ward of Coleorton, who noted:

> *'It was recorded in an article in the Leicester Advertiser dated Friday July 25th, 1975, that the headmistress of the school, who taught the girls, was the formidable Lucy Beckwith, a stickler for discipline. She wore – or so it is reputed – a whalebone corset from which she would whip a whalebone and rap any erring pupil. She reigned from 1817 to 1857 – 40 years of tyrannical female rule.*
>
> *Although her husband John Beckwith was the headmaster, who taught the boys, and would have taken the lead role, there is little recorded about him. This is presumably because Lucy was a feisty character who commanded the limelight.*
>
> *Of course, Lucy's approach to corporal punishment needs to be viewed in the light of Victorian values when discipline was seen as both necessary and indeed desirable and I think the whalebone story just adds to her character.*

Of interest is how their 10 children, essentially raised in a community, managed their lives having considerably more education than most of their contemporaries. I have described how eldest Ann helped on the farm as did Mary Ann. Neither married but had sufficient resources to live on annuities in their later years. The source of this capital is unknown. Upon her death, Ann left £653 to her brother James Edward: Quite a sum in those days. The source of the wealth is unknown. James left the family and became a brewer's clerk while John became first a police constable and later an Inn Keeper. Both left Coleorton, as did Charles who became a timekeeper on the railway. All but one of their sons left home. Was Lucy too overbearing??

The most educated of the children was Frances (1834-1877). She married well, to an army school master, a Thomas Walker who was born in York. Their first child, Thomas was born in 1855 in Malta: their second, John in 1857 in Arundel, Sussex. Army postings took the pair to Kercher, India, where daughter, Mary Louisa, was born in 1863. Then his posting returned them to England where son Frank was born in Aldershot, Hampshire in 1870. Frances Mary Walker arrived in Norfolk on February 16, 1872. Sarah Edith was born in Manchester two years later. After Frances witnessed the deaths of her parents in 1877, she too died on August 18 prematurely at aged 43. Frances and Thomas Walker had a life of travel to foreign territories: Certainly, the most different of all Lucy and John's children.

The story of your direct ancestor, Edward, will be told in the next chapter.

The final child, George (1842-1915), kept the books on his father's farm when he was in his 20s but by 1871, he had become a baker and a grocer, the only son to remain in Coleorton.

We have imagined the lives of John and Lucy Beckwith, your great Grandma Lucy's great grandparents, who offered a promising future to their children. John became sufficiently educated to receive prominence as a school master. And Lucy was a force of Nature! He responded to the emphasis on teaching during the mid-19th century, deemed necessary to produce an educated workforce. We know that colleges and institutions of higher learning: Eton, Harrow, Oxford, Cambridge existed for the wealthy. Rugby College was close by. But were they so far out of reach for this family? We know too state-sponsored Grammar schools and Secondary schools were also well established. Were they also out of reach?

Some of Lucy and John's children moved into middle class: all avoided working the land. Others became clerks and entrepreneurs. Only Ann entered briefly into service. With nine brothers and sisters, I doubt that any were well nurtured by their parents. They were, however, surrounded by a community of widows during their childhood. Three had numerous children: others none: some married, others not. They lived to varying ages with no discernible patterns. There appeared to be no predictability to their lives. None joined their uncles in London, a city I am sure seemed far away. But I can say for sure they looked after one another and were not plagued by poverty.

Lucy Beckwith died on December 18, 1876. A few months later, on April 1, 1877, John died. They were both 79 years of age. I think we can truly say they lived and worked together for 60 years.

With the passing of George, the Beckwith name ended in Coleorton from this side of the family.

Epilogue

I am so grateful to the historians in Coleorton, particularly Terry Ward, who enriched the story with photographs and anecdotes. Undoubtedly Lucy was the driving force in the relationship and the true mistress of the school. Their stories illuminate the characters of John and Lucy Beckwith.

(Photographer: Terry Ward)

(Photographer: Terry Ward)

From Terry Ward: Attached is a photograph of John and Lucy Beckwith's headstone and a photograph of St Mary's Church where they are buried. As you can see this is a very peaceful spot.

In affectionate remembrance of Lucy Beckwith who died December 18th 1876 aged 79 years. Also, of John Beckwith who died April 1st 1877 aged 79 years.

Endnotes

History of Coleorton and nearby Coalville, the family's new home.

Now spread over a fairly wide and hilly area, Coleorton boasts a long history of literature, arts, and industry. It played a major role in the English Civil War and was also the seat of the Leicestershire Beaumonts for more than 500 years. During the Civil War, the Cromwellian forces had their regional headquarters at a garrison on the site of Coleorton Hall. From this position, they were able to launch cannonballs towards the Royalist stronghold of Ashby Castle, two miles away. The current hall is Georgian in style and was completed by Sir George Howland Beaumont in 1807. It has far-reaching views over Charnwood Forest.

The Coleorton Colliery, situated between Coleorton and Swannington, is now closed; coal-mining came to an end in nearby Coalville during the 1980s, resulting in about five thousand men being made redundant. A woodland Coleorton Wood was planted in 1991-92 on the colliery site as part of the National Forest. Opencast mining operated between 1985 and 1995.[22]

---

22 www.coleorton.org.uk/coleorton.html

Chart 2. Family Group Sheet for John Beckwith

Husband: John Beckwith

Birth:	21 May 1797 in Castle Hedingham, Essex,
Marriage:	17 Jan 1817 in Essex,
Death:	01 Apr 1877 in Ashby de la Zouch, Leics
Father:	Edward Beckwith
Mother:	Sarah (Dobnam) Beckwith

Wife: Lucy (Sandford) Beckwith

Birth:	Abt 1798 in Walter Balshamp, Essex,
Death:	18 Dec 1876 in Ashby de la Zouch,
Father:	James Herbert Sandford
Mother:	Sarah Elizabeth (Dexey) Sandford

Children:

1 F
- Name: Ann Amelia Beckwith
- Birth: 1822 in Coleorton
- Death: 12 Jan 1907 in Burton upon Trent, Staffordshire
- Burial: 16 Jan 1907 in Staffordshire,

2 F
- Name: Emma Lucy (Beckwith) Irons
- Birth: 1826 in Leicestershire,
- Marriage: Apr 1848 in Leicester,
- Death: 07 Jul 1904 in Dorking, Surrey,
- Spouse: Wentworth Irons

3 M
- Name: John Beckwith
- Birth: 1827 in Coleorton,
- Death: Jan 1892 in Burton upon Trent, Staffordshire
- Spouse: Ann Beckwith

4 M
- Name: James Edward Beckwith
- Birth: 1828 in Cole Orton,
- Marriage: 18 Dec 1852
- Death: Jan 1915 in Burton upon Trent, Staffordshire
- Burial: 26 Jan 1915 in Staffordshire,
- Spouse: Mary Ann (Leggett) Beckwith

5 M
- Name: Charles Frederic Beckwith
- Birth: Abt 1831 in Coleorton,
- Death: 01 Feb 1923 in 3 East Street, Leicester,
- Spouse: Sophia Beckwith

6 F	Name: Birth: Marriage: Burial: Death: Spouse:	Frances Hannah (Beckwith) Walker 1834 in Cole Orton, 1868 in Ashby de la Zouch, 18 Aug 1877 in Stapenhill St Peter, Derbyshire, Sep 1877 in Burton on Trent Thomas Walker	
7 M	Name: Birth: Marriage: Death: Spouse:	**Edward Beckwith** 1836 in Coleorton 03 Mar 1859 in Birmingham, St Martin, Warwick 28 Sep 1889 in New Street, Coalville, Snibson; **Rose Caroline (Daniels) Beckwith**	
8 F	Name: Birth:	Mary Ann Beckwith Abt 1838 in Coleorton,	
9 F	Name: Birth:	Elizabeth Beckwith Abt 1840 in Cole Orton,	
10 M	Name: Birth: Marriage: Death: Spouse:	George Beckwith 1842 in Coleorton Oct 1862 in Ashby-de-la-Zouch Apr 1915 in Ashby de la Zouch, Mary (Cross) Beckwith	

3.

Edward (1836-1889) and son John Beckwith (1863-1938)

This story continues from John and Lucy Beckwith, the School Master and Mistress, to our direct ancestor, Edward, born in Coleorton, the sixth of John and Lucy's eight children, and then to his son, John who was your great Grandma's father. I wish I had asked her about her parents and members of her family; in those days we just didn't. But she indeed had a story to tell.

On the Leicestershire sketch on page 2 you will see the proximity of Coleorton, Coalville, Swannington and Ravenstone to one another.

I hoped that my research would lead to an academic career for Edward and his siblings. But that was not so. At a time when many of the classics we read today were being written in England, I wondered whether your ancestors read Dickens (1812 - 1870), any of the Bronte sisters, or Jane Austen (1750 - 1817). These were the family members who had the opportunity for a scholarship. I am disappointed that they failed to take advantage of a classical education. I have to wonder why they did not see this future for themselves and am disappointed.

In father John's lifetime and in Edward's, the industrial revolution in the UK was well underway, and education was being emphasized by Queen Victoria's government. There was a movement from teaching what was "useful," towards reading, writing, and mechanics. There was a grammar school in Ashby, only 8 kms from Coleorton, a school that seemed beyond the aspirations of this family: aspirations that would not change in our family until my generation. I was the first to attend the English Grammar school. Geoff was the first to attend University. When you three arrived, a university education was expected of you.

When Edward Beckwith married Rose Caroline Daniels in a solemnized ceremony on March 3, 1859, in the Parish Church in the Parish of St. Martin, Birmingham, he was 22 and Rose, 24. Edward's occupation is stated as an Inn Keeper. On the marriage certificate, his father John's occupation is stated as a grocer and hers as a maltster. Edward lived in Birmingham at the time of his marriage and she at her home in Coventry. We don't know the reason for his move from home in Coleorton to Birmingham or how he would meet a young lady from Coventry. But I can guess! Coventry and Birmingham are located south and west of Coleorton in the county of Warwickshire some 50 to 60 kilometres away.

At the time of the marriage, Edward's father, John had retired from his schoolmaster position, had a smallholding, and operated the farm shop on the farm. I note that Edward's elder brother John was an Inn Keeper. The connections were predictable, especially when we consider the in-laws!

The In-laws: The Daniels family

The Daniels family came from Foleshill, a suburb of Coventry, in Warwickshire on the canal system. Alexander Daniels had married Caroline Bryon in 1830 when they were both 19 years of age. While Alexander was able to sign his name, Caroline made her mark on the marriage banns. According to the Church of England tradition, Banns or announcements were made to the church congregation announcing the intention of a couple to marry. The congregation was asked to declare whether they knew of any impediment to the union. If there was no comment from the congregation, the marriage could take place. Alexander and Caroline started a family immediately. William was born in 1831, Rose in 1835, Cornelius in 1836 and Henry in 1837. I marvel at the early age these families accepted the responsibilities of a family: did they have a choice?

Alexander Daniels was a maltster, a task that involves creating malt from barley and other grains. The maltster could either sell the malt to a brew master or brew ale himself. Malting was a lucrative business, both for the maltster and the government: malt was heavily taxed. Since ale was drunk by virtually everyone, brewers needed huge quantities of malt. As a result, whether Alexander used a middleman or brewed the ale himself, he earned a good living. And his son-in-law was an innkeeper. We can, therefore, make the connection between Rose and Edward via the drink of choice for the English. We know that they chose to drink ale at the time because the water was impure. I suspect that water was boiled for children's consumption.

As a tragic side story, ten years before the nuptials between Edward and Rose, in 1849, Alexander Daniels lost two of his family members: on October 10, 1839, 8-year-old Henry Albert died of typhoid fever. His 13-year-old brother, Cornelius, was present at the death. Eight days later, Edward's 38-year-old wife Caroline also died of typhoid fever: again, Cornelius was present. How distressing for the teenager to witness the deaths of his family. Were they aware typhoid fever is caused by the bacterium Salmonella Typhi, growing in the intestines and bloodstream? Typhoid is spread by eating or drinking food or water contaminated with the faeces of an infected person. Death from this cause was common in those days when knowledge of bacteria and cleanliness was not associated with disease. It seems particularly sad to me that the young Henry and mother Caroline died while her husband was engaged in producing the popular alternative for water. William and Cornelius Daniels and their sister Rose survived this tragedy. They were 18, 14 and 13 years of age. Young Rose would have been called into action. The remaining family stayed together with Rose as their housekeeper. But they also had a servant, moving them into the middle class. The maltster died at the age of 77 in 1887.

From the evidence, we know Edward Beckwith married well, into the Daniels family, a truly middle-class family. Of interest is how he and Rose benefitted from this wealth.

Our story now moves to their lives.

Edward Beckwith (1836-1889) & Rose (1835-1913)

Rose was pregnant at the time of their marriage on March 3, 1859, at St. Martins in Birmingham. Their firstborn, Edward Alexander, named after both fathers, arrived in October that year. He was baptized in St. Thomas's Church in Coventry. At the time of his birth, the family lived at 21, Union Street, St. Thomas, Coventry. Edward senior was then a shopkeeper. The distance between Birmingham and Coventry, Warwickshire is approximately 50 kilometres which must have been an arduous journey then, so one wonders what took Edward to Warwickshire. We do know that the countryside was peppered with short rail tracks used for hauling coal short distances. These would eventually be linked together as the train transportation system grew. In those days, however, the canal system was the main transportation route. I suspect and surmise the Beckwiths used canals for moving around, a system in use today as a vacation opportunity.[23]

Rose gave birth to five children in the first eleven years of their marriage: Edward Alexander in 1859, John in 1864, Annie Amelia in 1867, James in 1869, and Rose in 1870. The couple set up home in Swannington and Whitwick, close to the Beckwith family in Coleorton.

By 1871, at the age of 34, Edward was employed as the Colliery timekeeper at the Coleorton Pit. He might have monitored the rhythm of the mine or kept track of employees' hours of work time which formed the basis of their pay. He might have prepared their weekly wages which would have been in cash. Or he could have provided safety checks concerning underground working conditions. We don't know exactly but I suspect the timekeeper kept track of employees and paid their wages. We simply know he had returned to home territory from Birmingham and Coventry.

Ten years later Edward worked as a bookkeeper: employer unstated but most probably at the Colliery. The family lived in Mantle Lane, Coalville. He died of pneumonia on September 28, 1889, aged 53, leaving no financial legacy. Was he too close to the unclean colliery air? His occupation was stated as rent and debt collector on his death certificate. His son, James, was present at his passing.

By 1891 his widow, Rose Caroline, at 56 was the head of the household, living on her own means. Since Edward left no legacy, I wonder whether her wealthy father paid her bills. James and Rose, by then 22 and 21, lived with their mother. The family had taken in a 30-year-old widowed boarder and lived on Belvoir Road, Hugglescote: a village on the River Sence about 1.6 kms south of the centre of Coalville. All the young residents had jobs.

Twenty years later in 1911, 76-year-old Rose lived with her firstborn, Edward Alexander, and his wife, Fanny, in their six-room house at 34, Lord Nelson Street, Nottingham: they had two paying boarders. Nowadays, Lord Nelson Street looks like a respectable row house development. Rose died in July 1913 at the age of 78.

Rose and Edwards' second son, John Beckwith was your ancestor, born in 1863 after the family had returned to his father's birthplace: Coleorton. More about him later.

---

23   http://www.canaljunction.com/canal/coventry_ashby.htm

Your great Grandma's grandfather, Edward appeared to have married well. He had a skill for numbers and certainly was not a labourer. His premature death at 53 must have devastated the family.

Moving on a generation to Edward and Rose's son John: our direct ancestor:

John Beckwith (1863-1938) and Elizabeth (1865-1902)

John, Edward and Rose's second son, was baptized in the parish church in Coleorton on May 10, 1863. The ceremony would take place very shortly after birth as was the custom: Church of England of course.

He became a carpenter, which would involve an apprenticeship programme for at least five years. He would likely have completed the programme when in 1887, at the age of 24, he married 22-year-old Elizabeth Woolley. This pair had seven daughters. Their first child, your great Grandma, Lucy Caroline, born on February 14, 1888, was named after her great grandmother, Lucy the schoolmistress, and her grandmother, Rose Caroline. Both names never seem to go out of fashion. She and Elizabeth, born on April 6, 1889, and named after her mother, were born in Ravenstone, a small rural cluster village between Coalville and Ashby-de-la-Zouch, in North West Leicestershire, and within the National Forest close to the Derbyshire border. I would drive through Ravenstone on my way to London airport via the M1 from Stathern without knowing that I had roots there.

In 1891, John, Elizabeth, and their daughters lived in Swannington with a work colleague, another carpenter, and his wife. I hope that pregnant Elizabeth had help with the children from her boarder, Ellen Dumloe. Alice arrived in March that year: along with Lucy and Elizabeth another name that never goes out of fashion and the only one of your great Grandma's sisters I knew. Her name came out of the blue. When I knew her, she called herself Annie.

John and Elizabeth continued with their family: Florence Mary arrived in 1895 and Fanny in 1897. Ethel arrived in 1898 and Gertrude in 1900. These names are currently unpopular and not in the family either. Where did they come from, I wonder?

During her early childhood, Elizabeth, known as Lizbeth, had moved to Ravenstone to live with her grandparents, the Woolleys. I note that the Woolley son was a framework knitter at the time. We will learn about framework knitting later, from the paternal side of this family.

At the turn of the century, John had been a carpenter at the Colliery for 20 years, a skilled tradesman. He and Elizabeth with six of their children lived together at 170 Mantle Lane, Coalville. There were two 24-year-old male boarders also in residence. I wonder whether Elizabeth was responsible for all the laundry, cooking, and cleaning? But we know she was, probably with the help of her elder daughters, Lucy and Alice.

Then tragedy: John's beloved 36-year-old wife Elizabeth died suddenly on June 17, 1902. I was sufficiently curious to order her death certificate which stated cancer of the uterus and exhaustion as the causes of her premature death. She was interred at Coalville Cemetery on June 21st. John, the journeyman carpenter, was present at the death which took place at home on Mantle Lane. He was too heartbroken and traumatized to sign his name, merely leaving his mark on the certified entry of death, a certificate that acknowledges he was present at her passing.

So, John, at the age of 39 was left with seven daughters between the ages of 14 and 2. Your great Grandma would have been called into action as the cook, housekeeper, and nurturer to Alice, Florence, and Fanny as well as her distraught father. Life would also change for the Woolleys and Lizbeth when the two younger children, Ethel and Gerty, moved in: the Woolleys were then in their late 60s.

Henry Woolley was a local, a threshing machine engine driver. Lizbeth, already in residence with Woolleys, would become the carer of her younger sisters. Ethel and Gerty were still living with the Woolleys as a family ten years later in Ravenstone. The Woolleys in their 70s with two teenaged granddaughters: imagine! Lizbeth had moved on and was in service.

By 1911, John, then aged 49, had been married for two years to Sarah Ann Price. He was still a carpenter but out of work. I have no way of knowing whether the unemployment was temporary. But then he was a journeyman, work would have been sporadic. The pair lived in Tan Yard, Swannington, and had had a child together who did not live. Also in the household was Sarah's 60-year-old widowed mother Hannah Hodgkinson and 15-year-old niece, Lillian Price. The census, unfortunately, provides only a glimpse on one particular day: On that day though we see a foursome having no income on which to live. Sarah and her mother likely tended the garden, took in laundry, and cleaned houses.

John Beckwith lived to 74. His death is registered in the Ashby-de-la-Zouch registry in March of 1938.

This is a disappointing and sad story of missed opportunities and one premature death that affected your dear great Grandma and her father. He lost a wife far too early which most probably left him weak and vulnerable. But then the stress of constant childbearing as well as caring for family and lodgers was too much for her. John's work as a carpenter would have been strenuous, exhausting, and unpredictable. His premature death from pneumonia paints a picture of a man too sad and depleted to continue life.

Your great Grandma lost her mother at the age of 14 and would have hesitantly assumed the motherly role herself, at a time in her life when she had been exposed to child-rearing but not the responsibility. I am certain she rose to the occasion as she was the sweetest, gentlest person imaginable. Your great Grandma's father and grandfather were employed in the colliery but were thankfully not miners. I surmise money was not plentiful and life would have been difficult for these families for multiple reasons.

Your great Grandma will narrate the next story as I imagined she would. And you know the back story.

ENDNOTES

Coalville is a product of the English Industrial Revolution. As its name indicates, the former coal-mining town was a centre of the coal-mining district of north Leicestershire. The *Leicester Chronicle* of 16 November 1833 reported: "Owing to the traffic which has been produced by the Railway and New Collieries on Whitwick Waste, land which 20 years ago would not have fetched £20 per acre, is now selling in lots at from £400 to £500 per acre, for building upon. The high chimneys, and numerous erections upon the spot, give the neighbourhood quite an improved appearance. We hear it is intended to call this new colony appropriately, 'COALVILLE'".[24]

Transportation

The Ashby-de-la-Zouch Canal is a 50 km long canal in England which connected the mining district around Moira, just outside the town of Ashby-de-la-Zouch, with the Coventry Canal at Bedworth in Warwickshire. It

---

24   https://en.wikipedia.org/wiki/Coalville

was opened in 1804, and several tramways were constructed at its northern end, to service collieries. Driven by the force of the Industrial Revolution, supplies and personnel needed to be on the move. The Midland Railway originated in 1832 in Leicestershire/Nottinghamshire, to serve the needs of local coal owners.

The Journeyman Carpenter

A journeyman carpenter designation is an occupational title given to an individual who has completed a formal apprenticeship programme. They work for new home builders, commercial construction companies, government agencies, remodeling firms, or are self-employed. Journeyman carpenters work in a variety of environments such as office buildings, mills, residential homes, underground mines, and tunnels. Hand-to-eye coordination, mathematical skills, project management abilities, strength, and stamina are important attributes for a journeyman carpenter.[25]

A Maltster[26]

The Master's Association of Great Britain offers us a description of the malting process: Malting is the controlled germination of cereals, mainly barley, followed by a termination of this natural process by the application of heat. Further heat is then applied to 'cure' the grain and produce the required flavour and colour. A basic rule is that for malt to be made, the barley must be capable of germination, so maltsters source their barley with a minimum germination of 98%. The malt is then used to produce beer.

End of the Victorian Era-1901

This time heralded the end of the Victorian era, remembered for modesty, lace, frills, demure long skirts and much more. Queen Victoria had ruled over an Empire that covered a quarter of the globe with 400 million subjects for 60 years. She, and particularly her husband Prince Albert, energized the British industrial revolution: the railways linking cities, a formal education system, coal and steam power, and the Victoria and Albert Museum. These initiatives provided a variety of new employment opportunities for men and women, allowing them to leave the land and service to work in the new industries, providing they had the education and skills. Queen Victoria died in 1901.

---

25 https://careertrend.com/journeyman-carpenter-job-description-2373.html
26 http://www.ukmalt.com/barley-growers

Chart 3a. Family Group Sheet for Edward Beckwith

Spouse: Edward Beckwith

Birth:	1836 in Coleorton
Marriage:	03 Mar 1859 in Birmingham, St Martin, Warwick
Death:	28 Sep 1889 in New Street, Coalville, Snibson;
Father:	John Beckwith
Mother:	Lucy (Sandford) Beckwith

Spouse: Rose Caroline (Daniels) Beckwith

Birth:	1835 in Foleshill, Warwick
Death:	Jul 1913 in Nottingham,
Father:	Alexander Daniel(s)
Mother:	Caroline (Bryon) Daniels

Children:

1 M
- Name: Edward Alexander Beckwith
- Birth: Oct 1859 in Coventry, St Thomas, Warwick, A porter
- Marriage: 16 Nov 1879 in Newton Heath, All Saints, Manchester,
- Death: 04 May 1926 in Nottingham,
- Burial: 08 May 1926 in Nottinghamshire,
- Spouse: Fanny Musson Beckwith

2 M
- Name: **John Beckwith**
- Birth: Apr 1863 in Cole Orton, Leics
- Death: Mar 1938 in Ashby de la Zouch,
- Spouse: **Elizabeth (Woolley) Beckwith**

3 F
- Name: Annie Amelia Beckwith
- Birth: Jan 1867 in Ashby De La Zouch,

4 M
- Name: James Beckwith
- Birth: Abt 1869 in Birmingham,
- Marriage: 1891 in Ashby-de-la-Zouch,
- Spouse: May (Palmer) Beckwith

5 F
- Name: Rose Beckwith
- Birth: Oct 1870 in St Mathews Engte, Warwickshire,

Chart 3b. Family Group Sheet for John Beckwith

Husband: John Beckwith

Birth:	Apr 1863 in Cole Orton, Leics
Death:	Mar 1938 in Ashby de la Zouch,
Father:	Edward Beckwith
Mother:	Rose Caroline (Daniels) Beckwith

Wife: Elizabeth (Woolley) Beckwith

Birth:	Oct 1865 in Coleorton,
Death:	17 Jun 1902 in Coalville,
Father:	Henry Woolley
Mother:	Ann Wild

Children:

1 F
- Name: **Lucy Caroline (Beckwith) Heathcote**
- Birth: 14 Feb 1888 in Coalville,
- Marriage: 12 Jul 1919 in Melton Mowbray,
- Death: 20 Sep 1972 in Melton Mowbray,
- Spouse: **Albert George Heathcote**

2 F
- Name: Elizabeth "Lizbeth" (Beckwith) Lewin
- Birth: 06 Apr 1889 in Ravenstone,
- Marriage: Oct 1911 in Leicester,
- Death: Oct 1967 in Leicester,
- Spouse: John W Lewin

3 F
- Name: Alice (Annie) Beckwith
- Birth: 04 Mar 1891 in Coalville,
- Death: Oct 1960 in Leicester,

4 F
- Name: Florence Mary Beckwith
- Birth: 12 Mar 1895 in Coalville,

5 F
- Name: Fanny (Beckwith) Cobley
- Birth: Abt 1897 in Whitwick, Leics
- Marriage: Jun 1926 in Leicester,
- Death: Mar 1968 in Leicester,
- Spouse: Samuel Cobley

6 F
- Name: Ethel (Beckwith) (Blowfield) Griggs
- Birth: Jul 1898 in Ashby de la Zouch,
- Marriage: Jul 1947 in Leicester,
- Death: 27 Aug 1949 in Leicester Infirmary
- Spouse: Charles Samuel Griggs

7	Name:	Gertrude (Beckwith) Gwinnett
F	Birth:	18 Apr 1900 in Coalville,
	Marriage:	Oct 1943 in Marylebone, Middlesex,
	Death:	30 Jul 1965 in Camberley Surrey,
	Spouse:	Thomas Henry Gwinnett

4.

Great Grandma Lucy Heathcote's Story

Lucy Caroline Beckwith Heathcote was your grandfather's mother. Since I knew her, I feel I can help her tell her story. We have the facts: dates, names, and locations. The stories surrounding the facts are being told as I imagined she would tell the story. I will recall her memories as she would have recounted them, sometimes repetitive and disjointed, making space as they appear to the fore of her mind.

Your great Grandma, Lucy Caroline, was the gentlest of souls, simple and cheerful: a grannie with an aspidistra in the window of her house. I would visit her with my father but not very frequently. She seemed so pleased to see us whenever we showed up! This is how I imagine she would tell her story. ……..

You have asked me to tell you about me life, so I will have to think about what happened during the last 70 or so years. That is a long time. Where will I begin?

Start at the beginning! I was born on February 14, 1888, in Ravenstone which is near Coalville and Leicester. That is Valentine's Day I think although we didn't make much of that in them days. I was the eldest, y'know. After me came Lizbeth, and Annie. Then me mam had Florrie, Fanny, Ethel, and Gertie. As a youngster, I was expected to help me mam with all the washing, cleaning, and cooking. And watching the little ones.

Me dad, John, was a carpenter at the Colliery. We lived at 170 Mantle Lane in Coalville. It was a little house and we were crowded. Perhaps that is the reason Lizbeth went to live with the Woolleys. Grandad Harry Woolley was a threshing machine driver so he worked on the land. Their children had left home when Elsbeth moved in so they were glad of the company. I cannot remember why Lizbeth left us and went to the Woolleys who were me mam's folks. They lived in Ravenstone which was nearby so we saw one another often. But then Lizbeth had her own room and lots of attention from Grannie and Grandad Woolley.

Me mam told me she was 22 when he married me dad: October 1887 she said. They got married in a hurry because I was on the way. She was glad because me dad loved her.

I don't remember much about me Dad's side of the family. His dad, Edward, died just after I was born and his ma, Rose Caroline, moved away. So, we didn't see her. I was told stories about the Beckwith family though. There was a story about the schoolmistress in Coleorton who was quite a woman, very well-known there. I was named after her but am not at all like her. Me grannie on me dad's side was Caroline. So that is how I got me other name.

I did go to school but not for very long because I was always needed to help me mam with the younger kids, or the washing or the cooking. I did learn to read and write but not very well. I still have a hard time putting me thoughts on paper. But then I never 'ad time for any of that.

I won't ever forget the day me mam died even though it was years ago but I was only 14. I had finished me schooling and was wondering what I should do next. Going into service was what all we girls did in them days. But I was really busy at home with the little ones. Fanny was five, Ethel was only four and Gertie was two. June 17, 1902 was the day me mam died. She was only 37. Me dad was in a state and couldn't do anything. He had lost his sweetheart, was so upset and could not sign his name on the death certificate. It pained me to watch him. I had to move myself as the eldest and help the family stay together. I took on the cooking, housekeeping, and doing what I could for me sisters, Alice, and Florrie. Me dad was stressed out for a long time. We girls did what we could for him.

Everything changed that day at the Woolley's house and for Lizbeth an'all. Me grannie and grandad Woolley were quite old then but agreed to take in our Fanny, Gertie, and Ethel. I was glad they did because we could not have looked after them. Me little sisters stayed with our grannie and grandad Woolley for a very long time. Lizbeth went into service somewhere sometime after that.

Some days stick into memory, don't they? For me, it was the sad, sad day when we all said goodbye to our mam at the Coalville Cemetery. It was a lovely June day but we were all crying. We three girls, Alice, Florrie, and me, became close over the next few years.

Let me see: Lizbeth went into service. She was a servant to Mr. Rogers at the Gypsy Lane Nurseries in Leicester. He was a florist and so much older than Mrs. Rogers or so Lizbeth said. Lizbeth had only one little baby girl to care for. But then she worked hard as a general servant. She was 22 when she married John Lewin. Just before I had Reggie, she had a little girl named Florence. After our Florrie I suppose. They lived in Leicester. We didn't see much of them.

Alice became a servant an'all at 41 St. Stephens Road in Leicester. She had two toddlers to look after. I think that was a lot of work for our Alice who was not used to little ones! Her boss, Mr. Ingamells was a florist and fruit seller. But Alice had dreams. She was determined to travel and have some adventures. And she did. She become a lady's maid with a difference. She travelled the world. She had a black trunk for storing all her clothes and things that she used on her voyages. She reminded me of Frances Beckwith Walker, our great aunt, who also travelled a lot with her schoolmaster husband. A few in the family left their homes to go far away. But when they did, we heard all about it! I was very proud of me sister Alice who called herself Annie then. We became close as we grew older.

Me poor dad did not do well as a single man. He married me mam so young and needed to be married. He was not yet 40 when we lost me mam but he aged quickly. He married Sarah Ann Price in 1909 and lived in Tan Yard in Swannington with some of her family. The next year they had a baby, John Albert Edward who was born in April but died in July. Imagine all those names! I was not around then but felt for him. He seemed happy enough with Sarah Ann although I am not sure they had enough to live on. He never seemed to have steady work as a journeyman carpenter.

I stayed around our house until me sisters all left and me dad married. Then off I went. I had no choice; I had no home. Oh, me sisters were close by somewhere in Leicester but all in service. Let me see, I was 21. I went into service when me dad married in 1909.

I was in service at 21 Highfield Street, Leicester. It was a huge house, a 10 room Edwardian-style terrace home. Mr. Thomas Henry Crumbie, was my boss with Mrs. Crumbie. He was a young man in his early 40s I would say. Much younger than me dad. There were seven children in the family and Mr. Crumble's sister who seemed older than Mr. Crumbie.

Their daughter and two sons went to school but four little girls needed caring for and a baby. Poor Mrs. Crumbie had lost two other babies. I was sad for her. Miss Crumbie and I worked hard to make the household work properly. Mr. Crumbie was a printer, and employer – a very important man y'know.

Soon after that and while I was with the Crumbies, I met Albert who was 16 years older than me and married. I don't remember where we met but a friendship came about. He explained to me at the time, he had moved the family from Countesthorpe to Leicester because of his job on the railway. He was a railway wagon repairer. His wife, Ann became ill soon after that. He was caring for his two sons because his wife was ill in hospital.

So, I moved in with him to help with his sons. There was Tommy who was about ten years old and another younger little boy, Harold Lemon, who had been adopted. It was a by chance adoption, unplanned, but at the time Ann was healthy but couldn't have more children. Sadly, then for Albert, Ann, died in January 1915.

We four moved together as a family to 227 Thorpe Road in Melton Mowbray again because of Albert's railway job as a railway wagon repairer. We lived with Albert's sister, Florence who had met a man from Melton, no doubt introduced to her by Albert. They married just before the Great War started. George Watkin, Florence's husband, worked for the local railway. After that, the inevitable happened. I fell pregnant.

Florence had Cathy just a bit before I had Reggie. So, we helped one another with babies. Their daughter, Marion was born just before the war ended.

So, on November 20, 1915, I had a son of me own. I think I will never forget that day! But I was not married even though Albert was me man I felt the shame of bearing a child out of wedlock. We could not marry because we had to wait a respectable time after Ann died. After all, that was the way things were done in them days. Oh yes, here I am with me Reggie. I was about 28 then. Reginald Leslie: named after no one in particular.

(Photographer: Unknown)

Then Florence had Francis born a couple of years after the war ended. Her husband, George returned home in the summer of 1919. He said he was disabled. He certainly was shell shocked and not the same man who left us. But he was able to return to work as a platelayer eventually. We were a bit crowded at 227 when George came home and their son Frank was born.

Albert was in what they called "essential service" and so was not too concerned about being called up to fight in the Great War. But that was all we talked about in them days. That and the rationing and the shortage of food. I was glad to be pregnant before the war started and to wait until it was all over to start again. But feeding everyone during rationing was not easy.

Oh, I remember, our Fanny went into service when the rest of us did. She went to 15 Welland Street in Leicester to the Cullen family. Mr. Cullen was a shopfitter. There were a couple of children but she was the only servant so she would have worked hard there as a domestic servant. That was what we did in them days. Fanny waited a long time to marry Sam Cobley. He was a metalwork press operator. They lived at 39 Laxton Street in Leicester and didn't have any children. I was pleased to see she wasn't doing domestic work in her later years. She was able to come be with me when I married Albert. But then we didn't see much of one another because we were living in Melton. I was then very far from all me sisters.

Y'know I really cannot remember what happened to little Harold……….. No, I really cannot remember.

Let me see……. Our Ethel was so, so young when we lost our mam. She would not remember her and me Grannie Woolley would be her mam. Gertie too. Ethel married John Blowfield when she was about 17. That was while I was pregnant with Reggie. John was 31 which seemed old for her. He was too old to fight which was a good thing for them both. The next year she had John William and then Freddie James and then so soon after that she had Dennis Reginald. Oh no the story is not good for them. Poor John died when he was only 45. Ethel had to look after the family. She worked as a charlady because that was all she knew. Life was hard for Ethel. But then she found Sam Griggs or perhaps he found her! We heard he was a decorated war hero from the second world war but we didn't hear much about them. I think Annie, as we called her, kept in touch because when Ethel sadly died, Annie received a nice little surprise. No details mind! Ethel got sick and died in 1949. So young.

Gerty was a servant for most of her life. Being a parlour maid in 1939 sounded so posh! Then she married Tommy Gwinnett but by then she would have been well into her 40s. He was a boot and shoemaker. He had been a driver in the Great War and got a medal, so we were told. He was from the south of the country. The pair lived in Camberley, Surrey. I was sad to hear she died when she was 65 but it was my turn for a surprise because she left me £400 then. A real surprise.

I can barely remember me wedding day: we did get married in the big church so I really should have remembered better. July 12, 1919, when Albert was 46 and I was 31, at the Parish Church in Melton. Me dad was there to sign the Marriage Certificate as a witness. He signed saying he was a carpenter. Our marriage was also witnessed by 19-year-old Tommy and me sister Fanny. I was really glad she was there.

Then we had a home of our own. When we were offered a Council house at #9 Springfield Street, Melton Mowbray we took it. We would have a new house with indoor plumbing! I set about making a home for us simple and cheerful. Yes, we had an aspidistra in the window of our house.

I set about cleaning houses while Albert prepared the meals for us. He was good at fixing things. I think we were a reasonably contented pair.

We went through the Great War with little Reggie as a baby. We had shortages so life was ….. y'know. We made do.

After Reggie came Edwin in 1921 and then George in 1923. Everything became better for Edwin and George. Tommy was working so we were all alright. I always thought of Tommy as me own son. The people of Melton did not know any different: we didn't say anything. He was a timekeeper on the railway. After the Great War, he married Rebecca Fisher. They were both 22. That would be 1922, I think.

(Photographer: Unknown) Yes, there they are with Reggie. They must have been on an outing before the Second War broke out. They all looked happy, don't they? It is a pity that would not last! This was before Sandra was born. She came along just as the next war started. They had been married a long time by then.

(Photographer: Unknown)

Oh, this is Reggie and Kathleen's wedding: January 1941. It looks cold and no one was dressed for the weather. I was surprised when Reggie told me he wanted to marry. We knew he would be going overseas along with George. We all knew tough times were ahead. Then I heard I had another granddaughter. It was a very long five years but both Reggie and George returned. Sadly, George lost a leg.

(Photographer: Unkown)

Oh, this is me granddaughter, Sandra's wedding picture. There I am in blue. Tommy is on the far left. Becky is next to Sandra. Doesn't Sandra look quite lovely? Becky looks as though she was having trouble with her leg. I see a bandage. We had lost Edwin by then. I think I see Reggie on the back row behind you and Kathleen.

Oh, me mind is wandering around!

(Photographer: R. Heathcote) Oh, this is an old photo! We are outside of our house on Springfield Street. In this photo, Albert looks like an old, old man and would have been close to 80, I think. He had been told he had a weak heart. He was not advised how he should live with his complaint. So, he sat in his chair by the fire all day long, moving very little. This frustrated me! He died in September 1954 at the ripe old age of 82.[27]

I was alone but I did have me sons all around me. I was cozy and comfortable at 9 Springfield Street, Melton Mowbray.

During his life, me Albert told me he was glad he did not follow in his father's footsteps as a knitter. He would talk a lot about his mam and dad: Cath and Joe in their little house in Countesthorpe which seemed so far away. He didn't see them very often. They both died just before I met Albert. He was glad he became a railwayman. When he was born, rail tracks were being laid across the country to move things and people around from city to city.[28]

---

27 This happened while I was visiting his sister-in-law, Auntie Annie, in Camberley.
28 Railway stations were being built in many towns and focal points in villages connecting them to cities, especially London. Stathern had a station with a link to Melton Mowbray, Nottingham and to the coast. They looked like this. Sadly, the village stations closed: only the main lines are now open.

Left: (Photographer: Unknown) So, I have remembered all of me family, all of me sisters. Oh no. Except for Alice who called herself Annie. She had the most interesting life of all. I am glad we have pictures. She was such a pretty girl. Here she is in the 1920s with her dog. Annie became a lady's maid y'know. She travelled the world. Once she went on a voyage to India on H.M.T Neuralia. She sent me a Christmas/New Year Card from the ship with the message "With all good wishes from your loving sister Annie." We were always very close. Annie was then in the employ of a Mrs. Chatfield of Cockermouth in Cumberland. I wrote to her an'all.

Right: (Photographer: Unknown) Oh yes. Here we are on a boat somewhere. I am in the middle of this photograph My hair is a mess! There is Annie on the right. [29]

I remember Albert's eldest sister who was named Lucy like me. She married Edwin Immins who was a policeman in Clarendon Park in Leicester. After he died, Lucy moved to Melton to be closer to us. She died a couple of years after the Second war ended.

Oh, I remember Albert's elder brother, John an'all. He was a railway train examiner first in the Leicester area and then he moved to Melton and lived near us at 215 Thorpe Road. Then off he went to Yorkshire.

(Photographer: R. Heathcote)
Edwin and Betty's wedding

---

29 Auntie Annie took the opportunity that presented itself to her: to travel. As such she received a different kind of education. She was worldlier, displayed more energy but was no less gentle. Why didn't I pay more attention?

Oh yes. This is when me son Edwin married Betty. Edwin and George look so alike! I liked Betty. She was such a gentle person. Reggie and Tommy are missing. I expect Reggie was taking the picture.[30] Don't I look smart standing there next to George? Albert is smart too, next to Edwin, but looks his age. Yes, this was June 1950, outside the church in Melton.

I remember we all met at 9 Springfield Street before the wedding so the bridesmaids would know what they had to do. That was when they all joked about Isle, Altar, Hymn. The little girls did not understand that of course!

Left: (Photographer: R. Heathcote) The next year after Edwin and Betty married, in September, I think, Sally Ann was born. I had another granddaughter. This would be the last photo of that family. We didn't know Edwin would soon be gone although he did not look well in this picture. Oh, so sad. Edwin was a bricklayer y'know. He died of cancer so young. He was only 39. I could not bear to see him waste away at home. Betty was so strong and took care of him. Little Sally Ann was only 10. That would be in the early 60s.[31]

Right: (Photographer: Unknown) Oh yes. A couple of years later George married June. They had two sons, Adrian and Stephen so I had two grandsons to add to me two granddaughters. George lost a leg during the war. He was in Ordnance. We were very glad to see him home.

After Edwin died, I did not know that I was soon to lose another of me sons. It isn't right when sons die before their mothers. I thought of Tommy as me son as he had been for so many years. Tommy died of a heart attack when he was only 64.

---

30 I am the bridesmaid on the right. I recall being prepared for the wedding including my duties.
31 I saw him in the later stages of his disease and was horrified how ill he looked. A skeleton of a man. He looked yellow. The first really ill and dying person I had every seen.

Here I am in Stathern celebrating a birthday. This is the last picture you have of me!
(Photographer: R. Heathcote) Grandma Heathcote, Auntie Olive Brown, Auntie Becky Heathcote and Auntie Beat.

I remember fondly your great Grandma Lucy Heathcote who died on September 20, 1972, in Melton Mowbray, not too long after the photo was taken of her with the family. She was 84. She had outlived three of her four sons. Little did we know how close she was to outlive them all. But that is another story.

So now we move to the grandad Heathcote's side of the family. But first, the female side: the Warburtons.

ENDNOTES

The Heathcotes were not a close-knit family which is the reason I know so little about them. I had no idea that your great Grandma Lucy Heathcote had brothers and sisters, except for Auntie Annie. We just didn't talk to her about them. A great pity.

During his life, your great-grandfather, Albert, had the wisdom not to follow in his father's footsteps in a dying industry. You will learn about them next. Rather, he took advantage of the opportunities offered by the industrial revolution. When he was born, rail tracks were being laid across the country to provide transportation of raw materials and finished goods produced as the new factories kicked into gear. I am certain as a young boy he engaged in train spotting and perhaps aspired to be an engine driver. While that was not to be, he did acquire skills that supported the new and growing means of transport. He learned new skills: he could fix things. Again, he wasn't talking and neither were we.

I feel I have minimal memories of this grandfather. He neither influenced, nor inspired. I cannot say that he had any effect on my life.

(Photographer: Unknown) With your Nana and our beloved dog, Suzie. These are all the photographs I have of Auntie Annie. I was close to her but again did not ask her about her family. I visited her in Camberley when I was 12. It was there that she took me to have my ears pierced. For that reason alone, she is always in my memory. I have no evidence that she married even though she did talk about a man. She said she worshipped the ground he walked on. I think he must have been killed in the Second World War. Auntie Annie died sometime in the early 1960s. When I moved to London, I was given some of her furniture: A lovely round table that was stackable on a stand and two easy chairs. I recall your grandfather helping to clear out her house in Camberley and delivering them to me in London.

I was unable to locate any travel documents recording the travels of my Auntie Annie. I suspect that she travelled before the Great War as she would have been in her twenties and highly desirable as a maid.

(Photographer: Unknown) Younger Annie looking smart with her dog.

(Photographer: Unknown)

(Photographer: Unknown) Auntie Annie on a trip to Torquay dated 1949!

CHART 4
LUCY CAROLINE (BECKWITH) HEATHCOTE

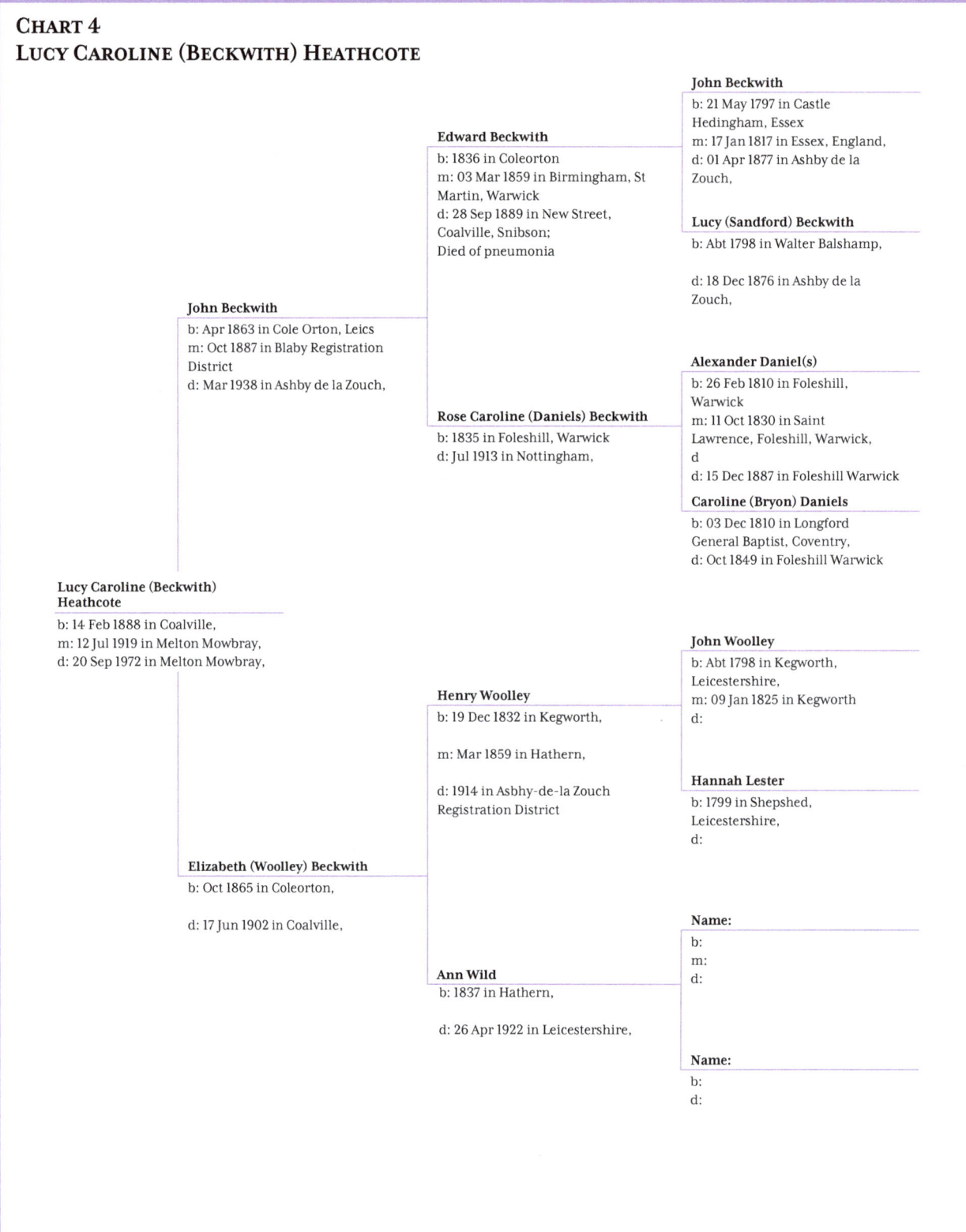

John Beckwith
b: Apr 1863 in Cole Orton, Leics
m: Oct 1887 in Blaby Registration District
d: Mar 1938 in Ashby de la Zouch,

Edward Beckwith
b: 1836 in Coleorton
m: 03 Mar 1859 in Birmingham, St Martin, Warwick
d: 28 Sep 1889 in New Street, Coalville, Snibson;
Died of pneumonia

John Beckwith
b: 21 May 1797 in Castle Hedingham, Essex
m: 17 Jan 1817 in Essex, England,
d: 01 Apr 1877 in Ashby de la Zouch,

Lucy (Sandford) Beckwith
b: Abt 1798 in Walter Balshamp,
d: 18 Dec 1876 in Ashby de la Zouch,

Rose Caroline (Daniels) Beckwith
b: 1835 in Foleshill, Warwick
d: Jul 1913 in Nottingham,

Alexander Daniel(s)
b: 26 Feb 1810 in Foleshill, Warwick
m: 11 Oct 1830 in Saint Lawrence, Foleshill, Warwick,
d
d: 15 Dec 1887 in Foleshill Warwick

Caroline (Bryon) Daniels
b: 03 Dec 1810 in Longford General Baptist, Coventry,
d: Oct 1849 in Foleshill Warwick

Lucy Caroline (Beckwith) Heathcote
b: 14 Feb 1888 in Coalville,
m: 12 Jul 1919 in Melton Mowbray,
d: 20 Sep 1972 in Melton Mowbray,

Henry Woolley
b: 19 Dec 1832 in Kegworth,
m: Mar 1859 in Hathern,
d: 1914 in Asbhy-de-la Zouch Registration District

John Woolley
b: Abt 1798 in Kegworth, Leicestershire,
m: 09 Jan 1825 in Kegworth
d:

Hannah Lester
b: 1799 in Shepshed, Leicestershire,
d:

Elizabeth (Woolley) Beckwith
b: Oct 1865 in Coleorton,
d: 17 Jun 1902 in Coalville,

Ann Wild
b: 1837 in Hathern,
d: 26 Apr 1922 in Leicestershire,

Name:
b:
m:
d:

Name:
b:
d:

5.

THE WARBURTONS

This story tells of the Warburtons, the maternal side of the Heathcotes, and introduces the industry in which they toiled: their story starts in the tough years of the English 17th Century. These then are the earliest ancestors into whose lives we peek. The Pedigree Chart for Benjamin introduces the earliest Warburtons I could find in 1610. The second chart continues the Warburton line. As you see the male line is easier to trace.

The Norman Conquest of England in 1066 brought substantial change to the island nation, including many immigrants with new names, status, and occupations. Among these were the ancestors of the Warburton family, who lived in Cheshire, in the village and parish of *Warburton*. The earliest known person to adopt the name lived in the 13th century. He was descended from a follower of William the Conqueror.[32]

Robert Warburton, born in 1800 in Wigston Magna in north Leicestershire. Robert's father, William, grandfather, William, great grandfather Benjamin, and great, great grandfather John all lived and died in the area. Wigston Magna was a very old, well established large village at that time.

I am grateful to Robert Warburton who contacted me as a result of my research, via Ancestry, into our mutual ancestors. He provided me with an invaluable family tree. We share a common great, great, great grandfather.

---

32 https://one-name.org/results/#Km01rEx2ubmClPRo.99

The Warburtons of the 17th Century had moved south from their ancestral home in Cheshire to Leicester and then to Wigston Magna. The sketch on page 2 indicates its location and proximity to Leicester. Also of interest is the nearby village of Countesthorpe to which your ancestors eventually moved.

At this point in the 17th Century, I wish to further set the scene. We know that the Warburtons were engaged in the production of clothing for men, particularly their hose. But we don't know when this occupation started. Initially, they would have worked the land.

Whereas women wore long dresses which covered their legs, for men the long coat was gradually giving way to doublets, and balloon-shaped knickers: showing as much leg as possible was fashionable. Thinking of Henry VIII, we can immediately picture his wearing a large full ruffle around his neck, a tight-fitting doublet, puffy gauntlet, and fancy stockings above his buckled shoes.

Somewhere around 1560-1590 stockings made from fine silk, rather than from coarse wool, became much desired. While silk, often elaborately embroidered, was becoming a favourite material for the upper classes, it was, however, a Royal and a rich man's material. Commoners were forbidden its use: they wore wool.

From the earliest records I can locate, the Warburtons were involved in producing these leggings using Framework Knitting Machines. Their wives and children were seamers, who sewed the pieces together to produce the finished garment, or they were winders of the yarn. Knowing this tempted me to research this industry further providing a glimpse into their lives. See more in the Endnotes

William (1610) and Elizabeth (1615) Warburton

The earliest Warburton on record is William born in 1610 and his wife Elizabeth born in 1615. We know little about their early lives but do know that in 1648, when she was 33 and he 38, son John was born in Leicester. According to the church records, he was baptized on June 29, 1648. The occupations of these early ancestors are unknown but we can guess: most probably they were farm labourers. Neither do we know whether John was an only child. So, our story moves to he and his wife Ann.

John (1648) and Ann (1660) Warburton

John Warburton married Ann Sargent, a native of Melton Mowbray, in 1681 when she was 21 and he 33. From Church records provided we know this couple had four children in eight years while living in Leicester: William, Margaret, Anne, and John: Their fourth child, John, born in 1688, is our direct ancestor.

The Normans originally began the construction of the Cathedral Church of Saint Martin in Leicester, which was where Ann and John's children would have been baptized. The church was extended and rebuilt over the centuries and was nominated to cathedral status in 1927. As is the tradition, to achieve status as a city, there must be a cathedral situated within its boundaries.

Beyond knowing the family lived in Leicester, how they lived and how they supported themselves is unknown. Similarly, I can find no trace of the other children or the couple's whereabouts after 1688. So, our story moves to our ancestor, John.

John (1688-1745) and Grace Vice Warburton (1691-1745)

John, the fourth child of John and Ann Warburton, married Grace Vice from nearby Blaby on September 12, 1709, in the Parish of Saint Mary in Leicester. She was the daughter of Deborah and William Vice. This couple had four sons: John (1702-), Charles (1725-1762), George (1727-), and Benjamin (1730-1785) who was our direct ancestor. All were born in Wigston Magna. Since I have no information about this family, we move to Benjamin.

Benjamin (1730-1785) and Mary Marten Warburton (1735-1785)

Benjamin Warburton married Mary Marten on March 25, 1754, in Wigston Magna where they established a home. They were blessed with 8 children: John, Robert, William, Anne, Benjamin, John, Elizabeth, and Mary. Two babies died within a year of birth. Benjamin Warburton's family group sheet will help you follow their story.

Mary might have looked lovingly at her first daughter, Anne, during her baptism on April 3, 1761, in the 13th Century All Saints Church in Wigston Magna. The church bells would have signalled the joyful occasion; a new child had been born, named, and welcomed into the church community.

What would life offer her? Mary may have wondered.

Mary had nurtured Anne for only one year before Anne's brother Benjamin arrived, followed too quickly by Elizabeth who sadly died within the year. Another baby was born in 1770 and named John even though there was already a John, aged 16, in the family. George was born much too soon after John in 1771 and died later that year. Almost as if a child was being replaced, another baby, born in 1772 was named Elizabeth. Mary's last child, a daughter named after herself, was born in 1775, when she was 40 years old.

Could she have imagined Anne marrying her beau, John Pallatt in that same church some 20 years later?

On that occasion, she might have felt her husband's hand resting on her shoulder, their grown sons, John, Robert, and William, dressed in their Sunday best, sharing this momentous occasion, their Anne marrying. Young John might have shot his mother a cheeky grin: she might have smiled in return. She felt proud of her handsome twelve-year-old with the lovely brown eyes.

Mary witnessed Anne's nuptials announced by the joyful sounds of melodic church bells in 1783 followed in 1784 by the birth of her first grandson, John. Sadly Anne, pregnant again, said goodbye to her 55-year-old father the following year. There is no further trace of mother Mary who may also have died in the same year. Typhoid fever may have been the cause. The church bells would toll a different tone, sorrowful and sad to mark their departure. Anne bore 13 children in 16 years; at least four did not reach adulthood. My heart goes out to this woman. She must have been permanently exhausted, sleep-deprived, and stressed: constantly pregnant and in the state of grief. Or was there relief when a child did not live resulting in fewer mouths to feed?

"What's wrong, Mum?" Sam Pallatt, Anne's eight-year-old son might have asked his weeping mother. "Your uncles: John, Bob, Will and Ben. All gone." She responded shaking her head at the sudden loss of four of her brothers.

The date was December 15, 1800, as they were preparing for Christmas. An unimaginable tragedy shattered the lives of four families as they faced the premature death of four grown men, all on the same day, leaving two grieving widows and seven children without a father. John died (aged 46); Robert (aged 44) leaving a wife,

Elizabeth, no children; our ancestor William died (aged 42) leaving Anne with seven children. 30-year-old unmarried Ben also died on that day. I am unable to confirm whether there was an accident or illness that caused the heartbreak in the family. Death certificates are unavailable.

When this family tragically lost their father, William's widow Anne was not yet 40, with mouths to feed. No doubt her two teenage sons willingly helped. We also know that the village of Wigston Magna was heavily populated with Warburtons. A support system would have been readily available for this family because that is how they all lived. Moreover, each child would have had Godparents, usually three. The status of a Godparent was taken seriously for spiritual support as well as emotional and financial assistance. Anne lived only 12 more years.

Our direct ancestor, William, was Benjamin and Mary's third son and is the subject of the next section.

William (1758-1800) and Anne (1761-1499) Warburton.

William married Anne Eltington on January 6, 1783, in Wigston Magna when she was 21 years of age and he 24. William and Anne would have four sons, William, Thomas, Benjamin, and Robert, and three daughters, Elizabeth, Anne, and Mary in 14 years. All survived to adulthood. Their first son, William arrived soon after the nuptials on April 11, 1783, and was our direct ancestor. He will be the subject of the next story.

While researching this period, I found confirmation of the occupation of the Warburtons as Framework Knitters, an activity in which all the family members participated, and one which could be carried out at home. I tell you more about Framework knitting in the Endnotes.

The Ruddington Museum in Nottinghamshire, displays what life would have been like for framework knitters, life that revolved around the knitting frame with every adult member of the family taking turns to operate its intricacies if they possessed sufficient strength and dexterity. A cottage industry indeed.

Since considerable physical effort was required, men usually operated the frame. Strength and good eye-sight were essential. The machine required frequent adjustments. It produced a flat piece of material, which would be removed from the frame and seamed, forming a fully fashioned stocking. Women and the elder daughters usually seamed the hose. Younger children or women wound the thread from hanks onto bobbins.

All four of William and Anne's sons became framework knitters. Their eldest daughter, Elizabeth did not marry but stayed home we assume as a housekeeper until her death at age 39. Their second daughter, Anne, born on March 29, 1789, married a Thomas Humberstone. He too was a framework knitter, a local.

The year 1800 would have been life-changing for Anne without her husband. But cope she did.

Our story continues with a glimpse into the lives of Anne and William's son, William, and his wife Elizabeth.

William (1783-1866) and Elizabeth (1782-1861) Humberstone Warburton

William was just 17 when his father suddenly died along with three of his uncles. The disruption to the family would have been unimaginable. William became the head of the family assuming responsibility to help his traumatized mother sustain the family. That year a little boy had been born to a local girl, presumably to William's sweetheart. During the first few years of his life, he remained in the care of the family of Elizabeth Humberstone, his mother. The Humberstones were locals, framework knitters, already related by marriage. For whatever reason, William did not marry Elizabeth until January 29, 1804, when they were both 21 years old. Did her parents and his mother believe they were too young to marry earlier? Was William needed at home? We do not know. We do know that this child was our ancestor, Robert, much loved I am sure by the whole family who had endured a heart-breaking loss.

William and Elizabeth would have 11 children in 19 years. Anne, born shortly after they married, did not marry and lived to aged 33. A daughter, named Mary was born next but lived only months. But Elizabeth, pregnant again gave birth that same year to Thomas who lived to 26. The records indicate that Elizabeth's next child, a daughter named Elizabeth, was married at 15 to a 20-year-old Richard Newby on September 16, 1823. Sadly, Elizabeth died on December 6, 1826, at the age of 18. We can surmise she died in childbirth. In 1811 Elizabeth gave birth to another daughter she named Mary, who on March 16, 1830, married a local man, a William Leach, both aged 19. He was a Framework Knitter. Elizabeth's next child was named William after his father and grandfather. I tell you this so you can imagine the turmoil. This was a time when too many children were being born because of poverty and the conditions in which they all lived. Many babies died as was expected. Women suffered stress in their bodies and hearts while trying to nurture and feed their families, a wretched time to live. And yet some did live long lives.

Within the next few years, William, Elizabeth, and their family moved a few miles away to the village of Countesthorpe where son John (1815) and daughter Hannah (1817) were born. I believe the family then returned to Wigston Magna where Elizabeth then gave birth to two more girls. Elizabeth died in 1861 at the age of 78. William then lived with family members for five more years.

Delving further into this framework knitting culture, the report by the Royal Commission on Children in Factories, in 1833, described the work as drudgery where children contributed to the labour force: This report of the framework knitters' states:

> *…they are, many of them, unhealthy and dyspeptic; …from the long period of labour endured in a close and confined atmosphere…. I can tell a stockinger well by his appearance; there is a paleness and certain degree of emaciation and thinness about them. Wages have fallen in each branch of the framework knitting trade during the last 30 years, about thirty percent. The workmen… are physically deteriorated; they are mentally depressed and too often morally debased. Ill fed, ill lodged, and ill clothed… they are a class… easily distinguishable from most others by their personal appearance… hopeless poverty is producing fearful demoralisation…*

(I have been given permission to use this image by Andy Nicholson, Thornton Society/Nottinghamshire Heritage Gateway)

The Warburton family living room might have looked as in this picture, extracted from the Framework Knitters Museum in Ruddington, Nottinghamshire, where framework knitting was a family affair with three generations working happily together. But I doubt it!

The Warburtons and many like them in the same trade were forced to deal with a change in conditions: firstly, men's fashions had undergone drastic changes between the late 1700s to the mid-1850s. Men needed more practical garments that would provide greater freedom of movement, warmth, and better protection of their lower body. Besides, they no longer wanted to have to contend with putting-on stockings or tights and holding them up. In 100 years, there was then a progression in men's fashion ranging from different styles of breeches to the creation of trousers. Instead of drawing attention to their family jewels, the new tighter fitting trousers emphasized men's legs. Sproles and Burns (1994) refer to the theory of shifting erogenous zones where changes in fashion "occur because of changes in perceived erogenous zones of the human body." Does this mean that since the 18th century, men's legs and possibly their posterior and frontal views, although covered, have become the focal points for defining their manliness?[33]

Secondly, they contended with the effects of the Industrial Revolution: Machines capable of making several items at once were developed. This ability drove down the value of the product and caused more economic hardship to the workers. Frame owners rented out more and more frames—without an increase in the demand for stockings. As the industry progressed, with more automated wider frames, the frames moved out of homes and into factories. Though machines for weaving and spinning began using water and steam for power by the late 18th century, knitting was one of the last areas of textile production to benefit from industrialization.

Read the story of a Mr. George Rippington who lived and died a framework knitter in Blaby, Leicesershire, near where our ancestors lived. He died of diabetes and exhaustion. He provides a glimpse into the lives of our Warburton ancestors.

I have painted a picture of the frame knitter's life as being gruelling, poorly paid, demoralizing even. *Life as a framework knitter was tough. The hours were long and working conditions cramped, uncomfortable, and dangerous.*[34]

Merchants, the middlemen, took their cut while wealthy frame owners rented out the machines and drove hard bargains. Knitters paid rental for the frames whether there was work or not.

This was a century of poverty and wretchedness for this side of our family, the stockingers of the Leicester area. Did they have any time for fun and joy? Did they sing and dance? Did the children have time to explore the countryside, climb trees, bird watch, search for bird's nests, forage for food items, collect kindling and play games with stones? We hope so but......

The lives of William's son, Robert, and his family, will be the subject of the next story.

ENDNOTES

What is Framework Knitting?

Knitting using a frame, as opposed to by hand, was known as framework knitting. The frames were the height of a man, built of heavy timber, operated by foot pedal, and needed stamina and concentration: it was physically demanding, backbreaking work. Days were long, as many as seventeen hours at the frame. Both feet were used to operate the pedals and the weaver used his arms to move the heavy iron carriage in its frame. A stocking-frame used bearded needles, which have long stems with ends that curve backward to form a simple hook. Using a series of treadles and plates, loops are formed by laying a thread over the stem of all of the needles. Then small metal plates were pushed between each needle until loops are formed and pushed into the hooks. The hooks close and as the carriage of needles is released new loops are formed and pulled through the previous row of stitches.

The wool, cotton, or silk used in the process was first spun into yarn using a spinning wheel; then wound onto bobbins which would be placed in the knitting frame. The yarn was usually collected by the weaver from

---

33 (https://www.bloomsbury.com/uk/changing-appearances)
34 https://www.frameworkknittersmuseum.org.uk/about-us/history/

a local merchant when he went to sell his output and collect his pay. Pay was very poor, materials had to be bought, rent for the frame and accommodation had to be found. A buyer would reject faulty work.

Besides narrow band ribbon weaving, wider broadband material was also produced using a similar but different type of frame. The name 'piece work' comes from the price paid to the broadloom weaver for a 'piece', or length, of the material. The measure of length of broadband material was the 'el', the distance between fingers and elbow.

Origin of the Framework Knitting Machine-the Stocking Frame

Following the demands of the prevailing fashion, particularly in men, in 1589 an entrepreneurial sort by the name of William Lee, living in the small Nottinghamshire town of Calverton, invented the stocking frame. As in all good stories there are subplots and unconfirmed facts and this one is no exception. It is said that Lee's inspiration to create a device to speed up the act of knitting was a woman. In some versions of the story the woman is a sweetheart who paid more attention to her knitting than to Lee; in others it was to help his poor overworked wife, as he was distressed to see how diligently she toiled over her handwork. On the other hand, perhaps his endeavours were motivated more by money than by love.

Lee, like any savvy businessman, decided to take advantage of the wealth that the industry was producing. Lee provided Queen Elizabeth 1 with a pair of stockings woven on his frame but she refused to grant him a patent because they were coarser than the French silk stockings she used. The Queen, apparently, bowed to the pressure of the knitters' guilds for fear of putting hand-knitters out of work. Lee packed up his machine and headed to the town of Troyes in northern France where he benefitted under the patronage of Henry IV: his frame gave rise to a flourishing industry there. Henry's assassination in 1610 put an end to Lee's success: he died in poverty. His brother James, however, returned to England, improved the frame and slowly established a framework knitting industry.[35]

By the outbreak of the English Civil War (1642-49) there were only a few hundred knitting frames in use. The Company of Framework Knitters was formed in London in 1657 enabling the trade to be regulated.

Training as an apprentice to become a journeyman led to the designation as a master framework knitter which took seven years. The trade at this point was focussed in London but, as the activity became closely regulated, knitters started to move their businesses to the Midlands: The counties of Leicestershire, Nottinghamshire, and Derbyshire in particular, where hand-operated stocking frames were first used.

While fashions for wealthy women of the time were intricate, elaborate, and also included knitted leggings, peasant women would have sported a more practical dress. They wore long skirts for warmth. They wore dark colours and owned very few clothes. Both wealthy and poor women covered their hair with some form of elaborate or simple cap, most probably made by the ladies of the household. A woman's status was defined by the hat or head covering she wore. Following demand, English knitters stopped making caps, previously a highly sought-after item, and started stitching stockings. This led to hosiery becoming a very important export trade, especially in the East Midlands.

Framework knitting was the first major stage in the mechanization of the textile industry and played an important role in the early history of the Industrial Revolution.[36]

---

35 https://en.wikipedia.org/wiki/Stocking_frame
36 https://en.wikipedia.org/wiki/Wigston

Pedigree Chart for Benjamin Warburton

Benjamin Warburton
b: 1730 in Wigston Magna,
m: 25 Mar 1754 in Wigston Magna,
d: 17 Jul 1785 in Leicestershire,

- **John Warburton**
  b: 1688 in Wigston Magna,
  m: 12 Sep 1709 in Saint Mary, Leicester,
  d: Unknown
  - **John Warburton**
    b: Abt 1648 in Leicester,
    m: Juy 10, 1681
    d: Unknown
    - **William Warburton**
      b: Abt 1610 in Unknown
      m: Unknown
      d: Unknown
    - **Elizabeth Warburton**
      b: Abt 1615 in Unknown
      d: Unknown
  - **Ann (Sargent) Warburton**
    b: Abt 1660 in Melton Mowbray,
    d: Unknown
    - **Peter Sargent**
      b: Melton Mowbray
      m:
      d:
    - **Name:**
      b:
      d:
- **Grace Vice (Warburton)**
  b: 1691 in Blaby,
  d: Unknown
  - **William Vice**
    b: Abt 1659 in Blaby
    m: Unknown,
    d: 12 May 1718
    - **Name:**
      b:
      m:
      d:
    - **Name:**
      b:
      d:
  - **Deborah Vice**
    b: Unknown in Leicestershire,
    d: Unknown in Leicestershire,
    - **Name:**
      b:
      m:
      d:
    - **Name:**
      b:
      d:

CHART 5B
ROBERT WARBURTON AND HIS ANCESTORS

- **Robert Warburton**
  b: 1800 in Great Wigston,
  m: 14 Apr 1822 in Countesthorpe,
  d: 26 Jun 1875 in Blaby,
  - **William Warburton**
    b: 1783 in Wigston
    m: 29 Jan 1804 in Greater Wigston,
    d: 26 Mar 1866 in Leicester,
    - **William Warburton**
      b: 05 Nov 1758 in Wigston Magna,
      m: 06 Jan 1783 in Wigston Magna,
      d: 15 Dec 1800 in Wigston Magna,
      - **Benjamin Warburton**
        b: 1730 in Wigston Magna,
        m: 25 Mar 1754 in Wigston Magna,
        d: 17 Jul 1785 in Leicestershire,
      - **Mary (Marten) Warburton**
        b: 1745 in Wigston Magna,
        d: Unknown
    - **Anne Eltington**
      b: 1760 in Wigston Magna,
      d:
  - **Elizabeth (Humberstone) Warburton**
    b: 21 Apr 1782 in Greater Wigston,
    d: Abt 1861 in England
    - **William Humberstone**
      b: Unknown
      m: Unknown
      d: Unknown
    - **Catherine Humberstone**
      b: Unknown
      d: Unknown

CHART 5C. FAMILY GROUP SHEET FOR BENJAMIN WARBURTON

HUSBAND: BENJAMIN WARBURTON

Birth:	1730 in Wigston Magna,
Marriage:	25 Mar 1754 in Wigston Magna,
Death:	17 Jul 1785 in Leicestershire,
Father:	John Warburton
Mother:	Grace Vice (Warburton)

WIFE: MARY (MARTEN) WARBURTON

Birth:	1745 in Wigston Magna,
Death:	Unknown

CHILDREN:

1 M		Name: Birth: Death:	John Warburton Abt 1754 in Greater Wigston, 15 Dec 1800 in Wigston Magna,
2 M		Name: Birth: Death:	**Robert Warburton** 29 Feb 1756 in Greater Wigston, 15 Dec 1800
3 M		Name: Birth: Marriage: Death: Spouse:	William Warburton 05 Nov 1758 in Wigston Magna, 06 Jan 1783 in Wigston Magna, 15 Dec 1800 in Wigston Magna, Anne Eltington
4 F		Name: Birth: Death: Spouse:	Anne (Warburton) Pallatt 02 Apr 1761 in Greater Wigston, Apr 1847 in Wigston, John Pallett
5 M		Name: Birth: Death:	Benjamin Warburton 1762 in Wigston Magna, 15 Dec 1800 in Wigston Magna
6 F		Name: Birth: Death:	Elizabeth Warburton 1767 in Wigston Magna, Nov 1767
7 M		Name: Birth: Death:	John Warburton 1770 in Wigston Magna, 1850 in Blaby
8 M		Name: Birth: Death:	George Warburton 1771 in Wigston Magna, 1771 in Wigston Magna,

6.

THE WARBURTONS OF THE 19TH CENTURY

In the prior story, we glimpsed the lives of our ancestors, the Warburtons. We also delved into their work environment. We continue with the 19th century Warburtons.

The population of Britain boomed during the 1800s from 9 million to about 41 million people by 1900. The Warburtons made a significant contribution to this increase. Our story continues with our great, great, grandfather, Robert, born at the dawn of the 19th Century.

Our ancestor Robert was born in 1800 in Wigston Magna, four years before his presumed parents were married. His father, William, would have been only 16 years of age, and his mother Elizabeth, 17, when he was born. This was also the year of the tragedy in the family: Robert's father and three uncles suddenly lost their lives.

Robert was a framework knitter. He married on April 14, 1822, in the village of Countesthorpe. His bride Sarah Findley was a young lady from that village. The daughter of Nathaniel and Frances Findley, Sarah was born in May 1806. Shortly before their wedding, Sarah gave birth to a daughter she named Ann. Sarah's mother would have held the six-week-old child as her daughter walked down the aisle on that spring day. Ann was adopted by her father and took his name. Sarah was unaware nine years later she would lose both her parents.

"How did our village get its name, Grandad?" Ann might have asked her grandfather Findley one day. He may not have known that Countesthorpe originated from the 11th century when the area was part of the marriage dowry of the Countess Judith, niece of William the Conqueror. The 'thorpe' part of the name is a variant of the Middle English word thorp, meaning hamlet or small village.

In 1870-72, John Marius Wilson's *Imperial Gazetteer of England and Wales* described *COUNTESTHORPE, a chapelry in Blaby parish, in Leicestershire; on a branch of the river* [37] *Some of the inhabitants are stocking-makers.*

Robert was one of the most fertile of our ancestors. He lived with Sarah during his formative years and must have been concerned when she endured difficult childbirths and child losses. In January 1842, they mourned the loss of baby Eliza who lived only a few weeks. After giving birth to 9 children of which 3 did not survive to adulthood, Robert held his wife's hand tenderly as she quietly left him. The date was April 24, 1842: she was 38. As he looked at her face he wondered: How could I have prevented the life she had endured with so many lost children? How could I have prevented loosing her? He remembered too that Sarah had lost her parents 11 years earlier: Frances in April and Nathaniel in August of 1831. But he could not indulge in self-reflection too long as he had 5-year-old Robbie and baby Tommy to care for at that time. But then he had two elder daughters, Ann and little Lizzie who would have sprung into action despite their own sorrow.

After Sarah's death, Robert became aware of the Root family: no surprise since both families lived in Countesthorpe, a village with some 200 families. At the head of the Root family was Josiah, a widower. After her mother died in 1838, eldest daughter Jane at 23 became the main housekeeper to her 65-year-old father living in Little End, Countesthorpe, with brother, John, and three younger sisters. Josiah, a woollen hosier was on the voter's list. To vote, he must have been a landowner, possibly his home: a man then of substance.

On February 18, 1844, Robert Warburton married 28-year-old Jane. She would have been considered an old maid by that age, on the shelf indeed: but preoccupied with raising her mother's children and no virgin! She was well into her pregnancy at the time of her marriage and gave birth to a daughter, she named Catherine after her mother, in April that year. Did Robert have a relationship with Jane or was he gallant to help her out of an unfortunate situation? We will never know for sure who fathered the little girl. But I have assumed it was Robert, who connects our ancestry to the Warburtons. Catherine Warburton, known as Cath, was our direct ancestor. I note that this Catherine was spelled with an e, but then who cared in those days? Just details!

"Cath has boyfriend" proclaimed John Henry Warburton. Cath glared at her annoying younger brother. "I seen them too," added George, "Joey Heathcote". The two boys giggled their way out of the kitchen as 18-year-old Cath swiped at the two of them and then complained to her mother as she stirred the soup bubbling on the blackened stove. Cath was visiting the family for the evening while also seeing her sweetheart. She glanced at her father working on the knitting frame: He returned her look and winked. Elder brother Robert was about to relieve their father on the frame. Both men looked exhausted, she thought. John Henry and George had been winding yarn all afternoon after attending the school. Cath felt a pang of envy that she had not taken advantage of the schooling she had been offered. While Cath could not read or write, she could tell a good tale and listen too.

"Tell me about your Mam," she asked Jane who stopped stirring to remember her mother. "She married me dad on Christmas day 1811. She was 39 then so no one expected babies. But then our Will was born and then our Jane. Three years later there was John and then there was our Catharine and then Alice. Mam was really old then, about 50, I think. But to everybody's surprise, she kept going. Jimmy arrived! And then our Becky. We

---

37 https://en.wikipedia.org/wiki/Countesthorpe

were so overcrowded! We were all sad when Josiah Johnson died so soon after he arrived. But our Mam was tired and fed up with babies but still, she had our Ann when she was 62. I couldn't believe it."[38]

"You must have worked hard an'all Mam." commented Cath. "Aye I did. I was doing for everybody and had no time for meself. I became Mam to John then 20, Sarah, 17, Alice, 16, Jimmy 15, Becky 13, and young Ann aged 4. I remember when me mam died four years later in July 1838. She had 10 children after she was over 40." Jane smiled at her eldest daughter as she remembered her mother and her life with so many children. She thought then of her own. She had married Robert after he lost the love of his life, Sarah, who had tragically died in childbirth at a young age. Jane was 28 when she became an instant mother to his children: Cath was on the way when they married. She smiled to herself as she remembered seeing her daughter for the first time and looked at her now: A grown woman. Sadness crept over her face as she remembered giving birth to Henry followed by John and losing them both so quickly after welcoming them into the world. Happily, John Henry was healthy as were George and Eliza.

"Our dad had so many children" commented Cath. "I don't want to have that many." Her mother smiled a knowing smile and added. "Then make sure you don't my girl." Cath wondered how she could avoid the poverty associated with framework knitters and heart-breaking baby deaths. Joe was a framework knitter. She felt she would be stepping into a life she knew but times were changing. She hoped they were ready.

Your great, great grandmother, Catherine Warburton, daughter of a framework knitter, married Joseph Heathcote, a framework knitter on January 8, 1865, in the Parish of St. Mary's, Leicester. And that is another story. I wonder why they did not marry in Countesthorpe in the local church!

Many of Robert's children became framework knitters. The lure of the knitting machine appeared to be in their blood. But did they have alternatives? Then another occupation appeared: that of asylum attendant.

The Warburtons of the 19th Century rode the wave of Framework Knitting while their descendants witnessed its decline: fashions were changing. Demand for their chief product fell sharply. Framework knitters would have responded to this change in fashion by producing half hose for the aristocrats and socks for men, women, and children. Worsted socks became popular.

Then during the 1880s and 1890s, with the wide adoption of steam power, factories in all areas of the textile industry were extensively developed. This sealed the fate of the hand-operated knitting frames, the precursor of the new textile weaving machines: they were relegated to history. Lee's machine for making stockings came into existence a good 200 years earlier than other mechanical devices for textile manufacturing. The spinning Jenny, for example, didn't come along until 1764; the power looms invented by Richard Arkwright and Edmund Cartwright appeared in 1769 and 1784, respectively.[39]

From the mid-century onwards, Queen Victoria's government began to introduce acts to improve the conditions in factories and also an education act requiring children to attend school until age 10, preventing them from being available for labour in the framework factories. This added pressure on the industry hastened the demise of the hand-worked frame.

---

38 I have verified that while giving birth naturally at that advanced age is rare it is not unheard of. (*The Lancet Medical Journal reported in 1887 the case of an English woman who had given birth, at the age of 62 years and 6 months, to three boys, real triplets, her 11th, 12th, and 13th children with her husband.* https://en.wikipedia.org/wiki/Pregnancy_over_age_50tps://en.wikipedia.org/wiki/Pregnancy_over_age_50)

39 http://www.intriguing-history.com/spinning-jenny-industrial-revolution/

Sadly, Cath Warburton did not take advantage of an education: she was illiterate, being unable to sign her name to her marriage certificate. Cath, almost ready to give birth to her 6th child visited her mother one afternoon on a winter's day. "Did you hear about cousin Bill?" She asked her mother referring to the son of Bob and Sarah's son William. "There was an awful accident at Mr Townsend's brickyard. We lost young Bill," she responded.[40]

In the next story, we imagine the lives of Cath and Joe Heathcote.

ENDNOTES

I recall there was a hosiery factory in Stathern when I was young. Now demolished and replaced with housing.

Living History

The museum in Ruddington, Nottinghamshire, provides a glimpse of how the framework knitters lived. There we find two cottages where the knitters and their families lived, a larger workshop building, and a few outbuildings. All are set out around a quadrangle of approximately 2,000 square feet. The workshop, where the machines were situated, is clearly identifiable by the plentiful windows on the upper floor, installed to provide the workers with light while they toiled. When it was fully operational this building was the workplace for dozens of knitters.

There is another Framework Knitting Museum in Wigston Magna, near Leicester.

History of Framework Knitting.

The following realistically describes a framework knitter's way of life.
- https://www.youtube.com/watch?v=rpZf7Tz_vXM

The following website provides historical context and describes the Framework Knitters of Leicester.
- https://www.le.ac.uk/lahs/downloads/palmervolume74-5vsm.pdf

A film made for Leicestershire Industrial History Society about Framework Knitting, once one of the most important industries in the East Midlands, UK, shows one of the few people today who know how to operate the frame working in his workshop and explaining how the machine works.

I hope you will take a look.

---

40 The following report was included in the Leicester Chronicle on Saturday 14th December 1878.
Fatal Accident at Countesthorpe - The borough coroner held an inquest on Friday at the Earl of Leicester Infirmary Square touching the death of William Warburton, 24, brickyard labourer Countesthorpe. Deceased worked at the brickyard of Mr. Townsend at Countesthorpe and on Thursday morning was engaged in carrying clay to a brick making machine. About seven o'clock in the morning Charles Page a fellow labourer heard a cry for help and going to the machine found the deceased had fallen into the machine and was held by two cogwheels. Assistance was obtained and after the machine had been reversed the unfortunate man was extricated and removed to Leicester Infirmary. It was then found that the right side of his chest was fractured and seven of his ribs were broken. He died soon after admission - Verdict "Accidental Death."

Leicester as a Centre of the Hosiery Industry[41]

Leicester became the most important centre of the hosiery trade. William Felkin's estimates of the numbers of frames in the various centres of the industry in 1844 show 18,494 hand-operated frames working in Leicester, a farming community, where the products would have been wool-based.

---

41 http://www.localhistories.org/18thcent.html

CHART 6. FAMILY GROUP SHEET FOR ROBERT WARBURTON

SPOUSE:	**ROBERT WARBURTON**
Birth:	1800 in Wigston Magna,
Marriage:	18 Feb 1844 in Countesthorpe, L
Death:	26 Jun 1875 in Blaby,
Father:	William Warburton Anne
Mother:	Eltington

SPOUSE:	**JANE (ROOT) WARBURTON**
Birth:	22 Oct 1815 in Countesthorpe,
Death:	05 May 1884 in England
Father:	Josiah Root
Mother:	Catharine (Lord) Root

CHILDREN:

1 F
- Name: **(Cath) Catherine (Warburton) Heathcote**
- Birth: Apr 1844 in Countesthorpe, Bap April 14
- Marriage: 08 Jan 1865 in Leicester, St. Margarets
- Death: Jul 1912 in Blaby, Leicestershire
- Spouse: **Joseph Heathcote**

2 M
- Name: Henry Warburton
- Birth: Jul 1846 in Countesthorpe, Leicestershire,
- Death: 10 Oct 1846 in Blaby, Leicestershire

3 M
- Name: John Warburton
- Birth: 04 Jun 1848 in Countesthorpe,
- Death: 05 Feb 1849 in Countesthorpe,

4 M
- Name: John Henry Warburton
- Birth: Jul 1851 in Countesthorpe,
- Marriage: 26 May 1874 in Wigston Magna,
- Death: Jun 1920 in Ashby de la Zouch,
- Spouse: Sarah Ann (Hubbard) Warburton

5 M
- Name: "George" Henry Warburton
- Birth: Apr 1853 in Countesthorpe,
- Marriage: 12 Oct 1887
- Burial: 19 Jul 1916 in Nottinghamshire,
- Death: 28 Nov 1916 in Blaby,
- Spouse: Jane Elizabeth Russell

6		Name:	Eliza (Warburton) Morris
F		Birth:	1856 in Countesthorpe,
		Marriage:	22 Apr 1878 in Countesthorpe,
		Death:	Mar 1937 in Leicester,
		Spouse:	David D Morris

7.

THE HEATHCOTE STORY: CATH MARRIES JOE

The Heathcote name originated when the Anglo-Saxon tribes ruled over Britain and literally means "Heath Cottage".[42] The location in Derbyshire was first recorded in the Domesday Book of 1086 as "Hedcote," and as "Hethcote" in 1244. There is a hamlet named Heathcote situated between Matlock and Leek in the Derbyshire Dales where our surname might have originated. Of interest and sad coincidence, this place of origin is close to Stoke on Trent where your grandfather's life ended. As I remember your grandfather with his mid-brown curly hair, his stocky build, and blue eyes, I think that was just how I imagine a Saxon to look. I conveniently forget the Norman blood on his mother's side!

So, we know our surname originated in Derbyshire. Some ancestors moved to neighbouring Leicestershire as did a Francis Heathcote, a farmer, who, in the late 1700s lived in Lockington, a small village in Leicestershire, close to the Derbyshire border. Francis was the father of John who initially apprenticed as a framework knitter but became sufficiently skilled and inventive to modify the frames to create more complex patterns. I have not yet discovered how close these Heathcotes were to our family. Nevertheless, I have included his story in the next chapter for your interest.

Other than knowing the Heathcotes were framework knitters in the 18th and 19th centuries and were Anglo-Saxon farmers before that, I could find no further information about our ancient Heathcote ancestors. The earliest Heathcote I could locate was David who, in 1841 at the age of 30, was engaged in the woollen hosiery business.

---

42 https://en.wikipedia.org/wiki/Heathcote_(surname)

David was born in Countesthorpe and was baptized in St. Andrew's Anglican Parish Church on April 28, 1811. His mother was Elizabeth and father possibly John, I cannot be sure. That they were related to the Heathcotes from Duffield in Derbyshire is very likely.

We know the Heathcotes, the Herberts and, the Warburtons all lived in Countesthorpe. Predictably, David found a sweetheart close by. James Herbert was in the hosiery business, a framework knitter, along with his wife Mary. The Herberts had been in the village for at least a century. Elizabeth (Betsy) Herbert, was the eldest of their six daughters.

The marriage banns were read for David and Betsy on April 27, 1834. The church bells merrily rang for them on July 14 in the church where both were baptized some 23 years earlier. Their first son, James arrived the next year and William two years later. William married into the Root family, the same family to which we referred in a Warburton story. William's wife, Catherine, gave birth to an amazing twelve children reinforcing the Root fertility phenomenon. Both James and William followed in their father's footsteps and looked no further for an occupation. They were all framework knitters, like a few generations before them.

Then Joseph arrived, another son for David and Betsy in October 1842 followed by a daughter they named Elizabeth and then a daughter, Florence Beatrice.

By 1861, Betsy, David, and son, Joseph, were all framework knitters living in Little End in Countesthorpe. There is no Little End these days. The life of a framework knitter as described in the Warburton story is one of hard work, drudgery, poverty, and poor health. Betsy died in 1873 at the age of 62. David, a widower, lived alone and continued to sweat his trade. Knitting was in his blood. He died at the age of 73 in January 1885 having lived all his life in Countesthorpe. His three sons too, James, William, and Joseph, allowed themselves no options. They continued in a dying trade.

Inevitably Catherine Warburton caught Joseph Heathcote's eye. On a chilly January day in 1865, Cath and Joe were married at St. Margaret's in Leicester. He was 21 and she 20. Perhaps Cath wished she could have worn white, just like Queen Victoria had on her wedding day. But Cath's new dress was of a darker, more practical colour. The distance is short: some 11 kilometres from Countesthorpe to Leicester. They must have ridden either in a horse-drawn carriage or by train. A new railway station had just opened in the village.

Here is a copy of their marriage certificate.

Cath and Joe wasted no time starting their family. Indeed, Cath and Joe rolled in the hay long before their marriage. Cath was three months pregnant when they tied the knot. Shortly after their marriage, Cath and Joe found a home at 10 Green Lane, Countesthorpe where Lucy was born in July 1865. She and Joe were fortunate to find their tiny two up and one down home with a scullery out back. Cottages often had mud walls, earth floors, and neglected thatch roofs. Perhaps their home was like that!

After dinner, we can imagine each sipping the small ale she might have brewed. Cath would have been curious about her new family: perhaps she asked about Joe's father. But Joe would have seen little of his father, David, because he was always working. His grandfather had moved the family to Countesthorpe long ago in search of work. Joe explained he never knew his grandfather: he never asked. He knew that his father had been born in the village.

She thought back to their chilly wedding day only a few months before. Cath might have looked wistfully at their marriage certificate. She was proud of her husband who was able to laboriously sign his name on the certificate whereas she could not. We see that Joe had learned the intricacies of cursive writing, an art he had not quite perfected. We see the witnesses to the marriage were David Bee and Mary Herbert. Whereas Mary was Joe's maternal grandmother, David Bee is a mystery.

Then Cath had more babies: After Lucy came John (named after Joe's grandfather perhaps), Robert (after Cath's father) and then Albert George arrived in July, 1872. His names appeared out of the blue! He was our direct ancestor.

Move forward thirty years to April 1911. A mysterious brown envelope appeared in the post: their 1911 census form (each household was required to prepare this census form for the first time in 1911). Cath and Joe were well into their 60s, thoughtfully looking back at their lives. The Census form provided the impetus. In the Endnotes you will see a copy of the census Joe completed. You will see over the years Joe had perfected his cursive writing techniques. The pair had been framework knitters for as long as they could remember. They frequently reminisced about those days, remembering the drudgery, the struggles, the heartbreaks. Joe had given up the frame some ten years earlier in favour of the less strenuous work of a glove-hand, that is glove making using animal skins or using a much smaller glove knitting machine.

Joe looked fondly at his wife of 46 years wondering where the time had gone. But then, time went both quickly and slowly while working the frame. There was no alternative but to work as quickly as possible to produce as many good quality products as they were able. Cath had worked hard putting food on the table, raising children, and keeping up with all the chores. Now only Florence remained at home. Joe watched her. At 22, she was a good worker at home as a hosiery hand. Joe looked around his four-room home in Anderson's Yard in Countesthorpe. Jane Wright lived with them too. She was a seamer, a good worker, yet he described her as feeble-minded: their niece and a little slow. They decided to give her a home, uncertain what would become of her. These two would be included on the form.

Joe and Cath would have examined the Census form which forced them to think of their children. Cath remembered all her nine pregnancies. Three babies died almost as soon as they were born: such a sad time. Lucy married Edwin Immins and moved Leicester way. She didn't have children. They didn't see much of her. John married Annie and also moved Leicester way. He told us he was a railway train examiner but we never understood what he was examining! They had two girls and three little boys and now live in Melton Mowbray, which seems a long way away. We shall perhaps not see our grandchildren.

Joe was thinking of their son Robbie who started in his teenage years as an enthusiastic knitter. After marrying Bertha, they had four sons: Dennis, Joe, Herbie, and Ernie. Both Cath and Joe felt tears fall as they remember their son dying at the age of only 29 leaving Bertha with four little boys. Fortunately, the family lived in Countesthorpe so they were able to help Bertha raise the boys. Oh, that was ten years ago. The boys are teenagers now. Quite grown up.

Cath thought then about her youngest, the one who lived with them now, Florence Beatrice. Cath remembered how she had Florrie when she was 45 and how very tired she felt. It was time she was married but Florrie was waiting. Florrie's elder sister Lizzie married Bill Heywood a couple of years ago. Florrie missed her sister. But the village of Cosby, where the newlyweds lived, was close by so the sisters visited often.

Cath thought about her son, Albert. He chose a different path, a servile life: he became not a domestic servant but a Company Servant, whatever that entailed. We were pleased when he chose the Gillam girl, from an old family who had lived in Countesthorpe for centuries. Cath remembered the lovely June day in 1899 when Albert married Ann Gillam, and remembered her own wedding day too on that chilly January day. Ann and her family were all framework knitters. Yes, and they all had huge families and lived in crowded conditions. Ann was the fourth daughter of William and Eliza (nee Herbert) Gillam. Indeed, yes there were intermarriages taking place in Countesthorpe! The Warburton, Heathcote, Herbert, and Gillam families had known one another for years. So, Albert's choice felt comfortable for us. We didn't think they would move away. They lived at 74 Foston Road, Countesthorpe, and soon had a family: We were so glad to welcome little Thomas who was born at the turn of the century.

Then we heard Albert had joined the industrial revolution: possibly influenced by his brother John, he had followed the growing transportation trend and become a railwayman. Albert's knack for fixing things came to the fore: he became a railway wagon repairer. Twenty-nine-year-old Ann was still a framework knitter.

Then suddenly, Albert and all the family moved to 16 Gorwell Street in Leicester and had adopted a son, Harold Lemmon. So, he left as well. Then we saw our Florrie become dewy-eyed for a young man that Joe and John had found for her! Who knew she would marry George Watkin and the three of them would disappear to Melton Mowbray?

Joe inevitably thought of his parents: David and Betsy who had lived all their lives in the village as he had. Most of his children had moved on as they should. His dear mother Betsy died in 1873 at the early age of 62. She did see four of her grandchildren and was able to help Cath with them. She missed the last two girls and would have liked being part of their lives. Dad David lived to the age of 74 and died in 1885. He was so exhausted. A small man who looked worn out from all the work. I will not be like that!

Cath was also thinking of her parents. Her mam Jane had been very active and helpful when Cath was having her children. Mam knew all about babies! As a widow, she especially wanted to be useful. Sadly, she died before Florrie was born. Sad day: May 5, 1884, when me mam died at the age of 68. Cath was inconsolable: She missed her mam so much. Dad had died already in 1875 at the age of 75. He was missed in the village as well as by us in the family.

Both Cath and Joe died the next year. She in July and he in October. He was 70 years old and she a little younger.

This story has been commingled with that of the Warburton story as they often do in our minds and thoughts. Before we move to your Nana's side of the family, we will imagine the life of a wealthy relative!

ENDNOTES

When your Nana and I visited Countesthorpe and made enquiries about the Heathcotes, we were told that Luddites had driven the framework knitters out of the area. Again, more research was required.

Under Queen Victoria's reign, Great Britain experienced unprecedented expansion in industry, building railways, bridges, underground sewers, and power distribution networks throughout much of the empire.

Queen Victoria continued in her duties up to her death. In keeping with tradition, she spent Christmas 1900 at Osborne House on the Isle of Wight, where her health quickly declined to the point that she was unable to return to London. She died on January 22, 1901, at age 81. Her son and successor King Edward VII and her eldest grandson Emperor Wilhelm II of Germany were both at her bedside.

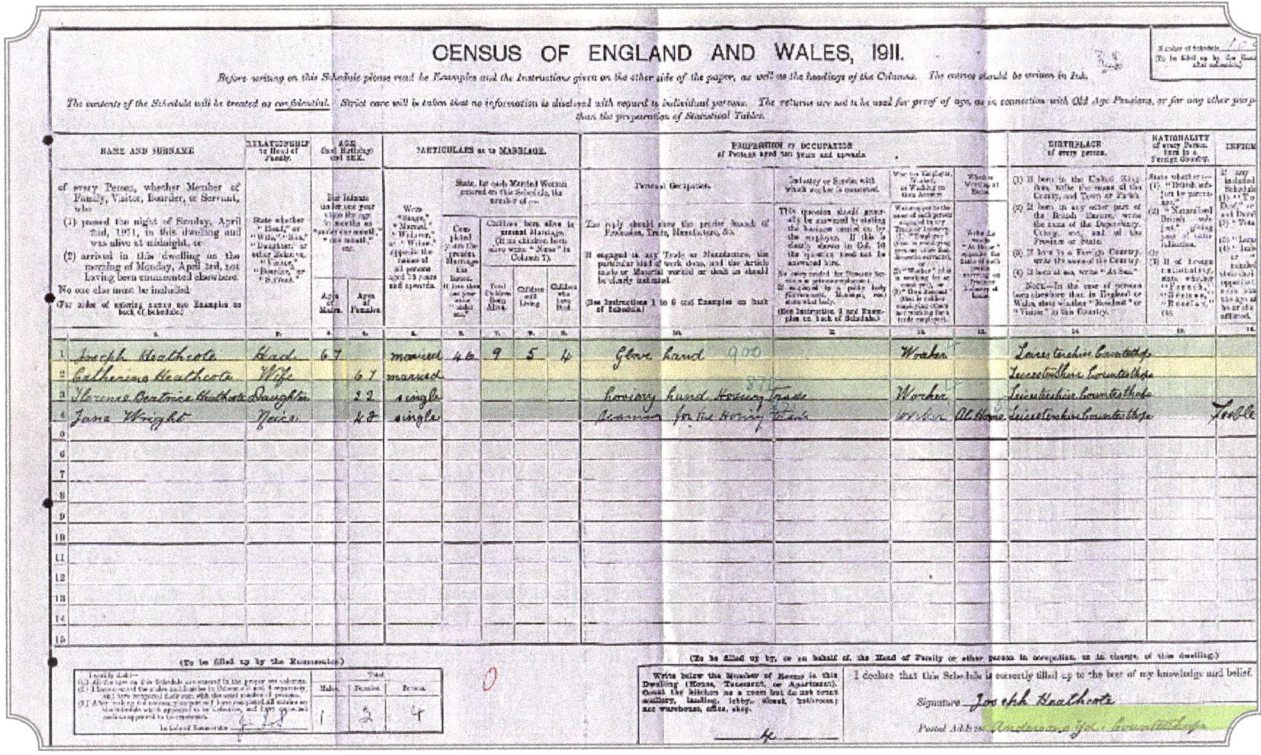

In the 1911 Census, Joseph's writing has improved!!

FAMILY GROUP SHEET FOR CATHERINE (WARBURTON) HEATHCOTE

SPOUSE:	**JOSEPH HEATHCOTE**
Birth:	Oct 1842 in Countesthorpe, ;Baptised April 14,1844
Marriage:	08 Jan 1865 in Leicester, ; St.Margarets
Death:	Oct 1912 in Blaby, Leicestershire
Father:	David Heathcote
Mother:	Elizabeth "Betsy" (Herbert) Heathcote

SPOUSE:	**CATHERINE (WARBURTON) HEATHCOTE**
Birth:	Apr 1844 in Countesthorpe,
Death:	Jul 1912 in Blaby, Leicestershire
Father:	Robert Warburton
Mother:	Jane (Root) Warburton

CHILDREN:

1 F	Name:	Lucy (Heathcote) Immins
	Birth:	Jul 1865 in Countesthorpe
	Death:	Mar 1947 in Melton Mowbray,
	Spouse:	Edwin Immins

2 M	Name:	John Heathcote
	Birth:	Jan 1867 in Countesthorpe,
	Marriage:	1891 in Leicester, Leicestershire
	Death:	Sep 1941 in Leeds, Yorkshire West
	Spouse:	Anne (Annie) (Myatt) Heathcote

3 M	Name:	Robert Heathcote
	Birth:	1871 in Countesthorpe,
	Marriage:	24 Dec 1892 in Blaby, Leicestershire
	Death:	Apr 1900 in Blaby, Leicestershire
	Spouse:	Bertha Ann (Boat) Heathcote

4 M	Name:	**Albert George Heathcote**
	Birth:	Jul 1872 in Countesthorpe,
	Marriage:	Jun 1899 in Blaby,
	Death:	Sep 1954 in Melton Mowbray,
	Spouse:	Ann (Gillam) Heathcote

5 F	Name:	Elizabeth Jane (Heathcote) Heywood
	Birth:	1874 in Countesthorpe,
	Marriage:	Sep 1897 in Blaby, Leicestershire, England
	Death:	Sep 1935 in Blaby,
	Spouse:	William Orange Heywood

6 F	Name:	Florence Beatrice (Heathcote) Watkin
	Birth:	04 Dec 1888 in Countesthorpe,
	Marriage:	01 Jun 1914 in Narborough
	Death:	Mar 1972 in Melton Mowbray,
	Spouse:	George Edward Watkin

Chart 7A
Joseph and the Heathcotes

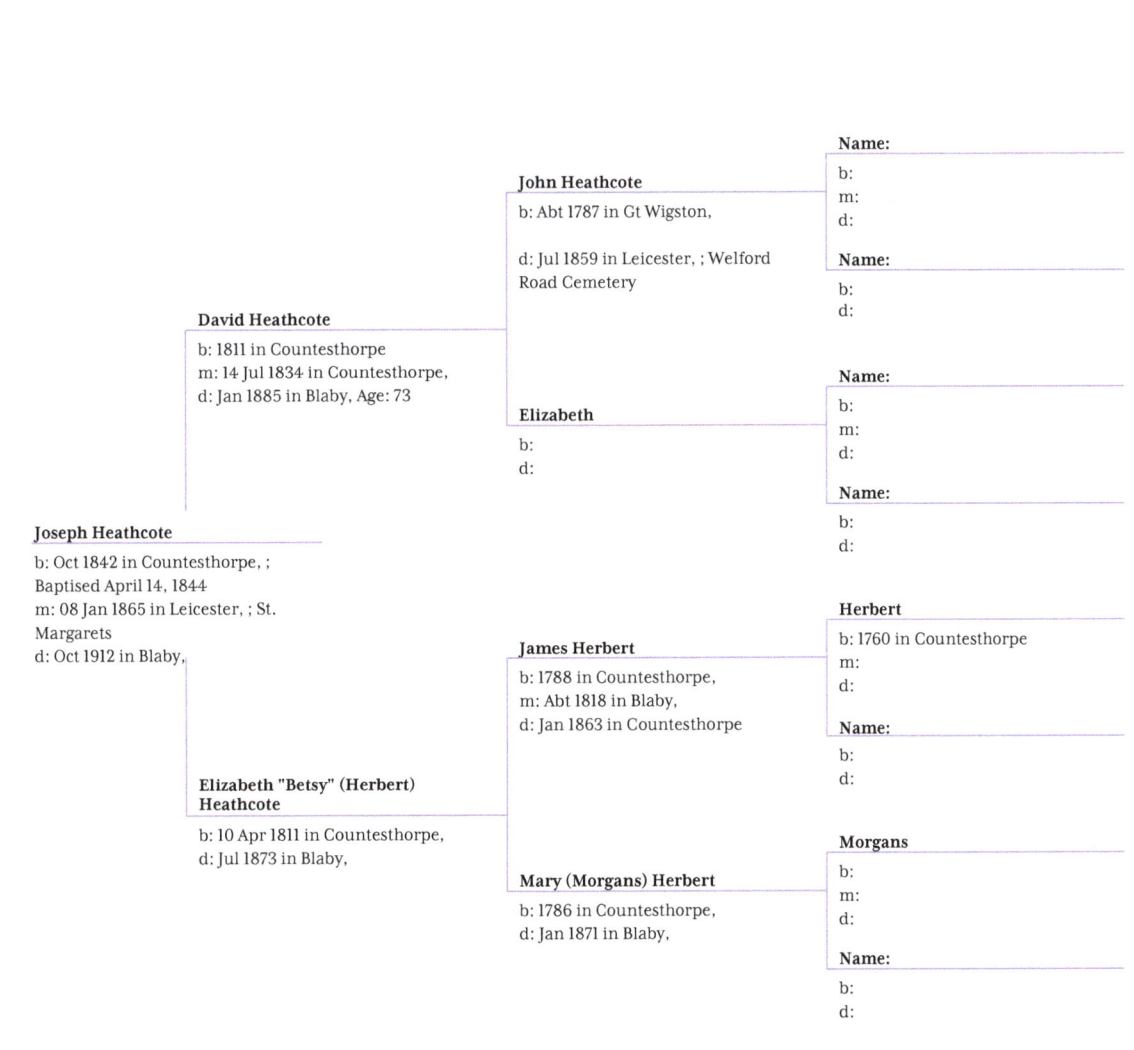

Joseph Heathcote
b: Oct 1842 in Countesthorpe, ; Baptised April 14, 1844
m: 08 Jan 1865 in Leicester, ; St. Margarets
d: Oct 1912 in Blaby,

David Heathcote
b: 1811 in Countesthorpe
m: 14 Jul 1834 in Countesthorpe,
d: Jan 1885 in Blaby, Age: 73

Elizabeth "Betsy" (Herbert) Heathcote
b: 10 Apr 1811 in Countesthorpe,
d: Jul 1873 in Blaby,

John Heathcote
b: Abt 1787 in Gt Wigston,
d: Jul 1859 in Leicester, ; Welford Road Cemetery

Elizabeth
b:
d:

James Herbert
b: 1788 in Countesthorpe,
m: Abt 1818 in Blaby,
d: Jan 1863 in Countesthorpe

Mary (Morgans) Herbert
b: 1786 in Countesthorpe,
d: Jan 1871 in Blaby,

Herbert
b: 1760 in Countesthorpe
m:
d:

Morgans
b:
m:
d:

Pedigree Chart for Catherine (Warburton) Heathcote

Catherine (Warburton) Heathcote
b: Apr 1844 in Countesthorpe,
m: 08 Jan 1865 in Leicester, ; St. Margarets
d: Jul 1912 in Blaby, Leicestershire

- **Robert Warburton**
  b: 1800 in Wigston Magna,
  m: 18 Feb 1844 in Countesthorpe, L
  d: 26 Jun 1875 in Blaby,

  - **William Warburton**
    b: 05 Nov 1758 in Wigston Magna,
    m: 06 Jan 1783 in Wigston Magna,
    d: 15 Dec 1800 in Wigston Magna,

    - **Benjamin Warburton**
      b: 1730 in Wigston Magna,
      m: 25 Mar 1754 in Wigston Magna,
      d: 17 Jul 1785 in Leicestershire,

    - **Mary (Marten) Warburton**
      b: 1745 in Wigston Magna,
      d: Unknown

  - **Anne Eltington**
    b: 1760 in Wigston Magna,
    d:

    - **Name:**
      b:
      m:
      d:

    - **Name:**
      b:
      d:

- **Jane (Root) Warburton**
  b: 22 Oct 1815 in Countesthorpe,
  d: 05 May 1884 in England

  - **Josiah Root**
    b: 1773 in Countesthorpe,
    m: 25 Dec 1811 in Countesthorpe
    d: Apr 1856 in Countesthorpe, South Wigston,

    - **Jane (Johnson) Root**
      b: 1737 in Countesthorpe, Leicestershire
      m: 03 Oct 1762 in Countesthorpe, Leicester, England
      d:

    - **Jane (Johnson) Root**
      b: Abt 1738
      d:

  - **Catharine (Lord) Root**
    b: Dec 1772 in Countesthorpe,
    d: Jul 1838 in Blaby, Leicestershire

    - **Thomas Lord**
      b:
      m:
      d:

    - **Jane Burley**
      b:
      d:

8.

John Heathcoat: Could we be related?

I note that the spelling of our surname was modified over the years. Perhaps the transcriber did not verify, or he/she made a mistake. I note either spelling is used inconsistently.

To date, I am still searching for a direct link to the family. One can dream.... Here is his story. I am grateful for the following article from The Victorian Web, "John Heathcoat and the Bobbin-net Machine", written by Samuel Smiles. It is a good read.[43]

When I first investigated the Heathcotes in Countesthorpe, I was told the Luddites had driven the family to Devon where they continued their business. I put this information to the back of my mind as I could find no evidence in the research of our direct family. Then a family friend directed me to stories about a John Heathcoat who had indeed moved to Devon from the Loughborough area.

Also perhaps check the following website:
https://museumcrush.org/john-heathcoat-the-industrialist-inventor-who-transformed-a-devon-town/

This story begins with Francis Heathcote, a farmer, who at the age of 18 married his sweetheart, Elizabeth Burton on May 16, 1773, in Lockington a small village in Leicestershire, close to the Derbyshire border. Their first son, Thomas was born in 1775 and registered as Heathcoat. Their daughter Ann, born in 1777 was registered as Heathcote, lived only three years. Their next daughter Elizabeth was registered as Heathcote. John was born on 7 August 1783, in Duffield in Derbyshire. In the registrar of his birth spelled his name as Heathcoat.

---

43 If you are interested in more read the article from The Victorian Web.
   http://www.victorianweb.org/technology/inventors/heathcoat.html
   John Heathcoat and the Bobbin-net Machine by Samuel Smiles

John was an excellent student whose education was curtailed when his father, Francis became blind and was obliged to give up his farm. John would have been around 10 years of age at that time: too young to take over the farm. Instead, he was apprenticed to a frame smith in the local hosiery industry. During his apprenticeship his imagination and propensity for all things mechanical were ignited. In his spare time, he made technical improvements in the construction of the warp-loom and was able to produce mitts of a lace-like appearance. John befriended a Thomas Bazley (1797-1885), some years his junior. Thomas and John were no doubt influenced and encouraged by Thomas's father, also Thomas, a Lancashire cotton manufacturer, mathematician and journalist (1773-1845). Young Tom entered the cotton-spinning business and subsequently became a yarn merchant in Bolton. He became an MP in 1858 and a peer of the realm in 1869. I wondered whether the pair held a life-long friendship.

In September 1802, at the age of 19, John married Ann Cauldwell of Hathern (Leics). I can only imagine the roller coaster life Ann would have led with her inventive husband as she supported his efforts, commiserated his failures with him and celebrated his successes.

In 1804 at the age of 21, after completing his apprenticeship the family moved to Nottingham where John became a journeyman to a Leonard Elliott, a frame smith. Then he took his first risk. He bought out Elliott's business with a loan of £10,000. In those days, this was an enormous sum. Who would have lent so young a man that amount? Did Thomas Bazley endorse the loan? John then set himself to mechanise the process of lace-making. But finding himself subjected to the intrusion of competing inventors he removed to Hathern (near Loughborough) in Leicestershire, the home of his wife's family.

In 1808 John Heathcoat designed and patented a machine for manufacturing lace which was described as 'the most complicated machine ever produced' at the time. This machine-made lace, an exact imitation of real pillow-lace, was also called 'English net' or bobbinet. After his machine was patented in 1809, he set up a factory in Loughborough, in partnership with Charles Lacy, a Nottingham manufacturer, which proved successful and profitable. He was able to charge royalties for the use of his equipment.

Then a tragedy: On a bright sunny summer day in1816 their factory was attacked by former Luddites, thought to be in the pay of the lace makers of Nottingham. 55 lace frames were destroyed. The local magistrates offered £10,000 of compensation, on the condition that he re-invested in the area. John, who believed his life had been threatened by the mob, declined the compensation and moved his operation to Westexe, Tiverton in Central Devon; many of his skilled workers are said to have migrated with him, embarking on the 200-mile journey on foot. I can find no evidence that any of your direct ancestors went with him. Did he not know them?

A Move to Tiverton

In approximately 1815 John had purchased an unoccupied woollen mill in Tiverton, Devon on the River Exe and proceeded to turn the fortunes of the town by not only introducing workers but also employment. He was overseeing work in Tiverton when the attack in Loughborough took place. He wrote to the Mayor of Tiverton, asking for protection for the mill there, and in the letter disclosed:

> *"I have great apprehension of an immediate attack at this place also. In fact, I believe the real cause of this mischief being done is principally, if not wholly, owing to the offence of removing here, and I have been informed upon undoubted authority that the Nottingham Lace Makers have sworn my entire destruction."*

Undaunted by his loss in Loughborough, John continued to construct new facilities and greatly improved machines in his new factory in Tiverton, propelling them by water-power and afterward by steam. I assume that the royalties he was receiving supported this endeavour.

He followed his great invention by others of much sophistication, as, for instance, the intricacies of ornamenting net, manufacturing ribbons and netting upon his machines, improved yarn spinning-frames, and methods for winding raw silk from cocoons. At that time in Tiverton, where there was severe unemployment, his successful and expanding mill soon made him popular with the townspeople.

When his wife Ann passed away in 1831, John was 49. Because of his popularity, the following year John was elected a Member of Parliament (MP) for Tiverton: he seldom spoke in the House of Commons but was constantly engaged on committees, where his thorough knowledge of business and sound judgment were highly valued.

John continued to make technical improvements in the lace-making process until his retirement in 1843. At that time his equipment was by far the most expensive and complex textile apparatus then existing.

John the philanthropist paid for the building of Tiverton British Schools in 1843. In 1854 he gave the site for St Paul's Church, Tiverton, and in 1856 paid the cost of installing the organ.

He retained his parliamentary seat until 1859, and after two years of declining health, he died on 18 January 1861 at Bolham House, Tiverton.

I found yet another enduring legacy: a website for Heathcoat Fabrics, which reads: *Founded by John Heathcoat in 1808, Heathcoat Fabrics has evolved over 200 years into one of the most innovative and forward-thinking fabrics manufacturers, with an international reputation for high quality and brilliance. Heathcoat Fabrics is based in beautiful, rural Devon UK where our all-encompassing hi-tech site resides.*

John Heathcoat was so much more than a pioneering English inventor of lace-making machinery. He was clever, imaginative, tenacious, optimistic, and creative: a courageous leader, highly principled and a risk-taker, a man of integrity: a genius in business activities with a ceaselessly fertile brain. He was self-educated, a linguist. And he was the son of a farmer, humble beginnings indeed yet he rose to the top and became exceedingly wealthy. He appeared to see possibilities and searched beyond his own generation. He created a company that endures today.[44]

---

44 (http://www.heathcoat.co.uk)

He was willing to relocate to take the opportunities that were offered. Why he selected Tiverton is anyone's guess. And he had a friend in Tom Bazley, an educated young man, the son of a family of substance. Both were no doubt guided by Tom's father, who was perhaps John's mentor. John was a leader who made a name for himself, an MP who earned the respect of his colleagues and employees. How did he view those who toiled, the workers, the other Heathcotes, and the Warburtons?

I wonder if he and our Heathcotes had a common ancestor in the distant past. I cannot prove it but I can wish and hope…

ENDNOTES

Read more about John Heathcoat if you wish before we move to your Nana's side of the family.

Appendix A

STILL REMEMBERED
From the Loughborough ECHO….
In 2006 in order to commemorate the departure from Loughborough to Tiverton to mark the 200th anniversary of the Luddite attack on John Heathcoat's factory, a Local historian Ian Porter organised the 200-mile canal walk to honour a valuable part of history.

Heathcoat had made a machine capable of reproducing the best hand-made pillow lace, putting many lace makers' livelihoods at risk and crippling the competition by extracting large sums of money in royalties. He also cut the wages of his own workers. Fuming with anger, a group named The Luddites stormed the pubs of Loughborough, blackening their faces and spreading their fury. They attacked Heathcoat's mill, now Iceland in Market Street, attacking 55 lace-making machines and shooting one of the factory guards.

In 2006, the public was invited to dress up as workers including wives and children and take part in the first leg (around the park) of the walk the workers undertook down to Tiverton,

The Luddites[45]

The Industrial Revolution was a time in the early 19th century during which machinery began to replace hand production, water and steam power began to improve, and the factory system became implemented.

Methods and machines may have improved but the framework knitters themselves, who remained at the bottom of the industrial chain, enjoyed no benefit. By the beginning of the 19th century, low wages, high taxation, poor economic climate, and unfavourable working conditions drove many of them to rebel, blaming their unfortunate state of affairs on the factory owners and the middlemen. Angry mobs formed, but unlike today when workers march to raise awareness of their plight, these mobs were much more direct in their opposition. They stormed the factories and went to work smashing the machines contained within. Here again another fanciful character enters the story of the stocking-frame. Ned Ludd, more mythical figure than real man, was heralded as the leader of this movement. His very real flesh-and-blood supporters earned the nickname "Luddites" and are the origin of the term that today refers to somebody who is resistant to advances in technology. There

---

45   https://study.com/academy/lesson/luddites-during-the-industrial-revolution-definition

was a large wave of frame-breaking throughout the East Midlands in 1811-1812, and it seems it carried on sporadically until at least 1816. The perpetrators were dealt with severely, especially after it became a capital crime in 1812. In one trial six frame workers were hanged and three were transported, presumably to the penal colonies of Australia.

The workers, however, had prominent supporters such as Lord Byron (who lived in Nottinghamshire) as well as the government who attempted to assist with legislation by introducing a bill prohibiting the manufacture of cheaper, less labour-intensive cut-ups (stockings cut from cloth and seamed). Unfortunately, this bill was defeated, presumably after petitions by the wealthier frame owners. The framework knitters continued to live in poverty, often requiring charitable assistance to survive. The phrase "as poor as a stockinger" was very commonly used throughout the 19th century. When this disturbance passed, the workers returned to their toils, possibly they had too much invested in a trade or they had few alternatives. It appears that our ancestors took a stoic approach and resumed their tasks when the mayhem subsided.

9.

The Hubbards of Saxelby and Wyfordby

Your Nana's maiden name was Hubbard, so we now continue with her side of our family. Since their lives revolved around the town of Melton Mowbray, we will visit there too.

Firstly, the surname Hubbard is composed of the Germanic elements 'hug', heart, mind, spirit and 'berht', bright, famous. This popular Norman name was introduced into England following the conquest. The nursery rhyme, 'Old mother Hubbard', represents a feminine form of the given name.[46]

Amazingly, we can trace the first Hubbards to Saxelby, a small village in the district of Melton Mowbray, a village close to Ashfordby, and to Old Dalby where your grandfather worked. Saxelby is about six kilometres to the north-west of Melton Mowbray and is situated on the southern slope of the ridge that makes up the southern boundary of the Vale of Belvoir. The next generation moved to the village of Wyfordby, a settlement recorded in the Domesday Book, in the hundred of Framland, Leicestershire. Before 1600, who knows? I did find connections on the female line as you will see in the geographical context section.

Wyfordby had a recorded population of 45 households in 1086, one of the largest 20% of settlements recorded in Domesday.[47] The village is situated about six kilometres east of Melton Mowbray on the road to Saxby.

We know virtually nothing about these ancestors except their names, dates of birth and death, and the same information about their children. How they lived we can only guess. That they were farm labourers is a given.

---

46 https://www.surnamedb.com/Surname/Hubbard
47 https://opendomesday.org/place/SK7918/wyfordby/

The first Hubbard I could locate was Robert, born in Saxelby in 1600. He married Margaret Kevell. The couple moved from Saxelby to Wyfordby where the only child I could find, Walter, was born in 1634. Whereas Margaret died in 1650 at the age of 46, Robert reached the amazing age of 95, having lived most of his life in Wyfordby. We have inherited his genes and hopefully his immune system!

Without a doubt, these families worked the land. Both Saxelby and Wyfordby would have been an easy walk to the market in Melton for those burly farmers. That these families were involved in growing and selling produce and/or livestock is very likely. They might have had a cart pulled by a horse, one of low birth called a nag, or even a mule or donkey. Their employers may have provided housing or perhaps they rented a small drafty dwelling in the village. The climate? Damp! The 17th Century was a tough century in which to live, without power or running water.

Walter Hubbard married Catherine Hutchings from the village in May 1659. The pair had six sons and four daughters, including the first set of twins in our family. Both Walter and Catherine died in the year 1711, both aged 77. Read more about her later.

Their son, Edward, born on May 27, 1675, was our ancestor. He married Anne Downs from the village and set up home there. This pair had three daughters and two sons, one of whom was William, our ancestor, born on July 17, 1704. Edward lived to the age of 56 and his wife to 48. His grandfather's long-life genes were not evident in the case of Edward: or perhaps there was illness.

William Hubbard married Elizabeth Dennis from nearby Thorpe Arnold and set up home in Wyfordby. This pair had only two children: William born in 1736 and Elizabeth born in 1739. The children were named after their parents as was the custom. More lives lived in much the same way as their father and grandfather: meagrely with no luxuries.

Their son, William, married Elizabeth Prestin, who gave birth to a son they named William in 1770. Sadly, he lived only three years. Then three daughters arrived, one named Elizabeth after her mother, and finally a son, they named William in 1776: a replacement for an earlier lost little William. William and Elizabeth lived their lives in Wyfordby. William senior died at the age of 85 in 1821.

But towards the end of the 18th Century, this son William moved on. At the age of 20, he married Elizabeth Elston from the nearby village of Goadby Marwood on November 23, 1796 and shortly thereafter moved the family to the village of Eaton.

And what I know for sure: the Hubbard men smoked a pipe!

And this is what I don't know for sure!

Grandfather Walter's wife, Catherine Hutchins, was born into aristocracy! Her grandfather was Sir Thomas Hutchinson (1564-1618) of Newark on Trent, son of Baronet Thomas Christopher Hutchinson (1540-1598). One of Henry VIII's favourites perhaps if I can believe Ancestry! And I can dream! For sure we can say, Catherine married beneath her! And what she was doing in a small village in North Leicestershire is for us to wonder. But then only the firstborn son really mattered! He was the one who inherited everything: the title, the estate, and the cash.

There is back story regarding Catherine's mother Elinor Pierce, equally interesting. Her parents, John and Elizabeth Pierce were part of the group of Puritan immigrants who sailed to Boston, Mass. John was then a "Weaver farmer." While most of their children went with them or were born in the USA, Elinor remained in England. If we can believe!

Our story now moves to the next generation of Hubbards in the Eastwell/Eaton villages.

ENDNOTES

Melton Mowbray was the town at the centre of their world: mine too as I grew up.

The name of our town emanates from the early English word Medeltone – meaning "Middletown surrounded by small hamlets" (and therefore has the same origin as Milton and Middleton). Mowbray is a Norman family name.

(Photographer: D. Field)

The market looks like this today: commercial and social still. Your Nana loved a visit to the market.

The vibrant Melton Mowbray Cattle Market, where livestock brought in from the villages is purchased and sold under auction, thrives today. The Cattle Market is the largest town centre livestock market in the country. The livestock market serves over 2,500 farming customers and 350,000 visitors to the site annually. A must-see each time I visited the town. Recorded as Leicestershire's only market town in the 1086 Domesday Survey, it boasts the third oldest market in England. Tuesday has been market day ever since royal approval was given in 1324.

Most of the local inhabitants lived in one of the 50-some villages that clustered around this central town, including Wyfordby, Saxelby, and Stathern. Imagine homes and farms dotted over rolling hills, small woodlands, ordered hedgerows, and lush green pastures. In the early days the villages might comprise a few houses dotted along the main road, all with a distinctive church: Roman Catholic until the mid-16th Century but mostly Church of England (Anglican) after that date.

Prior to the Second World War, the villages surrounding the town were virtually self-sufficient. There may have been a store selling local produce, otherwise residents grew, caught, or made whatever they needed. While I was growing up in the village of Stathern, there was also an abattoir, a dairy, and a butcher's shop. The villages varied in size between 200 and 400 residents. They were all scattered around the territory approximately 3-5 kilometres apart. Even though the villages were relatively close together, residents did not necessarily intermingle. There was no public transport until after the Second World War. For that reason, although Harby, Eastwell, and Eaton were close to Stathern, I knew no one in those villages.

Our town is best known for its culinary specialty, the Melton Mowbray pork pie. It is also one of the six homes of Stilton cheese. Melton Mowbray is promoted as the "Rural Capital of Food".

Blue Stilton cheese was made in the traditional cylindrical shape. Stilton cheese originated near Melton Mowbray and is still made in the town today.[48]

Melton Mowbray pork pies are made with a specific "hand-raising" process and recipe. On 4 April 2008 the European Union awarded the Melton Mowbray pork pie Protected Geographical Indication status, following a long-standing application made by the Melton Mowbray Pork Pie Association. As a result of this ruling, pies made only within a designated zone around Melton, and using uncured pork, are allowed to carry the Melton Mowbray name on their packaging. I remember making those pies at home!

[49] (Photographer: R. Heathcote) St Mary's Church, Melton Mowbray where your great Grandma Heathcote as well as friend Heather were each married. St Mary's Church is the largest and "stateliest" parish church in Leicestershire, with visible remains dating mainly from the 13th-15th centuries. The stonework in the lowest section of the tower, which has Norman windows, dates from 1170, although there were certainly one or more Anglo-Saxon churches on this site before the Norman one. It is built on a plan more usual for cathedrals and the 100-foot tower dominates the town. It contains many notable monuments including the tomb of Roger de Mowbray, 1st Baron Mowbray, and others dating from the 14th to the 18th century; also a memorial tablet to equine artist John Ferneley (1782 to 1860).[50]

There were times when the Leicestershire market town must have felt like quite the happening place to be. Thomas Cromwell, Lord Palmerston, and Lord Carrington all lived here. The rich and reckless partied in the town, literally painting it red; it is said the Marquis of Waterford and a group of friends did so in 1837.

A little quieter these days, a couple of locals tell us that the "only decent pub" is the Anne of Cleves. Originally a 14th-century hall for chantry priests, it passed into the hands of Cromwell, only for him to lose his head in 1540 after advising Henry VIII to marry Anne. She fared rather better, getting the house in the divorce (although she never visited). Few middle-England towns sag under the weight of their history like Melton Mowbray. [51]

I have depicted Melton Mowbray as the focus of the community: socially and economically, today as it was in the 17th Century and long before.

As they grew in population, the surrounding villages all boasted key buildings. Firstly, there was always an Anglican church representing the Parish and administered by a Council. Secondly, there would be a public house: an alternate gathering place where gossip flourished and news was shared. Because Marriages and Baptisms were solemnized only in churches, church records offer us superior information about our ancestors before the days of the census.

By the mid-18th century, the Country was becoming organized. Schools were being built, education was mandated and care for the unfortunate was formalized. Melton Mowbray also assumed the task of providing

---

48   https://wikivisually.com/wiki/Melton_Mowbray
49   St Mary's Church, Melton Mowbray
     cc-by-sa/2.0 - geograph.org.uk/p/1275349 Copyright Stephen McKay and licensed for reuse under this Creative Commons Licence
50   https://en.wikipedia.org/wiki/St_Mary%27s_Church,_Melton_Mowbray
51   https://www.telegraph.co.uk/travel/destinations/europe/united-kingdom/england/articles/melton-mowbray-what-to-see-and-do/

accommodation for the homeless poor: a safety net for the ill-fated. I note they might be described as paupers or imbeciles.

By 1834 the Melton Mowbray Poor Law Union came into operation serving some 54 surrounding parishes. The objective of the Union was to provide for those unable to take care of themselves: a task previously assigned to the village church parishes. In response, municipalities built workhouses to accommodate these desperate individuals. In exchange for food and clothing, they would be given a mandatory workload either within or outside of the workhouse. One such workhouse was built on Thorpe Road in Melton Mowbray in 1836. All workhouses would have been unpleasant, offering the mere basic subsistence.[52]

Males and females were separated as were children from their mothers. The children were raised in nurseries. There would be an element of shame being admitted to a workhouse, shame that some of our ancestors experienced as we will encounter some of our ancestors who lived and died in the workhouses. The stigma of being a pauper and destitute, with no member of the family willing and able to offer accommodation, is unimaginable.

(Copyright David Hallam-Jones and licensed for reuse under this Creative Commons Licence)
This is a photograph of the Melton Mowbray Workhouse on Thorpe Road.

---

52 http://www.workhouses.org.uk/MeltonMowbray/

Chart 9.
First Hubbards

Robert Hubbard
b: 1600 in Saxelby,
m:
d: 09 Feb 1695 in Saxelby,

Margaret Kevell
b: 1604 in Leicester,
d: Oct 1650 in Leicester,

Walter Hubbard
b: 1634 in Wyfordby,
m: 23 May 1659 in Wyfordby,
d: 17 Feb 1711 in Wyfordby

Thomas Hutchings
b: 1607 in Devizes, Castle, Wiltshire,
m: 04 Nov 1632 in St John the Baptist, Devizes, Wiltshire,
d: 1669 in Wiltshire,

Elinor Pierce
b: 1608 in Devizes, Castle, Wiltshire,
d: 1667 in Wiltshire,

Catherine Hubbard
b: 23 Nov 1634 in Wyfordby,
d: 23 Dec 1711 in Wyfordby,

Edward Hubbard
b: 27 May 1675 in Wyfordby,
m: Wyfordby,
d: Jan 1731 in Wyforby

William Hubbard
b: 17 Jul 1704 in Wyfordby
m: 15 May 1733 in Wyfordby,
d: Mar 1768 in Wyfordby

10.

THE HUBBARDS IN EATON - JOHN STAYED BEHIND

Your Nana's side of the family, the Norman Hubbards, have been in Leicestershire for at least five hundred years. Sometime in the early 1800s, the family moved from the village of Wyfordby to Eastwell and then Eaton. From where did they originate? We don't know!

From the prior story, we know that at age 20 William married 22-year-old Elizabeth Elston on November 23, 1796, in nearby Goadby Marwood. Their first daughter, Elizabeth, was born in Long Clawson in 1798. They had relocated to the Eaton/Eastwell area by the time of their son William's birth in 1801.

Eaton and Eastwell are approximately 13 kilometres north of Melton Mowbray and 5 kilometres from Stathern at the top of Stathern Hill. Your Nana and I would enjoy many a Sunday lunch in Eaton at The Church Restaurant.

As I entered the Eaton area having been away for a while, I saw the red hue to the soil. Unnoticed when I lived there.

First a look at our Elston ancestors. When Elizabeth's grandmother, Elizabeth Pick married Vincent Elston on February 19, 1744, she faced tough times. Elizabeth lost her first two children in 1748 before their third

(Photographer: Kate Jewell) This is of the sleepy village of Eaton. The surrounding land has at least ten known springs and is the source of the River Devon. It is full of sandstone and in the past, a large quarry was found outside the village. The quarry has since become a woodland area. The land is full of iron ore and was a famous source of iron during the 1800s, supplying two local ironworks. The railway bridge under which the iron was transported is still in Eaton today.

birthday. Sadly, as we are aware, infant losses were common. Then son John was born in January 1748 and survived. Imagine dealing with a new-born and the death of two young children at the same time? Vincent and Elizabeth lost another child, William, in 1750. Then she delivered three more children. But this is not a happy story. The family, who lived in Scalford, a village between Stathern and Melton Mowbray, lost their father in November 1761 when their youngest son James was not yet one year old. Vincent would have been in his early forties. Elizabeth was left with three young children and 13-year-old John. This was farming country: John would have been working hard at 13. Records do not show whether Elizabeth had family close by to help her.

In 1772 24-year-old John Elston married 19-year-old Ann Bartram in nearby Long Clawson. Ann would bear 12 children over 23 years. Their eldest daughter, Elizabeth was our ancestor. She was born in Long Clawson and baptized there on November 1, 1774. On marrying William Hubbard, Elizabeth entered our field of vision. Her family background provides us with a glimpse into the intense struggle of their lives.

Elizabeth Elston and William Hubbard raised their family of a daughter and four sons in Eaton. Their second son, William, born in 1801 in Eaton, was our ancestor: more about him later in this story.

As a side story which also illustrates the times, William and Elizabeth's fifth child, Richard, died in infancy. The last child of their family, a son was born in 1819 and baptized as Richard. Naming a new child, the same name as a child that died too early might have enforced the illusion of continuity or perhaps minimized the loss. One wonders how the knowledge that he was replacing another affects the life of the second Richard who remained in the household until he married Mary George on August 31, 1846, in Melton Mowbray. The pair moved to Melton where there were more opportunities. But Richard failed to take advantage of these. Mary and Richard had two children: Sarah, and William ten years later. With 10-year-old William, they lived in Bridle Yard, Melton Mowbray. Mary was a charwoman, William a labourer.

But life did not go well for Richard and his family. Twenty years later Richard, designated a pauper at the age of 72, resided in the Melton Mowbray Workhouse. Other residents were described as vagrants: one little pauper, I noted, was only four years old. One cannot imagine the shame of being obliged to enter a workhouse because of ill health, old age, mental illness, or poverty. Indeed, knowing no family member was willing or able to assume responsibility would have been particularly heartbreaking. Richard died in the workhouse in April 1895 at the age of 75.[53] From this family then, one died in the workhouse: unimaginable personal shame. Wife Mary was still alive at the time. One wonders how they became parted. Unable to help her father, daughter Sarah had died before him on January 27, 1892, at the age of 42. She died as a result of pyloric cancer and exhaustion at home with her husband Edward.

Our ancestor, William, son of William and Elizabeth, married 21-year-old Elizabeth Riley on November 25, 1825, in nearby Thorpe Arnold. William, an agricultural labourer, was 24. This pair settled in Eaton and raised their family of five sons, John, Thomas, William, Henry, and Jonathan, and four daughters in the village. The eldest, John was born in 1825: another pregnant bride! Elizabeth's childbearing years extended over 20 years.

But four of the five sons were not destined to remain in Eaton as labourers, farming land that was not theirs. The eldest, John Hubbard, however, did not break with tradition like his four younger brothers who had the inclination and the courage to move away from what they knew. Equally bravely, John stayed home to take care of the family. One can imagine the scene as Ma Hubbard tearfully whispered farewell to first Thomas, then William,

---

53 Out of interest, I located Richard's death certificate. The cause of his death at the age of 75 was stated as Old Age. Did he simply not wish to live in the Union Workhouse? Was 75 considered old age in those days?

and lastly Henry and Jonathan. Their father would have stoically and gruffly stifled his feelings as he wished them all well, no doubt relieved that John had decided to stay home to make a life for himself in the village. Perhaps a young lady named Mary had entered his life. The next story will tell of the four sons who left the nest.

In April 1853, John married Mary Ann Tyler, a local girl, daughter of Richard and Elizabeth (Rodwell) Tyler. Mary's mother Elizabeth Tyler was from Ashby Folville, a nearby village. Mary lost her father in 1846, so mother Elizabeth was widowed long before her daughter married and had children. In the six years following their marriage, John and Mary had four sons: James, Thomas, Arthur, and Edward. After the children arrived, Grandma Elizabeth lived with the family. Three sons were living with her when John and Mary welcomed daughter, Emma, into the family. Mary was then 39.

John worked the land as an agricultural labourer all his life. Sons James, Thomas, and Arthur started their working lives as labourers whereas the youngest, Edward worked at the local quarry. Our ancestor, Arthur Hubbard was born in October of 1858 in Eastwell. In 1871 we see 13-year-old Arthur as a farm boy possibly with his father. Ten years later, Arthur was still an agricultural labourer. Then he met a sweetheart in nearby Stathern and married Sarah Ann Smith on May 18, 1884. The pair set up a home in Stathern. You will read about Sarah Ann in a later story. Arthur eventually became an ironstone quarryman. The pair started their family. I note that at the time, William Brown, the blacksmith, lived next door to the Hubbards on Main Street, Stathern. Wait for his story!

I have mentioned in prior stories that the Hubbards demonstrated limited imagination when naming their children. This pair broke the mould. They themselves had nicknames: Arthur was always known as Bradley and Sarah Ann as Saran. When their first daughter was born, they entered naming mode. Her moniker was Trissie Maud Madeleine, names that came out of the blue. I wonder whether Trissie was as exotic as her names! I don't remember her. Their first son, John Henry, arrived in July 1888. Just to confuse me, he was my Uncle Harry! Next came my grandad, Wilfred Alec on July 3, 1890. He was known to all as Alec. A second daughter, Louisa Mary was born on August 30, 1892. She apparently looked much like her mother, Saran. According to your Nana she was the village gossip. Millicent Rachel, known as Rach, was born in January 1895. I remember Auntie Rach who remained in the village and married Percy Bellamy. They adopted Joyce who had a son, David whom they also adopted. My mother hinted that Auntie Rach was disappointed by Joyce's behaviour, bringing the first illegitimate child into the immediate family.

Bradley's father did not live to welcome his next grandchild, Bertram William who arrived in 1901 when Saran was 40. John Hubbard died at 72 in 1897. After his death, Grandma Mary lived with Bradley's sister Emma's family: the Pooles on Main Street in Eaton. George Poole had left the land and was working as an ironstone quarryman, like many of his generation: an alternative to farming emerged.

I remember trying to sort out this family with your Nana in her later years. She remembered only the short or nicknames. But I needed to know who was who! My grandfather was particularly close with his brother, Harry. But then he may have been close to his other siblings too: I would not have known because they all lived so close by in the village. He could have seen them daily.

Your Nana would tell me that her grandfather Bradley loved flowers, particularly geraniums which he had on his window sills. He also liked dogs.

This family of Hubbards seemed to be supportive of one another, each living with different family units as the need arose. After all, Eastwell and Eaton were small villages close by to one another. Families tended to live with one another every day. The wage earners all worked the land as was the custom in that part of England, until the next generation found work at the ironstone quarry. They would grow their food, keep chickens, gather berries, preserve food, and were great cooks. They made feather beds, hooked rugs, and sewed their clothes: a simple, unsophisticated yet resourceful life. I have yet to find a probated will in this family.

The next story is one of adventure as we follow the four Hubbard sons on their journey.

After that, my grandfather will tell his story.

Endnotes

Leicestershire Ironstone

Some background information

Leicestershire contains isolated outcrops of the Midlands ironstone deposits and opencast working was carried on by several companies around Eastwell and Eaton. Land worked was leased from the Duke of Rutland.

(Photographer: Unknown) Images of Eastwell Iron Ore Company.

Iron ore was quarried in the parish between 1884 and 1965. A mineral branch, known as the Eaton Branch, was built by the Great Northern Railway in 1884 to transport the ore. Its terminus was to the north of the Belvoir Road. Its nearest point to the village was a bridge passing under Stathern Road. The first ore was carried to a railway wharf to the north of that bridge by a narrow-gauge tramway in horse-drawn wagons. The horses on that line were replaced by steam locomotives in 1890.

The ore was dug by hand at first but from 1912 onwards steam diggers were introduced. From 1936 onwards these began to be replaced by diesel diggers. The Waltham tramway had steam locomotives from its opening in 1884. One of the tramways had a petrol locomotive from 1929 and a diesel locomotive from 1936. From 1946 onwards the tramways began to close and ore was transported from some quarries to the wharf by lorry. The last quarries to close were south of the Stathern Road and west of the railway and close to the Eastwell Road (east of the road). The last loads of ore were transported from these quarries to the railway wharf by lorry in December 1965. The Eaton Branch then closed and was lifted.

World War II saw intensive production replace the uncertain 1920s and 30s and the quarries were almost exhausted. Further quarries were cut requiring extension of the tramway system to over three miles from the tippling dock. Waltham Quarries closed in 1958, a year of depression in the iron ore industry.[54]

---

54 https://en.wikipedia.org/wiki/Eaton,_Leicestershire

CHART 10
ARTHUR "BRADLEY" HUBBARD

Arthur "Bradley" Hubbard
b: Oct 1858 in Eastwell,
m: 19 May 1884 in Stathern,
d: Mar 1943 in Melton Mowbray,

John Hubbard
b: Abt 1825 in Eaton,
m: Apr 1853 in Melton Mowbray,
d: 22 May 1886 in Eaton,

Mary Ann (Tyler) Hubbard
b: 1825
d: Oct 1902 in Leicestershire,

William Hubbard
b: Abt 1801 in Eaton,
m: 26 Nov 1825 in Thorpe Arnold Eliz. Riley 26 Nov 1825 Book:
d: 04 Jan 1887 in Eaton,

Elizabeth (Riley) Hubbard
b: 26 Jun 1804 in Melton Mowbray ; Christening date
d: 1870 in Eaton Hundred Framland, Leics

Richard Tyler
b: Abt 1796 in Leicestershire,
m: 04 Jul 1820 in Ashby Folville,
d: Jan 1846 in Melton Mowbray;

Elizabeth (Rodwell) Tyler
b: 1792 in Ashby Folville,
d: Apr 1875 in Eaton, ; Family Search. Registered in MM

William Hubbard
b: 1776 in Wyfordby, Leicestershire,
m: 23 Nov 1796 in Goadby Marwood,
d: Jun 1853 in Melton

Elizabeth (Elston) Hubbard
b: 1774 in Long Clawson,
d: Jan 1853 in Loughborough,

John Riley
b:
m:
d:

Name:
b:
d:

Tyler
b:
m:
d:

Name:
b:
d:

Rodwell
b:
m:
d:

Name:
b:
d:

11.

THE HUBBARD BROTHERS:
THOMAS, WILLIAM, HENRY & JONATHAN

Our prior story provided background to the Hubbard family and described where they lived. This story explains how four of your Hubbard ancestors left Eaton, the sleepy farming community where they were born. Their eldest brother, John, stayed home. Thomas (bn June, 1831), William (bn July, 1840), Henry (bn July 1842), and Jonathan (bn February 1845) embarked on an adventure in search of better lives. Whereas many of our family stayed close to where they were born, these four yearned for different lives. They all left the UK to settle in Northern Indiana, USA.

How Thomas Hubbard had the vision to leave Eaton to live far away is unknown. Likely he, like his brothers, was illiterate. He might have discovered the opportunities in Indiana by word of mouth or by church notices. How he reached the White and Pulaski Counties of Indiana where he settled to farm is unimaginable. Perhaps the government offered Thomas land there to farm. His journey would have started in Liverpool some 200 kms from Eaton. Reaching Liverpool would have been no easy trek involving cross country trips by pony and trap. The voyage would have continued by ship to New York. Upon reaching the USA, he would

(Photographer: Unknown) This photograph is of a pipe-smoking pair: Henry and Jonathan Hubbard.

have continued by train and stagecoach. But he would have had to not only manage the arduous journey with little cash, but also navigate the immigration rituals as well as a new currency. His courage continues to amaze. With his encouragement, this journey would have been repeated by William first and then Henry and Jonathan.

A look at Pulaski County at that time provides a glimpse of the social and physical environment Thomas would have faced as he settled. The land was ceded by the Potawatomi Indians to the United States on October 26, 1832. It was another 10 years before the Native Americans relocated, but before the ink had dried on the treaty, white trappers, hunters, and squatters moved into the territory. An 18-by-24-mile area (labelled on maps as "Indian Lands") was to be known as Pulaski County, in honour of General Casimir Pulaski, a Polish general. Four years passed before the county was populated enough to formally organize on May 6, 1839, making Pulaski County the 87th of Indiana's 92 counties.[55]

Thomas, at 21, immigrated alone to the USA in approximately 1852. I know this because he appeared in the 1851 UK census but on January 17, 1854 he married Lydia Ann Hughes, an American from Pennsylvania in White County, Indiana. I have no further information about Thomas and his life, except that he was a farmer. He died on October 7, 1894 at the age of 63.

By the early 1860s in Indiana, towns had been planned and were growing; the area was dotted with churches and schools to provide settlers with their needs. New railroads had taken the area out of its isolation. Four of the settlements later became incorporated towns: Francesville, Medaryville, Monterey, and Winamac. This describes the environment our ancestors would have found when they arrived.

Indiana was part of the USA, at this time comprising seventeen states in the northeast of the territory. On his arrival onto the land, Thomas would have been aware of the civil unrest that was growing to the east and south although there were no battles in Indiana. By 1862 William Hubbard, at 22, had arrived into Indiana and lived in Monon, White County: one county to the south of Pulaski. There was evidence that he was drafted into the Civil War between 1863 and 1865 which suggests he was Naturalized.

Then in approximately 1865, Jonathan and Henry Hubbard, the two youngest in the family, joined Thomas and William in their migration to the USA. The relief to see their brothers must have been immense as they shook hands, slapped one another on the back, and shared a beer. "How's the old man?" enquired

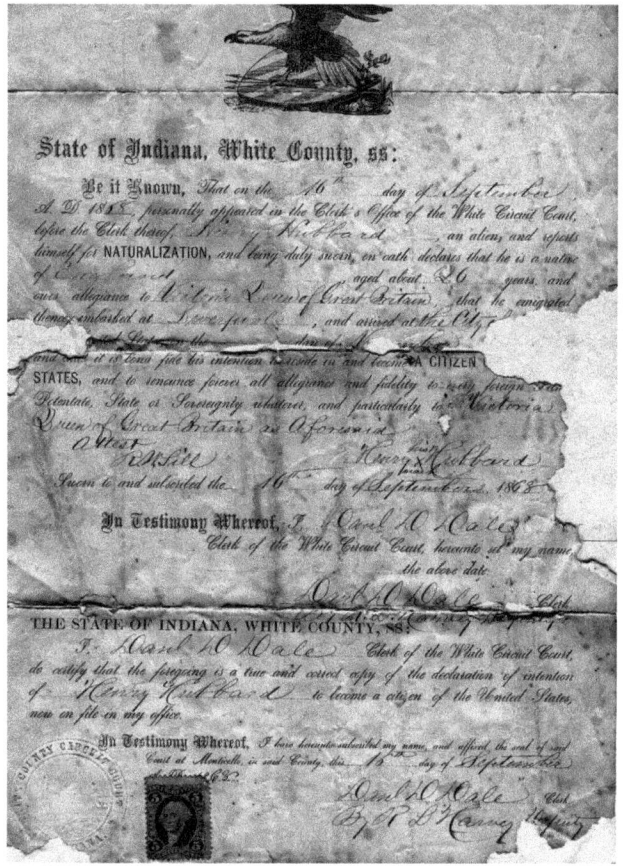

Henry renounced his queen. Initially, Henry worked on Thomas's farm when he arrived in Indiana in 1865. He was naturalized on September 16, 1868 which involved renouncing his allegiance to his queen, Queen Victoria. Being illiterate, Henry the 26-year-old made his mark on the document.

---

55 http://genealogytrails.com/ind/pulaski/pulaski_history.htm

Thomas. "Getting old. Worrying about who will take care of him in his old age!" responded Henry. "And Ma?" asked Thomas. "Her lumbago is bothering her. There were floods of tears when we left." Responded Jonathan. "For their sake, I am glad our John decided not to leave Eaton," added William.

The younger Hubbards arrived into their new country into an area busy becoming organized and settled so unlike the sleepy countryside they had left behind which had been the same for hundreds of years. Moreover, they witnessed Native peoples being displaced and former slaves attempting to find freedom and a new life. These country lads would have been unfamiliar with what they saw and were experiencing. For instance, they would never have encountered anyone who did not look like them, and they were illiterate. They would have been unaware of the idea of owning slaves. Indeed, they would have seen neither a Negro nor a North American Indian in England.

The brothers dispersed around the area. William married Elmira Weirick on October 30, 1866, one day after this brother Jonathan's wedding. William and Elmira had four sons to carry on the Hubbard name. I have not been able to confirm his occupation. He later moved to Plymouth, Marshall County where he died in 1887 at the age of 47.

Jonathan, the youngest, chose not to farm. I located a specific account of his life on the internet which reads like a biography:

(Photographer: Unknown) Henry, the farmer, left farming to work on railway construction of the Chicago, Indianapolis and Louisville railroad. In 1873 he returned to England to possibly introduce his Irish wife, Julia Shea whom he married on July 9, 1873, to his family. The family settled in Francesville, a town in Pulaski County. Here is Henry Hubbard smoking a cigar.

> *JONATHAN HUBBARD was born in Leicestershire, England, February 27, 1845, and is the son of William and Elizabeth Hubbard, who were the parents of nine children, named as follows: John, Mary, Thomas, Annie, Bessie, Eliza, William, Henry and Jonathan. Our subject, Jonathan Hubbard, the youngest of the family, came to America and settled in White County, this State, in 1865, and there engaged in railroading until 1879. He then came to this township and opened a restaurant in Star City, and has proved himself to be a worthy caterer and successful businessman. He was married at Badger, White Co., Ind., on October 31, 1866, to Elizabeth Phillips, a native of Champaign County, Ohio, born April 17, 1846, and the daughter of John and Catherine Phillips. Mr. Hubbard is a good citizen and is a member of the Independent Order of Odd Fellows.*
>
> *After his railroading days, Jonathan established himself as a businessman. I have not been able to confirm the date of his death.*

Henry lived most of his life in Francesville, Pulaski. He died on May 28, 1925, in Chicago at the age of 83. Henry and his wife had five daughters and one son, William John who became an entrepreneur, a furniture store owner, and a Charter member of the Lion's Club, its first President.

The Hubbard lads who ventured to Indiana in the mid-1850s were rough, illiterate country folk, who enjoyed smoking cigars. The culture shock must have been profound. Given more opportunities than they would have had in Eaton, they flourished. Thomas the farmer left first and established himself. He gave initial employment to his siblings. William did not live a long life and left little data. Jonathan became a well-respected citizen. I found little about Henry's life activities but see that his son became an influential businessman.

This is William John's DSS Registration card signed in 1941. He did not move far from his birthplace.

As I researched the Hubbards in Indiana, I located several families already living there. I have not been able to establish whether they were related to our four.

While these Hubbards are not our ancestors per se, we share their genes. Their story of courage and adventure is part of our story.

We continue now with your great-great-grandfather, Alec Hubbard.

Endnotes

Through Ancestry, I was contacted by a Bill Hubbard, a descendant of Henry. I was pleased to read his email below.

Hi Daphne,

Many thanks for your interesting email. Yes, these brothers were really something.

In some cultures, the eldest son inherits all the father's property. I don't know if that was the case with our family but that might explain why they needed to venture out. I would like to find out the role Thomas had with the Monon Railroad before and during our civil war. After the war, the brothers arrived and got jobs with the railroad. My great grandfather, Henry, seemed to have used his railroad money to start farming in Salem township, just south of Francesville Indiana. My father once stopped the car on top of the railroad track bed and pointed to a strip of land southeast of the track as the home of his grandfather before the family moved into town.

Indiana is beautiful this time of the year with all the crops in full bloom, yet short enough to still see the land expanse.

Hope you are enjoying Canada.
Regards,
Bill Hubbard, June 2, 2016

CHART 11. FAMILY GROUP SHEET FOR WILLIAM HUBBARD. FOUR SONS LEFT

SPOUSE: WILLIAM HUBBARD

Birth:	Abt 1801 in Eaton,
Marriage:	26 Nov 1825 in Thorpe Arnold; Wm. Hubbard, of Ab-Kettleby, & Eliz. Riley 26 Nov 1825
Death:	04 Jan 1887 in Eaton, Leicestershire,
Father:	William Hubbard
Mother:	Elizabeth (Elston) Hubbard

SPOUSE: ELIZABETH (RILEY) HUBBARD

Birth:	26 Jun 1804 in Melton Mowbray
Death:	1870 in Eaton Hundred Framland, Leics
Father:	John Riley
Mother:	

CHILDREN:

1 M
Name:	**John Hubbard**
Birth:	Abt 1825 in Eaton,
Marriage:	Apr 1853 in Melton Mowbray,
Death:	22 May 1886 in Eaton, Leicestershire
Spouse:	**Mary Ann (Tyler) Hubbard**

2 F
Name:	Mary Jane Hubbard
Birth:	29 Mar 1829 in Eaton,
Marriage:	22 Jul 1850 in Eaton,
Death:	15 Apr 1872 in Eaton,
Spouse:	George Shelton

3 M
Name:	Thomas Hubbard
Birth:	22 May 1831 in Eaton,
Marriage:	17 Jan 1854 in White, Indiana
Death:	07 Oct 1894 in Mississippi
Spouse:	Lydia Ann (Hughes) Hubbard

4 F
Name:	Elizabeth ('Bessie') Hubbard
Birth:	Abt 1836 in Eaton
Death:	26 Apr 1843 in England

5 F
Name:	Ann Hubbard
Birth:	Abt 1837 in Eaton

6 M	Name:	William John Hubbard
	Birth:	Oct 1840 in Eaton,
	Marriage:	30 Oct 1866 in White, Indiana
	Death:	1887 in Plymouth, Marshall, Indiana, USA
	Burial:	Plymouth, Marshall County, Indiana, USA
	Spouse:	Elmira (Weirick) Hubbard

8 M	Name:	Henry Hubbard
	Birth:	1842 in Eaton,
	Marriage:	09 Jul 1873 in Pulaski, Indiana, USA
	Death:	28 May 1925 in Chicago, Cook County, Illinois, USA
	Burial:	Pulaski, Pulaski County, Indiana, USA
	Spouse:	Julia

9 M	Name:	Jonathan Hubbard
	Birth:	22 Feb 1845 in Eaton,
	Marriage:	31 Oct 1867 in White, Indiana
	Death:	27 Jun 1888 in Indiana, USA
	Burial:	Star City, Pulaski County, Indiana, USA
	Spouse:	Elizabeth (Phillips) Hubbard

12.

GRANDAD HUBBARD'S STORY

Wilfred Alec Hubbard was your Nana's father, my grandfather, Grandad to me. This story is based on my research as well as my memories of my beloved grandad, a super male influence for me in the absence of my dad in my early years. I remember him as a kindly, mild-mannered man, gentle and hard working. I will never really know how he and my Nana lived but at least I know the location well and can remember how difficult life was without electricity, running water, and the amenities we have today. I recall the coal-burning fireplace, the outside toilets that had to be emptied, and the trauma of wash day.

This would have been how he would have told his story although I have taken liberties!

(Photographer: R. Heathcote) The second war was finally over when this photograph was taken. I am giving my favourite granddaughter a ride. We were trying to get back to a new normal.

You wish me to tell you about me life as I remember? You know I was born in 1890. When I arrived, there were already two children in the family: our Harry and Trissie. We lived on Main Street in Stathern. The Browns lived next door and so did me Grandad and Grannie Smith. The Browns had many children and so did we so we all grew up together. We went in and out of one another's houses as children, usually looking for something to eat. We all lived together on Main Street.

We were on a trip to Skegness with Kathleen, Reg, and Daphne. Rosie was in the hospital at this time. Kathleen insisted I came along with the family. It was a day trip to this popular seaside town on the Lincolnshire coast. Reg had a car by then. It looks a windy but nice day. 1946 perhaps. Skegness is a two-hour trip to the coast through the city of Boston. The sea is often miles out. It is usually cold but still is a favourite place to go for the day.

(Photographer: Unknown) I think the look on me face tells you how I am feeling. Another trip to the coast. I was again encouraged to join the family for a day trip. Missing me Rosie and feeling despondent about the future. Kathleen and Reg included me in their outings even though I felt so lost. I couldn't manage a smile on this trip to the seaside. Rosie would have been in the hospital when this was taken. I could do nothing for her.

(Photographer: A. Thompson) We did go to the coast often! Here we are with Kathleen's friend, Valerie and her daughter, Vivienne. You can just see the sea in the background. It looks like a warm day for a change. I am not dressed for the beach and most probably didn't want to be there! It was difficult for me to manage a smile for the camera on these outings. Kathleen had to be cheerful for her family. But really, she was so worried about her mother. Reg looks very thin here. He had not been home very long.

(Photographer: unknown) I spent a lot of time with this little girl who would not be destined as a horsewoman! This little pony belonged to a friend in the village.

We had relied on horsepower for many years. Those were days long gone. But I remember being told me Grandad Smith was a horse whisperer. Seeing the little pony reminded me. He died just after I was born. But me Grannie Smith talked to me about him. She died when I was about 20 and just settling into work. She lived with the posh Clamp family then in the village

Top: (Photographer: Unknown) This is a few years later. I had lost me Rosie and Geoff had been born. 1948 perhaps. I wonder why I am so dressed up for these trips. I am overdressed in all the pictures! This is us walking along the promenade again- Skegness. It doesn't look very warm! Daphne does not look well in this photograph and she wasn't. We had a scare. She had to go into the Children's Hospital in Nottingham for six weeks. We nearly lost her. But she did recover after her operation.

You look distraught but in this later picture you managed a smile.

Bottom Left: (Photographer: Unknown) I could not be happy without me Rosie. But I was happy to be with me grandchildren, especially to see that you had recovered. Oh, now you are taking me back in me memory!

Bottom Right: (Photographer: Unknown) This is me dad, Arthur, although everyone called him Bradley. As you can see, he liked dogs. So, I grew up with them. He was born in Eastwell, you see, close by Stathern. In 1858 he moved to Stathern when he married me mam. She was a Stathern girl. This photo was taken on Main Street, outside their house. He loved flowers, particularly geraniums which he grew on his window sills. He encouraged me to become a gardener and showed me the way!

(Photographer: Unknown) This is me mam, Saran Smith. She is the same age as me dad. She was born in Stathern. Me Grannie was Louisa Smith and Grandad was Andrew Smith. He was the one who worked with horses but I never knew him because he died just after I was born. We all lived on Main Street in Stathern. Me mam told me she went into service as a cook before she married me dad. Here she is in front of her house on Main Street with another dog and a little person I do not know.

My dad told me he became a farm boy when he was 13 although he did get a few years of schooling. His mother was Mary and his dad, John. Me Grandad and Grannie. We didn't see much of them. Eaton where they lived wasn't far but we always seemed to have other things to do.

Me dad had two older brothers and one younger. Me grandad told me all about his four brothers all leaving Eaton to go far away to America. Because of the distance, we didn't hear from them. I often wonder how they were doing. Not many would have the courage to go that far from home. Unfortunately, there is a saying "out of sight, out of mind" that seems to be how it was.

Me dad was an ironstone quarryman in Eastwell. That was the reason I went to work there with me friend and neighbour Edgar Brown. I was 17 then when I began to work at The Stanton Ironworks Company Limited not thinking I would work there all me working life. I was an Assistant Carpenter at the Ironstone quarry in Eaton about a mile walk from Stathern. But soon began driving the trains, which I liked a lot.

We lived next door to the Browns on Main Street. They had quite a few children. We all grew up together. Edgar was the eldest. He had three sisters, Lizzie, Beatie and Rosie. I remember those girls would play hopscotch on the road outside their house. I fell for the youngest, Rosie and was heartbroken when she had to leave to go into service. She had to look after a baby and was the general servant as well. She worked so hard: I worried about her. She was not strong, you see. I don't mean she was weak, just gentle and a little fragile. We didn't see much of one another when she first left Stathern. Then we started to write. With all those people around, we didn't have much privacy. Thank goodness we had Stathern Woods close by. We could go for walks and be on our own and explore. We found a lovely bluebell grove which we considered as ours.

I am glad Rosie had eyes for me. I wanted to marry her and so asked her father. He must have liked me because he agreed. Rosie's brother, Edgar, was me best man. I was pleased to have him there.

WEDDING.

A pretty little wedding was solemnised in the Parish Church on Monday afternoon, the contracting parties being Mr. Wilfred Alec Hubbard and Miss Ethel Rose Brown. The bride was given away by her father, Mr. W. Brown, and was prettily attired in a cream dress with grey hat. The bridesmaids were Miss Rachael Hubbard and Miss Gladys Hutchins, who were dressed in grey, and wore black silk hats, with pale blue sprays. Mr. Edgar Brown officiated as best man. The Rev. W. New, Rector, performed the ceremony. The happy couple were the recipients of many useful presents, and the bells rang out merry peals in honour of the occasion.

Left: (Photographer: Unknown) We married on Monday, March 15, 1915. Rosie looked so nice. I was proud of her. I think I always knew Rosie was the one for me. Wedding bells rang out for us on that day, a beautiful spring day. Yes, this is the Marriage Certificate we received. Edgar had just married Alice Bird from the village and I was his best man. We were close friends and workmates at the Stanton Ironworks. You can see pictures of where Kathleen was born on pages 13 and 14.

Finding a house was not easy but we did manage to find a tiny row house to rent up the street in the yard of a cheese factory, a tiny cottage, one down, two up, in a narrow lane, one of three, off the main street. The house was what you would call primitive. No water or electricity. Just a roof over our heads. But it was ours and our families were in the village as well. So, in a way it was perfect. Can you imagine three tiny houses on that bit of land?

I remember, Rosie was not a brilliant cook although I liked what she made. Perhaps she did boil the vegetables I grew too long, but that was alright. I bought her a treadle sewing machine which she used to make new clothes out of old clothes in the early days. She showed Kathleen how to sew too.

Because our new house had no garden, I rented a plot in the allotments to grow fruit and vegetables:

(Photographer: D. Field) We soon found another house, it was during the Great War, a bigger house on Main Street close to where Rosie and I had grown up next door to one another. It was a two-bedroom row house on the main street near the fork in the road where the road veers left and right, one toward Harby, the Station and Nottingham and the other toward Plungar, Granby, Belvoir Castle, and Grantham. Ours is the one with the red door although it did not have a red door when we lived there!

(Photographer: Unknown) On November 28, 1916 a brown-eyed baby girl was born in the cottage. Here she is. We named her Kathleen Elizabeth. Oh, but me Rosie suffered from her birth and could not face having more children. That was a great pity she didn't want to suffer like that again. So, we would have no more children. Rosie was so gentle and not at all strong in that way. Her mam and sister Beattie tried to help her but could not ease the pain.

about 10 feet by 30. I became a keen gardener with the help of me dad. We grew: potatoes, carrots, peas, cabbage, celery, black currants, red currants, and rhubarb. I gardened most of me life. I wanted to contribute to the family. Fertilizer was available too: I used to take care of sewage waste by emptying it into a hole I dug in the garden. No need for other fertilizers! The crops were good. Surprisingly it did not smell but no doubt increased our immune systems.

(Photographer: Unknown) Sometime before the Great War, bicycles began to appear as a means to get around instead of horses and the pony and trap. After I found a bicycle at a price I could afford, I biked everywhere. I liked to take it apart, clean and oil it often. It was the way to get around before Reg returned from Service and bought a car. Oh yes. This must have been me first bike. I was so proud to have wheels! It looks so clean. I am carrying a milk container on the handlebars.

I did not serve in the Great War because I was working in what they said was an essential service: The Stanton Ironworks Company Ltd during that War produced large numbers of shell casings. This continued also during WWII. I was very pleased I was not called to serve because I wanted to be with me family. Some of the young lads went off but I heard they had a rough time with the conditions, the weather, the awful food, and the fear. I heard there was a bad illness, the flu too but it did not reach Stathern. We were all eager to hear about Armistice Day: November 11, 1918. We wanted to forget the war and get on with our lives.

Soon after the Great War ended, Stathern Council built a War Memorial Hall on Main Street which we called "The Institute."[56] We enjoyed all indoor village events in the Institute, jumble sales, flower shows, produce competitions, and community feasts. As well, there would be dances every Saturday night with live music. These were good times for the villagers who liked to dance. As Kathleen grew, she loved to dance. The only music we had was what we created for ourselves. The Browns were musical, thank goodness.

(Photographer: Unknown) Oh yes, I liked the game of football. Here I am with the team standing: second from the left. I was not playing that day. I was small in stature compared with those burly fellows.

Oh I remember, Harry was me older brother by a year. I looked up to him, y'know. After he left home, Harry worked as a carter for a grocer in Mansfield near Nottingham and lived in lodgings with the Coupe family. We lost touch a little after that because of the distance. But wouldn't ye know, he fell for the eldest Coupe daughter, Lizzie. And married her in the summer of 1911. Then they had two boys: Vic and Billy. Elizabeth died in the late 1950s. I used to bike over to see them all in Kinoulton. They lived in a heritage cottage known as Stone Cottage with a large garden in Kinoulton, Nottinghamshire. The old house had a scullery and a small living room. He liked horse brasses and had many of them hanging in his house.[57]

I continued working at Stanton Ironworks on the road to Eaton. Young Kathleen brought lunch to me every day.

Rosie's sister Beatie got herself into trouble. Rosie thought we should offer her a home. So, we did. Her little one, Dorothy, went to live with her Grannie Brown. It was wartime: there were no houses.

Kathleen was good at school but refused to go to the Grammar School when a position was offered to her. That was disappointing because she would have been good there. But she said she would be out of place. So, Kathleen stayed at Stathern school until she was 14. Then she went briefly into service, a position I got for

---

56 There were public subscriptions. People could buy a brick for 2s 6d to help the building fund.
57 I was particularly fond of Uncle Harry. He and my grandad were so alike in appearance and demeanour. My grandad and I would cycle over to visit them in Kinoulton to their tiny farm house with a huge garden, a heritage house, which could not be renovated. I recall how basic it was in its design with its outside kitchen, a tiny living room and outside scullery, no door handles but latches. Certainly, there was no running water. Toilets were outside. The garden was ample with apple and pear trees, and a kitchen garden. There was no possibility of keeping the rooms clean. There would have been a damp odor, drafts and darkness. Oil lamps were used in the evenings, or they simply went to bed. I was mesmerised by the horse brasses that decorated the living room, which Uncle Harry would tell me were original and genuine. He taught me how to determine the real ones. I have a few of his brasses today.

her. But it didn't suit her. So, I fetched her home. She got a job at Woolworths in town. After the Great War, things had changed. Girls had more choices.

Then Rosie's sister, Beatie met and married Ernie Green. We all liked him and were pleased for Beatie. So, she left us. Must have been a few years after the Great War ended. Then she had a little boy she named Reginald.

Rosie lost her dad soon after that. He suddenly became ill, went into hospital in Nottingham, and never came out. All of the Browns were so upset. I was too as I had known the family all me life.

Then we found a new house we called Wood View which had three small bedrooms, a living room, kitchen and front room. Rosie liked that our front door did not open directly onto the street but was through the garden path. We had a cold room off the kitchen. Toilets were outside, round the back. We had no running water but we did have two electric lights. We had a coal-burning fireplace that had an oven attached and also a tank for heating water. We always had a pot of water boiling on the top! The fireplace needed to be blacked, just like cleaning black shoes, so it looked smart. We felt pampered as we sat around the fire on a cold evening. We had candles for upstairs which had no heat at all up there.

The house had a huge garden. I set about making flower beds and a vegetable garden and building a garden shed for me potting plants. Down the garden path beyond the wooden garden shed,

(Photographer: Unknown) When Kathleen was about 18, we moved to a bigger house, called Wood View, in the east of the village, near The Green, overlooking the fields and woods in the Heartland of England. This photograph is taken in the front garden of our new home. Rosie and I were about 44 years old. It would be '34.

me garden at Wood View spread about 30 feet wide by 75 long. Just behind the shed were the black currant bushes (me favourite fruit). I also had rhubarb plants because everyone like the early fruit. I struggled with a small strawberry patch because Kathleen liked them. But I preferred to grow vegetables: potatoes, carrots, peas, parsnips, runner beans, celery (in mounds), onions, cabbages, broccoli and Brussels sprouts. I didn't try cauliflower! I liked to have lots available so that we could eat something different each day. We would harvest what was ready that day to cook for our evening meal. That was what we villagers did. We would dig up only those potatoes we needed. They tasted good when eaten right away. We had plenty of herbs too. Mint, parsley, thyme and sage were always available.

The house was attached to another house that Rosie's sister Lizzie and her husband Phil moved into. So, Rosie had family all around her.

I think the thirties were good for us. We were contented. We were dealing with Kathleen as a teenager. All she wanted to do was to dance! There were dances almost every week at the Institute. We encouraged her. She had a job at Woolworths in Melton which she enjoyed. She cycled to work. I remember she went into digs for a short time too. She bought us a white rose plant from Woolworths. It bloomed in the front garden for many, many years. Kathleen knew roses were my favourite flower.

I would take Rosie into Melton market sometimes and treat us to an iced bun.

Kathleen took music lessons to learn how to play the piano which she did beautifully. We bought her a rosewood piano which we kept in the front room of Wood View. We didn't use the front room very often. That room was kept clean and tidy for when we had visitors. We lived in the back room next to the kitchen where we kept the fire going all the time.

(Photographer: Unknown) Then Kathleen met the dancing bus driver. He was much sought after as a dancing partner but took a shine to Kathleen. Yes. Here she is with Reg and his brother Tom. I think they went out for the day to the coast. Living inland we were often drawn to the sea as you can imagine. They are well dressed for the trip.

(Photographer: Unknown) Rosie and I went on a coach trip with a group to Yarmouth. I am smiling there in the centre. Me Rosie is on my left. We had a fine time. I was glad to take her there. She looks a bit unsure!

(Photographer: Unknown) Here we are later in our lives at the front garden gate. We would have been about 50. We are deep in conversation here. I wonder what that was about! So many memories.

(Photographer: Unknown) Rosie and I look so happy together in this photograph taken in the garden at Wood View, and we were. Rosie liked to take care of the flowers in the front and side of the garden. I grew vegetables in the back garden and still had the allotment down the street. I had built a garden shed in the back with the help of me dad and me friends. In there I grew seedlings and stored all me garden stuff.

1940 Reg was called up to serve in the Second World War as a driver. Although we were all expecting this to happen, we were devastated. I could remember the Great War and was afraid of what would happen to us and especially those who had been called to service. The young lads did not seem to be joining up as quickly for this war! They had heard too many stories about the last one!

Kathleen and Reg wanted to marry and so they did in January 1941. They married quickly when Reg had a weekend pass. Kathleen and Reg are smiling in this photo but there are no smiles from Rosie and me. Neither from Reg's folks. We were all worried about the war we had entered.

(Photographer: Unknown)

Reg was in training in Taunton, Somerset, for about a year then was sent overseas. A baby had joined the family. A welcome distraction. It was an unsettling time for us all. I set about keeping the family together. We had gas masks and a safe place to hide under the stairs should a bomb fall on us dropped from an aircraft overhead. Fortunately, none did. But we were all afraid, all the villagers. Looking back, we were not nearly as affected as the city folk in the south of the country. We did have enough to eat but no luxuries.

We knew more about what was going on with the war because Phil next door had a radio and was often listening to the news. There was an airport in Langar, a short distance from Stathern, where the Canadian forces were stationed. We villagers thought the airfield might become a target. But it didn't. The airmen often attended dances with the local girls. We encouraged Kathleen to go and enjoy herself. There was just too much loneliness and sadness and uncertainty while Reg was away. She needed to get out and forget for a little while. We were glad to look after Daphne for her. Rosie became a happy Nana to Daphne.

During the war years, I encouraged Kathleen to play the piano and we would have a sing-song. Pack up Your Troubles in Your old kit bag and Smile and of course: We'll meet again: Don't know where, Don't know When.

Oh yes, I liked to smoke a pipe just like me dad. That's what we men did in them days. Tobacco was bought in tins. I filled the pipe with the tobacco from the tin and lit it with twisted paper which was lit from the fire. I would puff away until the tobacco ignited. I loved the smell! I am not sure everyone else did!

Oh yes, these pictures are of me mam and me dad later in their lives, taken just before the war. They lived near us on Main Street. Everyone seemed to live on Main Street! No, they were not as stern as they look! They knew another war was coming. They both remembered the Great War and were not looking forward to another one. They remembered the shortages, the awful fear, the losses and sadness and did not want that again. But it came anyway.

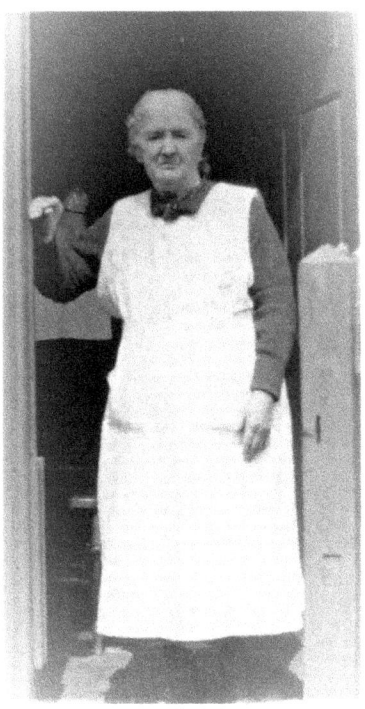

(Photographer: Unknown)

(Photographer: Unknown)

I visited them every day. They were almost next door to us. Me mam died just before the war got started but then she was about 80. Me dad died a few years after me mam but before the war ended.

But Rosie did not seem content in the village. She tried religion for a while which did not satisfy her. She would make apricot jam from dried apricots. Somehow, she became disconnected from her life, with Stathern. I was worried about her. She had her family all around her, her mam and sisters Lizzie and Beatie, for support. But she was such a gentle soul. Perhaps too sensitive. She was unsettled.

I cannot bear to think about it. A few years into the war, Rosie became ill: she had an awful cough. She had become infected with Pulmonary Tuberculosis, consumption. She was taken away from us so that we would not be infected. She had to be isolated from her family and neighbours to protect us all from infection.[58] It was all so sudden: so unexpected. I was unable to see her very often because I could not get to the hospital.

---

58 She was taken into The Carlton Hayes Hospital in Narborough which was the Leicestershire and Rutland County Lunatic Asylum. I wonder why she was taken there. Was there no other place for her? I have had intermittent images in my life of visiting her on a veranda in her bed. To reach her we went through a series of corridors which had gates. We had to wait for a staff member to unlock the gates so that we could go through and see her. Even though this would have been in the 1946/1947-time frame, I now know this would have been plausible. I would have missed Nana Rosie tremendously and would have felt a profound loss. She needed to be in isolation and needed the sunshine for recovery which explains the reason she would have been on a veranda.

(Photographer: R. Heathcote) Oh, this is the last picture I have of us. So, it is special. Rosie looked bonnie then. Here we are with May Brown, her brother Jim's daughter. It would have been in the spring of 1943. We are in a field in Stathern. My goodness, I am so dressed up! We must have been going somewhere. We were looking after Daphne for Kathleen while she worked in Woolworths. Me Rosie was happy doing this for Kathleen and became close with Daphne.

A couple of years after this photograph of us was taken, we lost Grannie Brown. We knew that Rosie's mam was ailing. That was in February 1945 in her house near us. Kathleen went to check on her and she had died. We had to decide what to tell Rosie.

(Photographer: Unknown) It looks as though I am painting a barrel outside the house. You can see me garden shed that me dad and I built at the top of the garden at Wood View. We collected rainwater that we used for washing clothes. Then I didn't have to fetch all the water we needed from the village well.

I was happy and content in the garden even though it was a bit solitary. But then I felt good providing for the family. My hard work was always appreciated. Yet I felt very alone. This was not how it was supposed to be.

After Reg returned we eventually bought the house from Mr. Rowbottom, who had built the house. Then Reg started renovations including connecting to the village water supply and the sewage system and installing more electricity. That was real progress for us. I wonder what Rosie would have thought to it all!.

Stathern was the first in the area to have electricity. It came about this way: Mr. Ernest Green, a toolmaker and engineer, persuaded us villagers in 1926 to lay aside our oil lamps and take a new fangled light from a wire. He installed a large National Gas Company engine run on crude oil in a former lace factory near the church. He built a storage house and supplied a network of poles and lines. It cost 30 shillings to have a light installed and 10 shillings every three months for the electricity.[59] So that is how we had our single electric light in our living room! Our church was the first in the Leicester diocese to have electric lights! First the businesses were connected and then the houses. Imagine!

Grandad Hubbard paused again to collect his memories before continuing…..

Me sister Trissie lived with Grannie Smith when she was 16 to make room for all my brothers and sisters in the house. Grannie Smith was alone because Grandad Smith had died. They were both lace workers. Trissie married William Palmer known as "Fruity" most probably because he was a greengrocer who later became a butcher. We kept pigs in their large yard on Main Street, Stathern.[60]

When Reg returned from service, he had his motorbike and then a car. We could then go to see me Rosie. But she grew weaker and didn't recover from her illness and died on May 17, 1947.[61] I cannot describe to you

---

59 Report from Jack Smith in undated copy of Melton Mowbray Times. Your Nana's friend Emily Jopling told me how she would read the meters, make up invoices and collect the money! At the time she told me, I didn't understand the significance of what she was telling me!

60 Although I do not recall his sister, Trissie Maud, I do recall that she married a butcher, Bill Palmer. We kept a pig in their yard, which we fed with table scraps. I would feed the pig with my grandad. Periodically, we would kill the pig and share the rewards. Who killed the pig? There was a slaughterhouse in the village. I do remember carving up the carcass placing bits if it on several plates to share with neighbours.

61 On May 17, 1947, she was one of 18,000 who died of TB that year in England. Her death certificate indicated she had secondary dementia. She was only 53.

(Photographer: Unknown) Oh yes. Here I am driving the train at the Stanton ironworks.

(Photographer: Unknown) In this picture with all the lads, I am the shortest! With the coveralls. In the middle of the picture.

my sadness that I would have to go on living without her. Kathleen was expecting another baby and missed her mother. Soon we would be five in the house. So many changes in such a short time.

Having Reg home, being part of the family for the first time, without Rosie at home was so difficult for me. I moved out of the front bedroom for them and moved to the back room. Daphne had the other front bedroom. There were many struggles at that time. Fortunately, we had another distraction. Another baby was born into the family and gave us reason to be joyful.

Grandad Hubbard again paused for his thoughts to surface, puffing on his pipe as he often did, before he continued.....

I remember showing Daphne how we plucked a chicken for our dinner. I would give the feathers to Beatie for making feather beds. Daphne was not too interested in its innards! Then she would watch me put a new sole on a pair of shoes. I cut out the leather using the old sole as a pattern and carefully nailed the new sole onto the shoe. I would set traps to catch rabbits. I wasn't keen to do this but we needed the food. Then I would skin the animal and remove its innards and prepare it for a rabbit pie. Daphne was both intrigued and disgusted. She and I were great pals at that time.

Before I retired, I worked in the garden but gave up the allotment. It was too much for me. Reg wanted to do things his way. But then fruit and vegetables became readily available in the shops. We didn't have to rely on the garden. I remember when we first ate frozen peas! They tasted so like the ones out of the garden. But potatoes out of the garden were delicious.

It makes sense to me that I would be close to the land like generations of Hubbards before me who were farmers. Me dad was the first to move away from farming but it was in our blood. So, you could say it came naturally to me.

Reg renovated the house and built a new kitchen, indoor toilets, and a bedroom for me above the kitchen. I was very glad when he connected the water supply and the sewage. That made everything easier for all of us. I didn't have to fetch water from the village well and carry it on me back! He put in electricity throughout the house as well.

I have taken a look at me life with photographs and remembering. I think you can see from the photographs everything changed for me when Rosie was taken from me. I never moved very far from Stathern and never wanted to. We went through an awful time during the war years, not knowing whether we would survive and who would return. I worked and looked after the family.

After I retired, I seemed to have no purpose. I felt in the way even though Kathleen included me in everything they did. So, I visited members of me in-law family in Nottingham frequently: Kate Slater. I seemed to stay away for long periods. I was lonely.

We move now to the Smiths. I have alluded to them before: Grannie Louisa Smith.

(Photographer: Unknown) Oh, this is a picture of me with Ernie Green, Beatie's husband. He is beside me. I have no idea where we were! Happily queuing up for something. And dressed up! Do you like our caps?

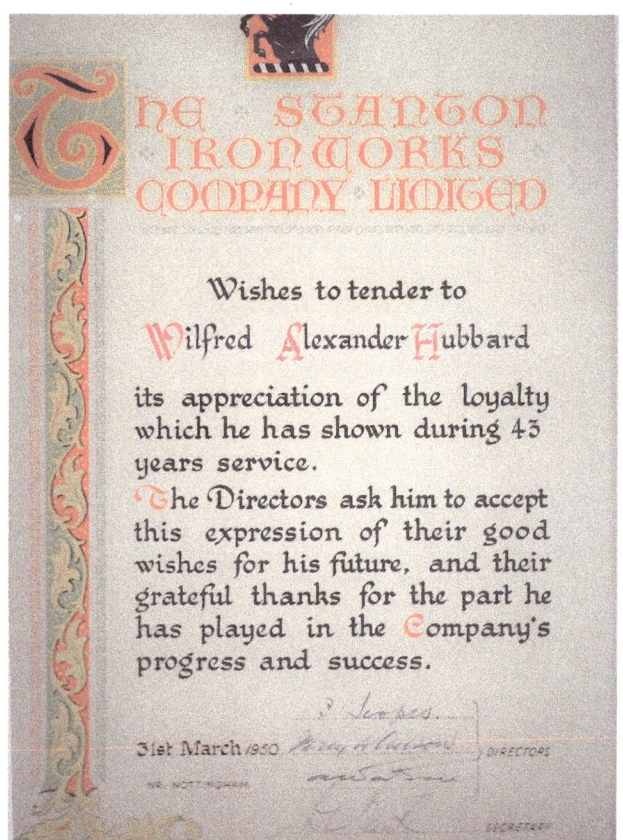

(Photographer: Unknown) I worked at the ironworks until I retired at 60. It was then 1950. I received a formal note of appreciation! Pity they didn't spell me name right! Fancy 43 years of service. I had forgotten I started working in 1907. Where has all the time gone?

(Photographer: R. Heathcote) I worked in the garden during the week and disappeared over the weekends to be with Kate Goodacre, who was part of the Rosie's family, and her family until Kate passed away in June 1945. I felt another loss.

ENDNOTES

I have painted a picture of a love story cut short which is my image having considered my grandfather's demeanour and what I learned from my Auntie Beat. Eventually, he met a woman who lived in Harby, an Irish woman, Violet O'Leary, who was glad of his company. Then he became ill: cancer of the stomach. I saw him in the hospital in Nottingham a short time before his death. I was desperately sad to see him ailing, knowing that we would lose him soon. When I heard the sad news, I drove quickly from London where I then lived.

(Photographer: D. Field) His body is buried in the cemetery on Tofts Hill next to Nana Rosie. We visited the graves often in the old days and took flowers. There is no one in Stathern now to do that. The graves will be abandoned and forgotten.

He died of stomach cancer on September 22, 1965. He was at rest in a coffin in the living room of the woman with whom he lived, Mrs. O'Leary, who was kind to him. She looked after him in his last days. He was where he wanted to be. We were grateful to her. His was the first dead body I had ever seen. But that was not my grandad anymore. I remember stroking his face, saying thank you, and putting a rose for him in the coffin. He loved roses. And so, another life ends. He was 75 years old. Tears swell in my eyes as I remember.

Certificate of Birth

YF 076451

1 & 2 ELIZ. 2 CH. 20

Name and Surname: Wilfred Alec Hubbard.
Sex: Boy.
Date of Birth: Third July 1890
Place of Birth — Registration District: Melton Mowbray.
Sub-district: Clawson

I, Richard Winters, Deputy Superintendent Registrar for the Registration District of MELTON MOWBRAY do hereby certify that the above particulars have been compiled from an entry in a register in my custody.

Witness my hand this 24th day of April 1958.

384/18

Grandad Hubbard's birth certificate

CERTIFIED COPY of an ENTRY of BIRTH.

Superintendent Registrar's District of Melton Mowbray
Registrar's Sub-District of Clawson in the Counties of Leicester & Nottingham

No.	When and where Born	Name (if any)	Sex	Name and Surname of Father	Name and Maiden Surname of Mother	Rank or Profession of Father	Signature, Description, and Residence of Informant	When Registered	Signature of Registrar
362	Twenty first June 1893 Stathern R.S.D. (Leicester)	Ethel Rose	Girl	William Brown	Caroline Brown formerly Slater	Blacksmith (Journeyman)	C. Brown Mother Stathern	Fourth August 1893	George James Registrar

I hereby certify that the above is a true Copy of an Entry of Birth in a Register Book in my custody.

Witness my hand this 27 day of June 1905.

E. A. Phinn Deputy Superintendent Registrar

Nana Rosie's birth certificate

CHART 12 GRANDAD
WILFRED ALEC HUBBARD

Wilfred Alec Hubbard
b: 03 Jul 1890 in Near The Green, Stathern,
m: 15 Mar 1915 in St. Guthlac's, Stathern
d: 22 Sep 1965 in Melton Mowbray,
; Age: 75 in Harby

Arthur "Bradley" Hubbard
b: Oct 1858 in Eastwell,
m: 19 May 1884 in Stathern,
d: Mar 1943 in Melton Mowbray,

Sarah Ann "Saran" (Smith) Hubbard
b: 06 Apr 1860 in Stathern,
d: Sep 1940 in Melton Mowbray,

John Hubbard
b: Abt 1825 in Eaton,
m: Apr 1853 in Melton Mowbray,
d: 22 May 1886 in Eaton,

Mary Ann (Tyler) Hubbard
b: 1825
d: Oct 1902 in Leicestershire,

Andrew Smith
b: 1828 in Stathern,
m: 12 May 1859 in Melton Mowbray R O, ; Louisa Rippin (widow) at time of marriage
d: Jun 1892 in Melton Mowbray, ; Age: 62

Louisa (Rippin) Smith
b: 1832 in Harby,
d: 27 Mar 1912 in Stathern,

William Hubbard
b: Abt 1801 in Eaton,
m: 26 Nov 1825 in Thorpe Arnold;
d: 04 Jan 1887 in Eaton,

Elizabeth (Riley) Hubbard
b: 26 Jun 1804 in Melton Mowbray,; Christening date
d: 1870 in Eaton Hundred Framland, Leics

Richard Tyler
b: Abt 1796 in Leicestershire,
m: 04 Jul 1820 in Ashby Folville,
d: Jan 1846 in Melton Mowbray; Family search

Elizabeth (Rodwell) Tyler
b: 1792 in Ashby Folville,
d: Apr 1875 in Eaton, ;

William Smith
b: Abt 1796
m: 1814 in Stathern, England
d: 20 Mar 1838,

Ann (Hawley) (Smith) Dyer
b: 1792 in Stathern,
d: Jan 1865 in Melton Mowbray,

Samuel Smith
b: Abt 1795 in Harby,
m:
d: 09 Aug 1873 in Melton Mowbray,

Sarah (Isam) Smith
b: Abt 1789 in Stathern,
d: Oct 1866 in Melton Mowbray,

13.

THE STORY OF LOUISA RIPPIN SMITH

Our story continues with your Nana's side of the family. Grannie Hubbard was a former Smith. So, we will look at our Smith ancestors.

Firstly, the origin of the name. Smith is an occupational name for a worker in metal, from Middle English smith, probably a derivative of smitan 'to strike, hit or hammer.' Metal-working was one of the earliest occupations for which specialist skills were required, and its importance ensured that this term and its equivalents were perhaps the most widespread of all occupational surnames in Europe. It is the most common surname in most of the English-speaking world. We see our Smiths did not follow this tradition.

(Photographer: Unknown) The fine lady you see here, dressed in her Sunday best, is Louisa Rippin Smith (nee Smith). Yes, her maiden name was Smith: she initially married Joseph Rippin but after he suddenly died at an early age, she remarried another Smith. She is your great, great, great grandmother... Sadly, the photograph is old and unclear.

Louisa will tell her story herself from her memories, written from my imagination of course but based on known dates, names, and places. This is how I believe she would tell her story…..

You want me to talk about me life. Let me see what I remember…. So far as I know me family came from the Harby area but I do know that me ma, Sarah, was born in Stathern in 1789. Me dad was born in Harby in 1795. We all lived in Harby: Charlotte, Harriet, Emanuel, Israel, and finally me. I was born in 1832. We stayed around Harby most of the time as kids. Me mam's mam lived in the village, the Isam family all lived in Harby, although mam was born in Stathern.

I remember Uncle Sam Isam took in our Emanuel about the time our Saran was born. Emanuel never married y' know and could never seem to find a home of his own. The news was not good for him either because he had to go into the Workhouse in Melton after that. He still worked but had nowhere to live. I lost touch of him really. So now you know about our Emanuel.

We used to go to Stathern sometimes to visit me Grannie's family. I don't remember much about them.

Stathern is a good walk through the fields from Harby. Or there is a track to walk on if the fields were too wet and muddy. It took me about half an hour in me young days. In them days, if you want to go anywhere you walk, or beg a ride with a carter and pony who is going your way and will give you a ride.

I remember there was a canal running through Harby where the village children would play. The canal was sometimes overgrown with bull rushes. We would collect them for decoratin'. The canal was used for moving things from place to place, anything that needed to be moved from chickens to vegetables. As children we would go there to watch the boats and wave to the drivers. The boats would be pulled by horses, walking along a towpath beside the canal.

I remember there were blackberry bushes along the towpath so we would pick them to make jam. Many of us would go as a group: mothers, kids, grannies. There would be as many blackberries eaten as picked on them days. The little ones came home with red fingers and faces and a few sore hands and arms from prickly branches. Once home we would set about making jam.

Me dad worked on the land and so did our Israel and Emanuel. Our Charlotte married a baker from Melton Mowbray: I was a lace runner as soon as me little fingers would work.

I had managed to not go into service and then I met Joe Rippin who was a miller. He told me he was born in Kinoulton. He had lived all over the place including Stathern. He was in lodgings in Harby with another miller for a short time. It was then that we met. I was 19, I think. Let me see, I was 21 when the Harby church bells rang out for us. August 22, 1853. Joe was almost 30 and seemed so mature! I will never forget me wedding day! I am not sure why but we moved to live in Stathern, most probably Joe found work there and a house to live in. I didn't mind because I knew the village. Me Grannie's family was there and made sure I knew everyone I needed to know. We waited so long for little Andy. We had been married for 5 years. But then after joy comes heartbreak. So suddenly, me Joe died in Melton Mowbray. He was only 37.

[62] (Photographer: J. Thacker)) So suddenly, me Joe died in Melton Mowbray. He was only 37. He is buried in St Guthlac's Churchyard in Stathern so I now visit him there often.

Being a young widow was hard with a little one, me mam and dad took me in and soon I started going with Andrew Smith from Stathern. Everyone knew everyone else y' know.

I loved to watch the fox hunts, so beautiful, so many hounds and horses and riders. The riders looked so smart in their red jackets. There was excitement in the air. Little Andy and me would go out to watch all the time. It was all

---

62 Churchyard and Old Rectory, Stathern Copyright Jonathan Thacker and licensed for reuse under this Creative Commons Licence

good fun for everyone. But then Andrew's family has lived in Stathern for many years. And I had known him for a while before we got together. There were so many Smiths in Stathern, I could not get them all straight!

Andrew decided we should get married and I agreed. I had been married before so Andrew and I chose to marry in the Registry Office in Melton on May 12, 1859. I think we always remember our wedding day even though we weren't married in the church. I was originally a Smith and was once again a Smith! I was so glad that Andrew adopted me son, Andy, into the family. He was known as Andrew Rippin Smith. We all loved horses: I remember how I spent me younger years at the Harby canal walking with horses as they pulled their load. We relied so much on horses to get around in them days.

Andrew and I was happy to have a daughter in 1860. We named her Sarah Ann. We both liked the name Sarah, me because after me mam. Ann was after Andy's mam. I spent a lot of time with me mam when Sarah was a baby. We talked and cooked and sewed and gardened. She helped me with Sarah and helped me do the washing. She would tell me how to keep Sarah warm and how to comfort her when she cried. We would sort out clothes we got from friends because we had not much of our own. Everything we women do. Andrew made me a little cart I could sit our Sarah in and push her around the village. I felt very proud as we would walk by the churchyard because we liked it there. Me mam and me would look at all the little houses in Stathern and talk about the people who lived in them. Not really gossip but just an interest in the people. Then me mam had to walk back to Harby to make me dad's tea.

Ma Dyer was Andrew's mam. She lived in the village but died when our Sarah was about 5. That was a great loss for me as well as for Andrew. There was a big hole in me life which got worse when me mam died the next year so I missed them both so much. Fancy losing both me mam and Andrew's mam so close together. Andrew was lost without his mam for a long time.

We waited a long time before we had Kitty in 1869, named after me sister, Charlotte who we all called Kitty. Me sister, she moved to Melton so I didn't see her very often. Then we had Sammy, named after me dad when Kitty was 1, and Sukie two years later. Imagine I had four little ones without me mam or Ma Dyer to help. Those two loved their grandbabies. I was so grateful to neighbours who would lend a hand.

It looks as though I named our children. But we both liked Susan who was called Sukie by all. I cannot remember the reason.

Oh yes, me dad died about a year after our Sukie was born. I missed me mam and dad. He was a rough sort but kindly. He was a labourer all his life. Hard work but he was close to the land and the animals. But not really into babies!

We were so glad to have a school in Stathern. All the children went to the school when they were six and learned their letters, to read and write. They learned their sums too and the scriptures. I was so proud of all of them. If the children could be spared from their jobs, they would go to school every morning. I don't remember how long they went to school. I did not have that chance to learn my letters and to read and so would have to ask one of the children to read Church Notices for me.

Our eldest, Sarah Ann, everyone called her Saran, wanted to leave home or perhaps she needed to leave the village for a while. There was not much to do in the village for youngsters finding their way. She went to work as a cook in nearby Gainsborough in Lincolnshire. Yes, the Platts family were drapers. She was a good cook. The family had a house maid so Saran didn't have to do all the cleaning and laundry. She was in the kitchen and looked after the herb garden. She helped Mrs. Platt with getting the food. She had a bit of company when the chores were all done of an evening. The servant girl there would chat to her. We pulled her leg a bit because we knew she was sweet on the boy next door! Her sisters would tease so much. Perhaps that is why she left home. I don't really know.

During this time, Kitty, Sukie and I were lace workers. We were living in a little house on Main Street in Stathern. We would sit around the fireplace and make toast with yesterday's bread using the toasting fork one of the blacksmiths in the village made for us. Mr. Elliott, I think. The toast tasted so good with our blackberry jam. We had a coal fireplace which was dirty but gave off a lot of heat. In this damp climate, we needed the heat.

Let me see, what do I remember about our Sammy? He liked to be around horses and went far away when he was so young. He really needed to leave the village. He had no fear. He went to be a groom at Glamis Castle in Scotland and was known as Smyth. I was once told the castle was a famous castle where Mary Queen of Scots once lived. I have heard of her! I was so proud of him for 'is courage and sad to hear he died so young. He was only 21 when he died. He had not really lived yet. But as they say, out of sight out of mind. I thought of Sammy a lot but he was not part of our lives when we lost him, so he wasn't missed so much. Isn't that an awful thing to say? Sammy just seemed to leave the village and not look back. The village was just too small a place for him.

Time for fun? Well, there was a skittle alley at the Plough Inn on Main Street in the village. The lads would throw a ball to knock down the skittles. It was very competitive. The village lads would get very excited and take it all seriously. Then they would have a game of darts. There was not much for the youngsters to do. Sometimes there would be a dance with lots of music.

Me sister Lottie married a baker and moved to Melton where they lived. I didn't get to see her very often. She and me sister Hetty were older than me. Hetty was 6 when I was born, the baby in the family. Hetty moved around a bit after she married Joe. Then she started having children. Lots of them. When they lived in Stathern I saw a lot of her. Even when she moved to Harby I would walk over to see her before I married Andrew and had Sarah. She had a Sarah too. Me mam was pleased.

Did I tell you about our neighbours? Elisha Brown was a maltster. His son Will and his wife Kitty were having their family at the same time as us. They lived a few doors away on Main Street. The Hubbard family also lived on Main Street. Our Saran and Bradley Hubbard grew up together in the village. Our Saran was sweet on Bradley Hubbard whose family came from Eaton. The family worked the land and so did Bradley. At least he started out that way. Maybe they missed one another after Saran left to go to the Platts. But soon Bradley asked Andrew if he could marry our Saran. And so: they did but not until they were about 25. Wedding bells rang for them on May 19, 1884 when Bradley married our Saran and set up a home in Stathern, almost next door to us. After that Bradley became an ironstone quarryman in nearby Eastwell. They were lucky to find a little house very close by on Main Street.

We had two weddings in our family that year. Our Andy Rippin had become a groom and a horse trainer just like his step dad. He then moved away, married Mary Jane an' set up home in Oakham. They had a little boy, called him Charles. But he did not live very long. So sad for them. He was about six when he died, I think. That seemed to be a turning point for young Andy.

Oh, but before little Charlie died, me Andrew died. So young he was, just after his 60th. I shall not forget that year. 1892, a sad one for me. Things were changing too. We saw the first bicycles come into the village. Funny looking things. You had to balance and work with your legs to turn the wheels. We could see that for getting places, they could be used instead of horses. I think that is the reason young Andy stopped working with horses and became a shop keeper.

Saran and Bradley had many children. They were our first grandchildren and made me happy. But they did give them such fancy names! First was Trissie Maud Madeleine Hubbard. I smiled to myself and wondered how Trissie would live up to her name. Where did those names come from? When I was in my 60s, Trissie came to live with me. That was after Andrew died. She would be no more than 16. But she was such good company. I was glad of that. We were both lace workers. Wow could she talk and was most entertaining. She was pleased to have a room of her own. Everyone was so crowded together in them days. For her it meant that she didn't have to go into service.

Then they had two sons: John Henry, known as Harry, and Wilfred Alec, known as Alec, arrived next a year later in 1890. Two lovely little boys were a handful for Saran. Kitty Brown lived next door to Saran and Bradley on Main Street. She was a good neighbour. We all helped our Saran. Neighbours would arrive with their babies and plop the little one into the playpen next to Saran, just like piglets in a pen.

When Saran had another daughter, she named her after me! Louisa Mary was born in 1892. Oh, did she ever look like her mother and seemed to look more like her every day [63]

Saran kept going. She had another daughter they named Millicent Rachel, and called her Rachel. And then Bertram William (Bert) was born in 1901 when Saran was 40 years old. I think she was done by then!

Our girls did everything they could not to go into service. Saran was kind of the exception but she had a good job as a cook. The other two were quite content as lace workers at home, especially Sukie after our Kitty left. I am glad we had enough room. Sometimes the girls had to leave to make room for others, you know. Our Kitty married John when she was 19. John was born in Eaton. He was a railway signal man. Those two had four girls.

Our little Sukie did very well. She caught the eye of a posh Stathern family, The Clamps lived in the big house on Penn Lane. Mr. and Mrs. Clamp were lace agents, real toffs. Their son George was in the business as well. He took a real shine to our Sukie. But he was at least 35, a real middle-aged man, for goodness sake, and our Sukie was not yet 20. But she accepted when he asked her. I think she realized she was on to a good thing. I remember the day, August 23, 1891, our Sukie married George Clamp in Stapleford, Nottinghamshire. Imagine a posh wedding. But I would have liked to see her married in Stathern with her kin. Oh, then I remember, Mr. Clamp's eldest died suddenly. John, I recon, He worked on engines. He died in the October the same year as our Sukie was wed to George. Very sad for the family.

Then in March the next year, old Mr. Clamp died. After that Mrs. Clamp moved out of the big house and moved to Edmondthorpe. She didn't live very much longer after that. Our Sukie became in charge of the big house. George took over as lace agent in the business. Oh, sad story though. George did not do well in the business. He wanted to be outside on the land: he became a grazier in the village, grazing cattle and sheep for market.

A couple of years after they married, Sukie and George had two children: Cyril and Gladys. Sadly, for them, they also lost a little one. But that happens sometimes. I was in me 70s then but so pleased to help Sukie with the children in her posh home. Sukie did not work after she married. I was glad for her. Fancy, she had her own servants. Everything was so posh. The furniture she got from her in laws was called antiques. I am not sure what

---

63 According to your Nana she was the village gossip.

that meant. It looked old to me. But was so fancy. Everyone had a chair to sit on. And everything matched, even her dishes, that were called bone china. And there was so many doilies. I had to be careful when I helped wash the dishes that I didn't break anything. Sukie wanted me to live with them in the big house, but I said no. Did I belong there?

Andrew was only 62 when he died about a year after Sukie married. He didn't live to see his grandchildren. He continued to do what he loved to the end: breaking in and training horses. He never would see that horses were going to be less important in our lives. Soon, all the young people wanted bicycles. Easier to take care of than a horse, less expensive and they didn't need feeding and grooming! After he died, I didn't like being alone and missed him a lot. That house was so quiet.

I look so smart in the photo. I have such a smart hat. I wish I could remember the reason I was so dressed up. I wish I didn't look so stern but see how straight I am standing! We did like pretty bows, didn't we? We would reuse them and borrow them until they had no wear left. We didn't have many clothes but tried to look nice especially when we went to church on Sundays when we wore our Sunday Best clothes. We always had hats and gloves for church. Do I look as though life has been hard?

I have had the chance to talk about, think about me life and all the people who lived their lives with me. I like to remember the people and what we did as children.

Now all I have are memories of me mam and dad, me grannies and grandads, me brothers and sisters. I also have me children and grandchildren to watch as they grow………….

And we move to Andrew……

ENDNOTES

Mother Louisa Smith did move in with Sukie and her family sometime before 1911, a 78-year-old widow. She died the next year on March 27.

Because of Louisa's great grandmother Mary Sills, we know our family was in Stathern from as early as 1729.

Wait for the Clamps to surface again in a later story!

Chart 13. Family Group Sheet for Louisa (Rippin) Smith

Spouse: Andrew Smith

	Birth:	1828 in Stathern,
	Marriage:	12 May 1859 in Melton Mowbray R O, ; Louisa Rippin (widow) at time of marriage
	Death:	Jun 1892 in Melton Mowbray, ; Age: 62
	Father:	William Smith
	Mother:	Ann (Hawley) (Smith) Dyer

Spouse: Louisa (Rippin) Smith

	Birth:	1832 in Harby,
	Death:	27 Mar 1912 in Stathern,
	Father:	Samuel Smith
	Mother:	Sarah (Isam) Smith

Children:

1 M	Name:	Andrew Rippin Smith
	Birth:	Jul 1858 in Harby,
	Marriage:	1884
	Death:	Jun 1933 in Melton Mowbray
	Spouse:	Mary Jane Smith

2 F	Name:	**Sarah Ann "Saran" (Smith) Hubbard**
	Birth:	06 Apr 1860 in Stathern,
	Marriage:	19 May 1884 in Stathern,
	Death:	Sep 1940 in Melton Mowbray,
	Spouse:	**Arthur "Bradley" Hubbard**

3 F	Name:	Charlotte (Kitty) (Smith) Darby
	Birth:	16 Aug 1869 in Stathern,
	Marriage:	10 Sep 1888 in Stathern,
	Death:	10 Jun 1948 in Waltham on the Wolds,
	Spouse:	John Darby

4 M	Name:	Samuel William (Smith) Smyth
	Birth:	Apr 1870 in Stathern,
	Death:	Abt 1891
	Burial:	14 Nov 1891 in Angus, Scotland

5 F	Name:	Susan "Sukie" (Smith) Clamp
	Birth:	Apr 1872 in Stathern,
	Marriage:	23 Aug 1891 in Stapleford, Notts
	Death:	27 Apr 1959 in The Limes, High Street, Ketton, Rutland,
	Spouse:	George Clamp

14.

ANDREW SMITH'S STORY

Stuart suggested great, great grandfather Andrew Smith, Saran Hubbard's father, should tell his story. Recall, Andrew Smith is Louisa Rippin Smith's second husband and great grandad Hubbard's grandfather. I have told the story as Andrew might have told it, based on facts but from my imagination, a life as he might have lived.

You have asked me to tell you what I remember of me life. You know all about me life with me wife Lou. I had a good life with her and me children. And horses were me life an'all.

I was born in 1830 in Stathern and me sister Clarice arrived in 1833. Then so sad: In 1838 we lost me dad, William who died of a disease of his brain, so they said. Me mam didn't know what that meant and neither do I. Me mam was 46, and alone with me and Clari to take care of. I think she went to live with her mam and dad then. I try to remember me dad sometimes but I was too young to really remember. I don't even remember me dad's family. They must have been around but I don't think they helped me mam much.

Me mam, she was born in Stathern. I know she was christened on September 21, 1792, in St. Guthlac's Church because she told me so. St. Guthlac's is a quite the church, very old, built of local soft ironstone. We villagers pay attention when the church bells ring: five church bells merrily tell of weddings and baptisms. They have a lovely sound. Everybody in the villages hear the bells. They call us to church service an'all of a Sunday. They seem to call us all to attend. Then there is the slow, mournful tone of death.

The church is important to us in the village. We went to church services of a Sunday, dressed in our best clothes, and had to be on our best behaviour! We had the chance to see our neighbours and catch up with the news. We kept to the rules.

There was no school in the village when I was a kid so I never learned to read and write. I didn't need to read and write for the job I did. I had to have a good memory because I couldn't write anything down about the horses I was working with. That would have made my life easier, I think. But I had my own way of keeping track.

I am glad that we live close by me mam now so I can keep an eye on her! I am glad that Lou and her get along and talk. Lou's mam lives in Harby and sometimes the three of them get together. Me mam helps with the grandkids. Both her and Lou had hard times in their younger days, being left alone.

Me mam's mam and dad, David and Frances Hawley, were both born in Stathern in the 1760s. So long ago. Me grandad David died when I was 10 years old so I don't remember him too well. But I remember me Grannie Hawley very well. She died in 1852 when I was 22. She was so missed. They were the Hawleys in the village who everyone knew. Stathern must have been very different then but the church was the same. It goes back years.

On me mam's side of the family were the Mussons. Great Grannie Musson's mother Mary Sills as was, was christened in the church in Stathern in November 1729. Me mam told me this many a time. I never knew Great Grannie Mary Sills because she died before even me mam was born. She died in her fifties but the interesting thing was that Great Grannie Mary was born in Stathern in 1729 and lived all her life in the village.

Me mam was on her own with Clari and me for a couple of years and then in 1840 she married a cottager from Stathern, a farm labourer, a neighbour, Mr. Samuel Dyer. He was from the village, born in Stathern in 1771 or so he told me. Everyone knew everyone else in them days in the close-knit community. But he was 69 when they married: a bachelor without children. He seemed old to us but then I was only 10. Me mam was too old to have more children. Mr. Dyer set about rearing us as a stepfather: we both kept our Smith surnames but me mam changed her name to Dyer.

I was glad I met Lou who came to me with a little fellow, little Andy Rippin. I am glad we found one another and liked one another. Lou and I were married at the Registry Office in Melton Mowbray. I was 31 and Lou was 27. She loved horses an'all. Whenever she could she would bring the children to the Meet. They all loved the horses and the hounds and the riders all dressed up in their red jackets. Life wasn't always grand like that! I worked hard with the horses.

Lou and I both wondered how the village had changed in the last 100 years since Great Grannie Mary lived here. We talked about that a lot. We think more than 500 people are living in the village. We know most of them. There are more than 100 houses, most of them very small. We did like to talk about the people and their lives.

Me horses were thorough breeds, treated carefully, majestic stallions some of them. They were not at all like the horses used on the farms. These were of low breed called nags and didn't get much care or respect. But they were strong and good-natured.

Young Andy moved to Oakham in Rutland to work with horses. He met a young lady there, Mary Jane. Those two married and had little Charlie. Last I heard he was still working with horses.

I remember me sister Clari was a lace runner which meant she embroidered patterns on lace. She worked so long hours and the light was not good. We had candles. Clari married Bob Osbourne and moved to Corby.

They had four children one after the other. That was so hard on her. But the latest news was that she had died. Let me see, she was so young. She was about 33, I would say. Too young to leave all those children without a mam. Perhaps she died while having a baby. That is so sad and sometimes happens. I think of her often.

Mr. Dyer died after 20 years of being married to me mam so she was alone again: she was close to 70 by then. She liked looking after the animals. We rallied around her to keep her company. Me mam became the cottager herself then taking care of sheep. She needed something to do other than taking care of her grandbaby. She was living alone in Watchorn's Row, at the bottom of Stathern Hill. But I lived not far away and we had Sarah Ann to keep her busy. Me mam died in 1865 when she was 73. I miss her still and think of her all the time.

I thought well of me mam because she did her very best to give us a home as meagre as it was. Mr. Dyer became our stepdad even though he was so old: he could have been our grandad. Me mam didn't seem to mind the age difference. Much later, she told me that she could have lived with Mr. Dyer as his housekeeper but Mr. Dyer was worried about wagging tongues. He didn't want us to be talked about. Mr. Dyer was a good stepfather. Under his encouragement I took to farming as a labourer then I realized I had a knack with horses. So, I worked with horses as a horse-breaker and groom. I trained horses and was involved with breeding. My bosses relied on me to take care of their horses. You could think of me as a horse whisperer! Stathern was a horsey place, a good place for me to be. I would help out when there was a Hunt nearby. I would make sure the horses were well taken care of and look after them if there was an accident. I was in the background you might say. I would have to be around the horses for a few days after all the excitement to calm them down!

I was glad to be around when little Andy grew. He would trail around with me when I worked with the horses. It was no surprise to me when he took to horse grooming and training. He helped me groom the horses and look at their feet for sores, inside their mouths for sores, into their eyes to make sure they could see, checking their knees for bone damage and their feet. Remember horses must stand most of the time. We would look at their shoes to see if they needed new ones. We might go over to the blacksmiths to get new ones made and then to the Ferrier to have them nailed onto the horse's feet.

I would also give Andy and our son Sammy the job of cleaning out the stables. They learned about how horses get along with us humans and how we get them to do our bidding. Both of them liked to ride them for exercise and would run errands for the villagers. Horses have eyes on the sides of their heads, y'know so they can see all around themselves. We trainers need to know that. Both little Andy and our Sammy came to work with horses 'cus that was what I did. They got used to the way we were with them. I was very fond of me horses, that were not really mine. But they were a lot of work to feed, to groom and keep healthy. I loved it when a young'un was born, a little pony for the young'uns. A new life to take care of.

In them days we relied on horses for so many things. They were really important for getting around. Without them we would have to walk everywhere. They pulled carts an'all so we could move things as well as people. Some people didn't treat them well but I talked to them and they would do anything I wanted them to do. There were many horses in the village so I was very busy. A workhorse was called a nag, y'know. These were not thoroughbred horses which the rich people had. No, the ordinary folks had the nags or even mules!

Lou has told you about all our children and about our lives in Stathern. Our Sukie married well. I was glad about that and hoped she would be happy in that posh family. I was used to being around them all but she and Lou were not! Andy, Saran, and Kitty had all married and were staying in the village. I heard that our Sammy had died so young….I will be working with horses until I cannot work no more…….

Our story now moves to the Browns who were the maternal side of your Nana's family.

ENDNOTES

Andrew Smith died at the age of 62 in June 1892 in Melton Mowbray. Louisa was 57 years of age then. She had her family around her.

The Smiths allow us to connect our family to Stathern from the year 1729.

(Photographer: B. Hopper) Your Nana loved the Hunt. Here she is with Heather. She is almost 90 in this pic.

Chart 14
Andrew Smith

Andrew Smith
b: 1828 in Stathern,
m: 12 May 1859 in Melton Mowbray R O, ; Louisa Rippin (widow) at time of marriage
d: Jun 1892 in Melton Mowbray, ;
Age: 62

William Smith
b: Abt 1796
m: 1814 in Stathern, England
d: 20 Mar 1838 in Stathern,

Ann (Hawley) (Smith) Dyer
b: 1792 in Stathern,
d: Jan 1865 in Melton Mowbray,

Name:
b:
m:
d:

Name:
b:
d:

David Hawley
b: 1763 in Stath ern
m: 04 Feb 1788 in Stathern,
d: Abt Aug 1838 in Melton Mowbray,

Frances (Musson) Hawley
b: 1769 in Stathern, Melton Mowbray,
d: Jul 1852 in Melton Mowbray,

Name:
b:
m:
d:

Name:
b:
d:

Name:
b:
m:
d:

Name:
b:
d:

John Hawley
b: 1748
m: 20 Oct 1768 in Long Clawson, L
d: Aft. 1768

Ann Kendall
b: 10 Aug 1744 in Long Clawson,
d: Aft. 1768

Joseph Musson
b: Abt 08 Apr 1734 in Barkestone- - Vale,
m: 19 Jul 1756 in Bakestone-le-Vale,
d: 12 May 1805

Mary (Sills) Musson
b: 1729 in Stathern
d: May 1783 in Stathern,

15.

THE BROWNS

The Browns were on your Nana's side of the family. Before delving into our Brown ancestors, we need to have a sense of where they all lived: an area in and around north Leicestershire, quite close to where the Hubbards lived.

Firstly, a look at the surname. Brown is an English-language surname in origin and would probably have been a nationalistic or tribal nickname for a person with a brown complexion or hair, although it may also have referred to someone who habitually wore brown clothing, such as a monk or cleric. It is one of the most common family names in English-speaking countries.

William Brown was your great, great grandfather. The story begins with his paternal great grandfather, William, and his wife, Anne nee Taylor. I can trace very little about this pair other than knowing they lived in Nether Broughton, north of Melton Mowbray on the main road toward Nottingham. They were born in approximately 1775.

Anne Brown gave birth to a son, John in August of 1789 and a daughter, Elizabeth in 1809 and then to Joseph in 1810 all in Nether Broughton. Joseph is our direct ancestor. I can find no trace of either William or Anne after that date. Their son, John emerges unexpectedly later in our story.

William and Anne's son Joseph married 17-year-old Sarah Brewin, a local girl, on September 23, 1833. He was a framework knitter and she a lace worker. We are familiar with framework knitters from the Warburton/Heathcote stories.

Nottingham lace is well known and enjoys a good reputation to this day. The area also became known for hose making, an industry that continued to the 1950s. There was a hosiery factory in Stathern when I was a child.

Joseph and Sarah Brown's large family comprised three sons: Edward, Elisha and George, and five daughters; Elizabeth, Isabella, Maria, Charlotte, and Emily. All the children were born in Nether Broughton over twenty years.

The family then moved to nearby Wartnaby some seven kilometres north of Melton Mowbray off the Nottingham Road and some five kilometres from Nether Broughton. The move was likely for employment reasons because, at the age of 51, Joseph was no longer a framework knitter but was a rural letter carrier while Sarah continued her lace-making. This new occupation begs the question: what was involved as a rural letter carrier? Joseph most likely delivered the mail on horseback since his territory would have extended to the surrounding villages: not long distances but certainly he would require some form of transportation. At least he was enjoying the fresh air and the opportunity for exercise rather than being in a confined space as a framework knitter: and he had a government position!

Other aspects also come to mind. Firstly, Joseph needed stables for his horse. Even in my day, stables were dotted around the villages. As a result, accommodating his horse would have been no problem. Its food would have been readily available too, grown by local farmers. Secondly, as Joseph travelled from village to village delivering letters and parcels, he would also have the opportunity to socialize, to share news and gossip, most probably within the local pub. As such he had become a valued member of a society with the opportunity to mix and mingle with the locals representing for them a world extending beyond their own back yards.

Thirdly, I questioned the commercial aspect of Joseph's job. Who paid?

Up to 1837, British postal rates were high, complex, and irregular. At the time the recipient normally paid postage on delivery, charged by the sheet, and on distance travelled.

(Photographer: H. Hopper from Brian Hopper's collection) To simplify matters, Sir Rowland Hill proposed an adhesive stamp to indicate the pre-payment of postage. Out of necessity, postage stamps emerged. The Penny Black was the world's first adhesive postage stamp used in a public postal system. It was first issued in Great Britain on 1 May 1840 but was not valid for use until 6 May. It features a profile of Queen Victoria. The Penny Black allowed letters of up to ½ ounce (14 grams) to be delivered at a flat rate of one penny, regardless of distance.[64]

Rare these days, Joseph must have handled many penny blacks. We wonder whether he also delivered parcels, all items strapped to his back in a leather bag.

Returning to family matters: in 1852, Joseph's eldest daughter 17-year-old Elizabeth presented the family with a granddaughter out of wedlock. Agnes was born in Nether Broughton, and was raised along with Joseph and Sarah's own children as was the custom in those days. Elizabeth was in service in the village. She married in 1857 and gave birth to Jemima in 1860. For whatever reason, this little girl also lived with her grandparents and was given the Brown surname. A few months earlier, another baby had appeared in the household. Isabella presented the family with her son George born in July 1859. Jemima and George, approximately the same age, were assimilated into the family. We will never know how reluctantly or enthusiastically these children were accepted or the extent of the disgrace brought to the family, the illegitimate children of two of his daughters.

Joseph and Sarah's second daughter, Isabella presents us with one of the saddest stories in our ancestry. At the age of 22 in 1861, she was a house servant in the household of a farmer of 300 acres, Thomas Ridge, in

---

64 https://en.wikipedia.org/wiki/Penny_Black

Hinckley Pastures only a few kilometres from Nether Broughton. She was the only female servant. In all likelihood, Isabella was a housemaid tackling in all the chores.

Then disgrace! Isabella became pregnant for the second time out of wedlock. She would have been dismissed by her employer and returned to her family: The Parish responsible for her welfare was Wartnaby. Her parents, Joseph and Sarah, had already assumed responsibility for her illegitimate son, George, and did not take her into the family fold this time. Thus, Isabella became the responsibility of the Parish as was the custom in those days: a version of the state welfare system. I note an imposing church built of local sandstone with limestone dressings at the epicentre of the parish. The 13th-century church of St. Michael and All Angels and its Council appeared unable to help Isabella within the parish.

Incredibly in 1871, we find Isabella residing in the Thorpe Road Workhouse in Melton Mowbray, working as a general domestic servant. Without the help of either her parents or her siblings, Isabella was designated a pauper, not as staff, living with 127 others of all ages of which 23 were labelled as imbeciles. Perhaps this was the best Wartnaby parish could offer her. Listed with her is her one-year-old son John William Brown. Seemingly Isabella, with nowhere to go, was sent to the workhouse to have her baby.

I presented the Melton Mowbray Workhouse in a Hubbard story. In fairness this workhouse was newly built when Isabella lived there and would not have looked so uninviting. The facility was later turned into St. Mary's Hospital now closed. I wish I had paid attention..................

http://www.workhouses.org.uk/MeltonMowbray/

Listed with her in the Workhouse, however, was 72-year-old John Brown, also a pauper. He had an unusual skill: he was a musician. While we do not know which instrument he played, we wonder whether he provided entertainment for his fellow inmates. He was Isabella's father's elder brother, her uncle. He had been in the workhouse for at least 20 years. He died in January 1876, still in the workhouse, still a pauper. But he brought music to the Brown family and his surroundings, a talent that endured.

The news is good, however, for Isabella. Whether she was obliged to work within the workhouse or outside to pay her way, we do not know. Neither do we know how she met her companion. Nevertheless, she did. She spent little time in the workhouse because on October 16, 1871, she married 38-year-old labourer John Creakwell, from Saxby, approximately six kilometres from Melton Mowbray in the direction of Grantham. The pair set up home in Wymondham, a village close to Saxby and fifteen kilometres from Wartnaby. They had a daughter, Charlotte. Isabella's son, John William was accepted into the Creakwell family but did not take the Creakwell name.

By 1881 Isabella's parents, Joseph and Sarah, had moved to 3, Soho Square, Melton Mowbray: she a seamstress and he at 71 a superannuated letter carrier. Joseph died in January 1883 at the age of 73: our first relative with pensionable employment.

This family of Browns were forced to deal with so many illegitimate children that when Isabella presented them with another, the camel's back was broken. After all Joseph and Sarah had raised three already and were then advanced in age. Fortunately, they had sufficient funds to assist their three younger grandchildren. We will never know for sure but understanding the living conditions inside the workhouse for a young woman and more particularly her young child is too much an image to discard lightly. Isabella chose an illiterate labourer as solace. That Isabella and John William found family life, however, is comforting to us all.

The following story continues with Elisha Brown, our direct ancestor.

ENDNOTES

I realize I would drive very close by Wartnaby on The Six Hills Road on my way to Stathern from Heathrow Airport. Until now I did not realize the drive would take me along an old Roman Road between Barrow upon Soar and Grantham. I can well imagine Joseph, then 61, still a Post Messenger, a mailman in our terms, travelling on those same roads, some 130 years earlier.

CHART 15. FAMILY GROUP SHEET FOR JOSEPH BROWN

HUSBAND: JOSEPH BROWN

Birth:	1810 in Nether Broughton,
Marriage:	23 Sep 1833 in Nether Broughton,
Death:	Jan 1883 in Melton Mowbray, Age: 73
Father:	William Brown
Mother:	Anne (Taylor) Brown

WIFE: SARAH (BREWIN) BROWN

Birth:	1816 in Nether Broughton,
Death:	1892 in Melton Mowbray
Father:	James Brewin Sarah
Mother:	Earl

CHILDREN:

1 F

Name:	Elizabeth (Brown) Ashton
Birth:	1835 in Nether Broughton,
Marriage:	25 Dec 1857 in Melton Mowbray, 20 Apr 1899
Death:	
Spouse:	John Ashton

2 M

Name:	Edward Brown
Birth:	25 Jun 1837 in Nether Broughton,
Marriage:	1862 in Melton Mowbray
Death:	1874 in Melton Mowbray
Spouse:	Mahala (Wade) Brown

3 F

Name:	Isabella (Brown) Creakwell
Birth:	Oct 1838 in Nether Broughton,
Marriage:	16 Oct 1871 in Saxby
Death:	Mar 1922 in Melton Mowbray,
Spouse:	John Creakwell

4 M

Name:	**Elisha Brown**
Birth:	1840 in Nether Broughton,
Marriage:	1861 in Nether Broughton,
Death:	01 Jan 1913 in Nottingham, ; Age: 72,
Burial:	29 May 1913 in Nottinghamshire,
Spouse:	**Sarah (Elliott) Brown**

5 F

Name:	Maria (Brown) Underwood
Birth:	Jan 1845 in Nether Broughton,
Marriage:	21 Mar 1864 in Melton Mowbray,
Spouse:	George Underwood

6		Name:	George Brown
M		Birth:	1848 in Nether Broughton,
		Spouse:	Elizabeth (Freeston) Brown
7		Name:	Charlotte Brown
F		Birth:	Oct 1848 in Nether Broughton,
8		Name:	Emily Brown
F		Birth:	1855 in Nether Broughton,

16.

Elisha Brown and the Elliotts

Our story continues with Joseph and Sarah's second son, Elisha, our direct ancestor.

By aged 20 Elisha had moved from Nether Broughton to live in a farm residence in Stathern. He was a Wagoner, a person who drives a wagon or transports goods by wagon, using a horse, of course. His employer, a James Bampton, farmed 140 acres. While I do not know exactly where the farm is located, I do recognize the names of farmers who lived there when I did. The Shipmans and the Bramleys, are in the 1861 Stathern census. I note there was a public house called the King's Arms, renamed in my day.

In 1861 21-year-old Elisha married 18-year-old Sarah Elliott from nearby Harby. They set up home on Main Street, Stathern. More about the Elliotts later. Sarah Brown gave birth to your great, great grandfather William Brown in 1863. He was the first of their ten children born over 23 years. Interestingly he did not live with his parents and family. Rather, William lived with his Elliott grandparents, a mere six doors away from his parents on Main Street.

Elisha continued farming while his family grew. But by 1880 Elisha had refined his occupation: he became a maltster. We know that up to Victorian times most water was unfit to drink, so brewing "small ale" was a very important necessity of life. Most families would have their brew. Even children drank beer.

We do not know whether Elisha sold the malt to a brewer or brewed beer himself. The grains and cereals he needed would have been readily available from local farmers. Those of you who enjoy a bottle or a glass, now know that the brew is legitimately in your past! There were maltsters in the Heathcote side of the family also.

In 1881, six children were in residence in the Brown household. With William never home and Mary Ann married, there were Charlotte, Joseph, Enoch, George, Ernest, and Florence Lily. Most were in school but I expect 14-year-old Charlotte, who everyone would have called Lottie, would have been assigned many household duties, as well as the care of one-year-old Lily.

Ten years later, six children were at home but not the same six as ten years earlier! Charlotte had left and married Frank Roadley, a railwayman. Joseph had also moved on. He had married Gertrude and was engaged in the shoemaking business in Leicester. The elder sons, teenagers, Enoch, George, and Ernest were working at the ironstone quarry nearby, the same quarry from the Hubbard stories. In addition to Florence, there were two new daughters in the family: Adeline and Emily. Emily Elizabeth Brown was born in 1886 when Sarah was 43 and most probably somewhat tired of bearing and rearing children. After all, Emily was number 10. Sarah died at 57 in the year 1900. Was she just too exhausted? Or old at 57?

In 1901 widower Elisha, a farm worker at 60, lived with his son Ernest who was then a railway labourer. Daughter Adeline was housekeeping for the pair. Also living only a few doors away was his son Enoch and family as well as Louisa Smith, his eldest son William and his growing family, and Bradley and Saran Hubbard and their family. You have heard about most of these families living on Main Street, Stathern.

The Elliotts

The maternal side of the family, the Elliotts played a key role in our history because they nurtured and sponsored your great, great grandfather, William. Moreover, they were responsible for moving this side of our family to Stathern for the next 200 years.

The earliest member of the Elliott family I could trace was patriarch William, born in 1796 in Bradmore, Nottinghamshire. Bradmore is situated ten kilometres south of Nottingham and overlooks a 'broad mere' or shallow post-glacial lake, now drained and farmed: thus, the origin of its name. It is now a commuter village for the city of Nottingham.

Sometime before the census started in 1851, William had apprenticed as a blacksmith and moved to Stathern where he had met a young lady. He and Bridgett Bland married and set up home on Main Street. William and Bridgett's daughter, Sarah Elliott, married Elisha Brown and as such entered the Brown family.

Sarah and Elisha's eldest son, named William after Sarah's father, was our direct ancestor. He lived with this family of Elliotts, his maternal grandparents. Their abodes were close by on Main Street in Stathern. Nevertheless, Grandma Elliott at 50 and grandfather at 65 must have appeared very old to the youngster. At age 18, William continued to live with his grandparents and was employed as a railway labourer.

Young William would have been accustomed to living around a blacksmith's shop, used to the heat, the techniques, the dirt, and the satisfaction of creating useful tools and therefore earning the appreciation of the villagers. As a result, his becoming a blacksmith's apprentice is no surprise. A blacksmith is a metalsmith, who creates objects from wrought iron or steel by forging the metal, using tools to hammer, bend, and cut. He would produce objects such as gates, grilles, railings, light fixtures, furniture, sculpture, tools, agricultural implements, decorative items, cooking utensils, nails, and chain links: all handmade. A blacksmith has a general knowledge of how to make and repair many items. A blacksmith is then a valuable resident in an isolated village, a most important craftsman. One of his tasks was to make shoes to protect the horses' hooves from wear and tear so that they could travel further and work harder. A Ferrier would attach the shoes to the horse's feet. He would have frequently assisted Andrew Smith, the horse whisperer. Blacksmiths also craft and repair iron farm tools.

The blacksmith's smithy would have been the hub of the village, where men would stand around swapping news while they waited for their tools to be repaired or created.

The Elliotts and the Browns had skills beyond farm work although the farm seemed to loom as a viable alternative when nothing else was available. By comparison with William's in laws, the Slaters, his life was peaceful, uneventful. Or was it?

Our story moves to the Slaters, the family into which William Brown married. Your great, great grannie Brown will tell us the story of her life with Will in the next chapter

Ancestry friend Julie sent me the following photographs of our cousins: her family of Browns.

(Photographer: Unknown) Julie with her daughter and granddaughter. The latest Isabel enters the Brown family.

Julie also sent me the following pictures:

(Photographer: Unknown; provided by Julie) Enoch with his son Henry Vincent, his eldest son Stephen Henry and his son Stephen Christopher Brown. Little Stephen looks about 2 so this would have been taken around 1947. Oh goodness. The Browns look alike!

(Photographer: Unknown; provided by Julie) William's uncle, Enoch Brown, with his pipe

Enoch, Grandad Henry and several of his sons all smoked a pipe, is that common in the Brown family I wonder?

17.

GRANNIE BROWN AND WILLIAM

On your Nana's side of this family, we imagine the life of your great, great grandmother Caroline Slater, known as Kitty, and great, great grandad Will. To everyone, Kitty was Grannie Brown.

I have decided that Grannie Brown will speak for herself Like our memories, hers are haphazard and random, disjointed, sometimes repetitive. She may take a few moments for her memories to develop, her recollections may be intertwined with stories she has been told and believes. Photographs have triggered her recollection. Here is my rendering of her story, as her mind meanders through her life using words she might have uttered. Only names, dates, and places are factual. The remainder is from my imagination and memory. Your Nana talked about her Grannie to me as did her second daughter, Auntie Beat. As such, I will take liberties and speak for her……..

I was born on May 10, 1868 in Granby.

I don't remember when I met Will Brown. He just seemed to be there. I recall Will loved to play the fiddle so most probably there was music in the air when we met. But once we did, we were always together. He loved me red hair and lively spirit. I liked his brown eyes and gentle nature.

(Photographer: Unknown) Here I am in me 70s, looking very grim for the camera, me red hair has faded. I am here in the lovely countryside in Stathern where I have spent most of me life. I think someone knitted that cardigan for me. Or I could have found it in the Church jumble sale! That dress looks a little big: I wonder who gave it to me!

It must have been while I was in service when I met Will. I was at the Rectory in Langar not too far from me home in Granby. Mr. Charles Wilson was a carpenter. I was a household servant and did the washing, cooking and cleaning for Mrs. Wilson. I had to do everything. There was a young boy there who went to school. I was only 13 when I was first put in service. I wish I hadn't left school so young. I was very lonely without me family but that is how it happened in them days. I would get up from me bed early to start the fires, empty chamber pots and heat water. Then I didn't stop all day, cleaning, tending fires, cooking, washing dishes, doing the washing and ironing. It would be very late when I had finished the jobs for the day. I would go straight to me bed. If I had time off, I walked to Granby to see me Mam and Dad.

Imagine having to empty chamber pots!

(Petr Kratochvil has released this "Chamber Pot Under The Bed" image under Public Domain license https://www.publicdomainpictures.net/pictures/380000/velka/chamber-pot-under-the-bed-1605274802WMn.jpg)

When Will and I got together, about a year before our Edgar was born. I was living in Langar. I fell pregnant then. I was glad Will wanted to marry me. He lived in Stathern and was working as a blacksmith at the Ironstone Quarry in Eaton, close to Stathern. The village was new to me but I was comfortable there because of Will. I was a free spirit then. I remember me wedding day as if it was yesterday. I put on me best dress. I was not showing yet so no one knew. The whole family came. July 1887, in Granby Church with the sound of the bells, celebrating just for us. Magical.

We were lucky to find a house to live in on Main Street in Stathern. I was 20 and Will was 25. Will white-washed the walls so that everything looked clean. We burnt coal and wood for cooking and heat. The room mostly smelled smoky. We had good neighbours, the Hubbards, a young couple, Saran and Bradley were also starting a family. Our children grew up together. Both men worked the Quarry; they walked to work together, up Tofts Hill towards Eastwell. So, we all became friends. We had other neighbours an'all. The Smiths were Saran's family. We all seemed to live together.

After I had the children, villagers would come to me for help with their own birthing. I grew herbs in the garden and made tinctures, salves and teas to help the mothers in pain and sooth their bodies. Sometimes they would fetch me in the middle of the night. I would stay for hours until she had given birth and was rested. I made sure the little one was alright as well and there was a cot for the babe to sleep, warm near the fire. The carpenters in the village always seemed to have a new cot at the ready. I remember, there would be a knock on the door. Any hour, I would find an agitated neighbour or a bewildered young person. Could I come to their missus or mam? They would come when a baby was on the way. I would be there for the anxious family before the doctor arrived, if he ever did. I would keep her calm, hold her hands and massage her back. I had salves and tinctures, y'see. There would always be pain and sometimes the poor little mite didn't make it. Sometimes, but not often, we lost the mother an'all. I was quite good at birthing: I had a bit of a reputation.

Reminds me of when our Edgar was born, December 1887. He was me first when I was 20. I was scared to death: I didn't know it hurt that much. But we all go through it, forget and then come back for more. And then sometimes they would keep coming, not always wanted: Another mouth to feed.

Sometimes there would be other small children around. I hoped that the new mam's mam would arrive to look after the family. Sometimes she did, or a neighbour arrived to take charge of the family. No need for them to see their mother moaning and screaming with the pain. Sometimes the new dad would be there but not often. The men folk considered this women's work! That was a good thing because the men would be in the way.

Will worked so hard as a blacksmith, an exhausting dirty job which he actually liked. His grandad William Elliott on his mam's side was a blacksmith so he was used to the work. He had finished his apprenticeship when we met. He made sure he cleaned himself up in the scullery before coming into the house. Will had lived with his grannie and grandad all his life. The Elliots, Will was named after his grandad, y'see. Oh, Will lost his grandad a couple of years before we met, so I never met him. I don't remember when his grannie died. Not living with his mam and dad was strange to me but he explained he had a room to himself and there was peace and quiet in his grannie's house. In any case, his family lived so close by in Stathern. He was always popping in and out to see them all.

When we had our first daughter in 1889, Will wanted to name her Sarah after his mam. But I liked Elizabeth so she got both names. Then we called her Lizzie! When we had another daughter two years later, we called her Caroline after me but Will liked Beatrice so she was Beatrice Caroline. We called her Beatie.

Then we had another sweet little girl in 1893 and named her Ethel Rose just because we liked the names. We called her Rosie. She was the gentlest of me girls, so sweet but fragile. I did not like having to send her away to Nottingham for service. She had to care for the little baby there and do housework. Rosie knew all about that because she took care of our Jimmy and Ellis who were babies when she was of an age to take care with them. And from me own time in service I knew how hard she would have to work and how tired she would be. I didn't want that for any of me girls but that is how it was in them days. Our Rosie must have caught the eye of a boy next door and was writing to our neighbour Alec, Saran's son, because before I knew she was his intended! Just after the Great War broke out, I think. Everything happened so quickly.

Grannie Brown paused for a moment as she rocked in her chair by the fire, waiting for the memories to bubble to the surface. Then she continued:

Earliest recollections? I suppose when I was about nine years old. Me mam seemed so old but then she was! She had me so late in her life. I never knew whether I was a wanted treasure or a burden. I think they thought they were finished having children. She was 46 after all when she had me. I have been with women that old in the village struggling to have their babies then with other children needing her time and milling around. Most of them think they are over all that. And then. Surprise! Sometimes they are so glad but often they are miserable depending on how many they already have. Sometimes the husbands particularly seem grumpy and less pleased. They should remember how the bairn got there!

Me mam told me nothing about having babies or how they came to be. Will and I figured it all out. We had to: no choice!

I remember when our Lizzie was married to Felix Jacques, he was called Phil. She was a serious girl and determined. We thought Phil was too old for her but Lizzie wanted to marry him. They married in Stathern in 1910 I think that was the year. He took her away from Stathern. Then she had a little girl, Nellie, and I wasn't there to help her. She was not in the village then; she was in Cropwell Bishop which seemed very far away. I rarely saw them. But very soon afterwards, they returned to Stathern. I don't think Lizzie liked being so far away from her family. Then very soon after that, she had Tommy. I was there to help her this time.

We were disappointed with Beatie. She went into service in Hose, not too far from home. But she was so young to leave home. But she was a good girl. Then she got into trouble and married a young man we did not like at all. Harold Hotchins he was. They were both about 19. We were right about him. He left her with a daughter, Dorothy. She had to leave service and return home to Stathern. She moved in with Rosie and Alec. Kathleen was a baby. Beatie was alone for a long time. But then, sometime before Will died, she found Ernie Green who was a real gentleman. We were glad when they married and then Reggie was born. Beatie was finally happy.

Our Edgar our eldest left home at 13. He became a farm boy in the village. He needed to go to make room in the house. He moved back into the house when he became an apprentice blacksmith and our girls had left. I was really pleased that he decided to become a blacksmith like his dad. I am not sure whether he finished or even liked the work because he became a loco driver like his friend Alec from next door. In 1914 he married Alice Bird and Alec was Best Man. That was the year the Great War started, I think.

Oh, I remember: on a Saturday night we all had a bath! Yes, in a tin bath in front of the fire. Not at the same time but we bathed the little ones first and put them to bed. Then we heated more water and took a bath ourselves. Just like me mam and dad used to do. We didn't have so much water so we couldn't each have our own. We had a rain barrel outside to catch rain from the roof. Heating it was hard and took a long time. But at least we were all clean once a week!

Doing the washing was the worst job, linens, towels, nappies an' all. We had to heat the fire under the copper and then fill the copper with water. We boiled the sheets and towels and of course the nappies and put a blue bag in to make them white. We had a wringer too. But the washing had to dry on the line outside. Oh goodness: sometimes it rained! Monday was always wash day. We ironed on Tuesdays. We heated a flat iron on the grate in front of the fire being careful not to get the bottom sooty. So that is how I spent two days. I also had to cook on those days. The washing and ironing took all day on Mondays and Tuesdays and was so tiring. Oh, me poor hands, red raw they were.

There was always the smell of cooking in me mam's house. I remember the smells from when I was very young. She made bread every day. We ate a lot of bread! We ate it with cheese she made or with jam. I like the smell of cooking so I cooked a lot too. Me mam showed me how to bake by feeling the flour mixture. Nothing was written down. Me mam had not gone to school so she couldn't read or write. I could read a little because I did go to school but not for very long before I went into service. We all made soups and stews depending on what we could get our hands on that day. Then we made jams and salted runner beans and made cakes and sometimes made beer. I made my concoctions to help new mothers as well. And to take care of blisters and scrapes and bruises.

I remember me dad and me mam were living with Grandad Robert just before he died. He needed looking after. I am remembering far back now! There was no houses anywhere to live. We had to go where we could. I don't remember me Grannie Mary because I was very young when she died. Grandad Robert died in the year I went into service. I had to make space for the others y'see.

After the children had grown a bit, I had time on my hands. I worked with the church warden washing bodies before burial. I liked to do this for the people of Stathern. But not until my lot had grown. So, you could say I handled hatches and dispatches for Stathern!

When I was having our family, I worked at home as a lace worker. It was tedious work but I needed to keep me hands busy. Me three daughters helped when they were old enough. We worked so hard doing things, making things. When it was too dark of an evening, we couldn't work on lace, we hooked rugs, altered clothes to fit us, knitted sweaters and socks and were constantly working in the kitchen. We had a kitchen garden for growing herbs and vegetables. Everyone did.

I remember when we would get a big bag of clothes, clothes from our neighbours and from our family. Mainly clothes for the little ones. We would pass bags of clothing around the village. I never had anything new. Someone else had worn everything before me. When I was very young, me sister Emma's clothes would become mine. Me mam would tell me there was wear left in that dress or pinafore. So, we altered everything or made something new out of it. I always wore a pinafore so me dress would not get dirty: all me life! If there was a nice piece of cloth, we would put it aside to use for hooking rugs. But most of all, I disliked doing the washing! We passed around our boots too. We all needed a good pair of boots to keep our feet warm and dry.

There was a new school in Stathern built long before I came to the village. All the children went there to learn reading, sums and scriptures when they were six years old. Our girls did not stay at school because they left to go into service. Our boys stayed longer until their apprenticeship started.

Me brothers and sisters? I barely remember me sister Mary Ann who was about eighteen when I arrived. She was not living at home. Me eldest brother was John Isaac. He was sixteen when I was born, so he was long gone from the house. Then came James who was eleven when I arrived. Y'know I think about our Emma sometimes and then there was poor Rosa. She was about four when I came along but she died when I was about five so really, I don't remember her.

I want to tell you about our John. He really wanted to stop farming which he said was a dying industry. When I was about ten, he married Mary. They already had a daughter, Gertrude, so that was proper. Then they had Harry and Tom who often lived with me mam and dad and me. Mary kept on having children: George, Mary Ellen and Rosa arrived! But only after I had left Granby.

John worked on the farm first then but soon found work at the Barnstone Cement Works. I knew he wanted to leave farming.

I was newly married and just had Edgar when we heard of the catastrophe that had happened on Tuesday August 21, 1888 at the Barnstone Cement works. Thirty-six-year-old John lost his life in an accident there, leaving Mary and their five children alone.[65]

Barnstone Cement Works - early crane workmen.
Back: ——, B Waring, T Haddon, H Parsham, A Sharp, W Pepper, G Freeman, S Johnson, W Patrick, ——, G Gibson, - Slater, L Wilcox, A Wilcox.

(Photographer: Unknown) Oh yes. Here is a picture of our John, bottom with that big pick axe. Oh dear, such hard work. He had hopes for himself and his family. It is such a waste that he died in an accident. I don't remember but have been told I had to compete for attention as a little one because me Mam and Dad had taken in our John's youngest children. I was never told who Tom and Harry were until much later.

---

65 *His death certificate reads: Died from injuries received by being accidentally run over by a Railway Wagon at the Barnstone Lime Works.*

Me mam and dad helped Mary after this tragedy. Harry and Tom already lived with them. Mary was strong and I heard she remarried and had a son. We lost touch after that.

Yes, some years just stand out to make you remember. We were all excited to reach the year 1900 and wondered what a new century would be like for us. I had just turned 32. We were happy in the village with our children but soon the passing bell would ring for us. Two deaths: me mam and Will's mam. Imagine both the same year. I will never forget the sad tone of the church bell signalled someone had died or was about to. I would then be asked by the churchwarden to take care of the body. I did that for the village for a long time.

Our old queen died soon after and we had a new king and queen.

(Photographer: Unknown) Here is me sister Emma.

After me mam died in 1900, me dad went to live with Emma in Granby. There was Hetty, George, Albert, John and young Adolphus and our dad. I know how hard Emma and Hetty worked! Emma's little Kate arrived in April 1903 when Emma was 43. But when she had Kate, there was just no room for our dad. I remember it well. We all simply had no room. He had to go into the workhouse. It wasn't that we didn't care about him, there was just no room. He died in 1904 in the workhouse in Bingham. I was so sorry we were unable to care for him and he ended his life like that. You cannot imagine the distress we all felt. We were unable to help him. And he died all alone in that awful place. The thought never leaves me! I am really sad when I think about what happened to me poor dad. We couldn't help him.

I was thirty-seven when Jimmy was born. It was 1904 same year as me dad died in Bingham workhouse.

But the passing bell tolled again for poor Emma: young sons, Adolphus and Albert died at thirteen and six in September 1905. I am not sure of the reason but I know those two years were very bad for Emma and all our family.

Me sisters and me had to leave home when we were twelve or thirteen to make room in the house for others. We all did. It seemed to me unfair that the boys in the family got to stay home longer when we girls couldn't. And it was the same in all families. But that was the way it was in them days. Just the same as when my turn came. Lizzie went and then Beatie. Rosie went to Nottingham to look after a baby girl. Not for long though because she wanted to marry Alec from next door. Mostly the work was very hard but everyone was treated well unless you got yourself into trouble. Our sons stayed home to start their apprenticeships. I left at thirteen which was very young. I was really lonely for me family. One of the good things that came out of that awful war was that the girls got to do real work.

There was talk of war, 1914, I think. We women felt fear, grief and sadness. But some local lads were excited by the idea of a good fight, mainly those lads were labouring. They happily volunteered because they were eager to leave home for some excitement. They would sing: Pack up your troubles in your old kit bag and smile. We wondered for how long they would be smiling.

Our boys were planning to be blacksmiths and so did not sign up. Will and I were pleased about that. Lizzie was married and Edgar and Rosie had sweethearts. Phil and Alec had no intention of volunteering, in any case they were doing what they called essential service. We were all glad. We weren't too concerned about Beatie's husband who had ran off and left her. We hoped he would get what he deserved, leaving Beatie like that! We all expected the war to last only a short time but it lasted years and years. We called it the Great War. Sometimes a husband and father suddenly left the village because he had been called to service in the middle of the night. We were devastated when the war ended and some of our lads did not return. All some had were memories.

I remember being told: the war would not last the year. But they were wrong! We didn't see any bombing but the price of flour went up and we could not get sugar. Everything else we went without or made do. Food was rationed. We never believed it would last all those years. We lost so many young men. But then the young women were given jobs, sometimes making bombs. So, they had more to do than be in service. By the time the Great War ended, I think the war changed everything for the girls! They knew they could do more than washing, cleaning, cooking, and doing for others.

Oh, I remember me dear sister Emma lost a son in the great war. About 1915 it was. He was only 25.[66] The loss of their eldest son who had sacrificed his life in the defence of his country, died not on the battlefield but by accidental drowning was agonizing for us all. Such a horrible waste of a life. Imagine! an accident.

Rosie and Alec, from next door on Main Street, liked each other as children. But Rosie at 13 had to go away to work. They must have written lots of letters to one another because we found out they were really sweet on one another. They decided they wanted to marry. Just as the Great War started, I think. Such a pretty little wedding took place in St Guthlac's church in the village. They all wore such pretty dresses. The Church bells rang just for them to celebrate their wedding. They found a tiny house further up Main Street. I remember when Kathleen was born. I helped our Rosie as much I could. Rosie had an awful time and declared she would have no more children! But then Rosie was sweet and a little delicate.

Sometime in August each year, we would decide the blackberries were ripe and ready for picking. They would be black and juicy. A whole gang of us women with our children would go out together to pick the berries. The sun would be warm and the hedgerows full of life and energy. We would carry pails to collect the berries and walking sticks to pull down the branches. We would chat and laugh and play with the little ones who would play tag around us. And eat blackberries! I remember seeing the children with red hands and faces, berries all over themselves. The berries bushes had thorns so sometimes we would have to soothe injuries and little arms by tying a rag around to stop the bleeding. We would carry the blackberries home to make jam, pies, and blackberry vinegar.

There was a skittle alley at the Plough Inn which kept the men occupied. There were tournaments I remember. I expect our boys were keen skittlers. They also kicked a ball around in the fields. They called this game, football. The ball was made from a pig's bladder. I am not sure there were any rules, but they seemed to have teams and the winners scored the most goals. This kept the teenagers and young men occupied. The young girls and women cheered on their teams and appeared to have fun.

Will loved to play the fiddle by ear. He said he could "feel" music. Our Jimmy, was the same, also musical and played the piano by ear. The two of them played at The Plough Inn on Main Street entertaining everyone. We heard the 20s called roaring and I suppose they were. Our clothes became freer, lighter, shorter. The young ones danced a lot. Really a lot. It seems that was all they could think about. But then they were happy, more so than at any time I could remember.

Do you know the saying: April Showers bring forth May flowers? That was the way it seemed to be each year. I looked forward to the Merry Month of May. On May the first, the children would dance around the May Pole, trying not to forget to hang onto their ribbons and to weave in and out. Oh, I remember we said: don't

---

66 Red haired son George, enlisted in the King's Own Yorkshire Light Infantry and served as a private in the 8th Battalion. He died in France in WWI in France and Flanders on September 12, 1915. He accidently drowned according to the UK Army Register of soldier's effects. He is honoured on the village War Memorial.

(Photographer: Unknown) Kitty and William Brown Oh! this is the only picture I have of the pair of us. I think I was about 45 in this picture and Will would be 50. We are so dressed up but I don't recall the occasion. Fancy looking so smart. We would put on our Sunday best for church every Sunday. Will used to wear a cap all the time. This photograph was taken just outside Wood View, Stathern, near The Green. Isn't it interesting that houses had names and not numbers?

(Photographer: Unknown)

cast a clout until May is out. You could never rely on the May weather. But I loved the pretty flowers that smelled so nice.

We liked going to church for Harvest Festival. The church would be decorated so nicely with fruits and vegetables and tree branches: we were celebrating a successful harvest that would keep us alive during the winter. So, the Festival would be after the harvest. I am not sure exactly when. In the autumn.

Look at the open farm fields and the horse wagons. I cannot imagine having a baby at the age I was in that picture. But me mother did. She had me. Was I wanted or a final nuisance?

Me Will became poorly sometime in 1927. He went to the Hospital in Nottingham. You cannot imagine how sad I was when he died at Christmas time. Let me see, he was 65 years old. We had been together for 40 years.

I had seven children y'know and all lived. I didn't lose any babies or children. I was very glad. Many babies and little ones died in them days.

Oh, one more thing…. We knew quite early on that our son George was not growing up properly. He just didn't get taller. He was like a man but the height of a child. We called him Gidge. I have no idea why.

Oh, this is Jimmy's wedding. He married Olive Miller from the village: a couple of years after Will died. There I am with my hands on Gidge's shoulders. Nellie was the second bridesmaid on the left. Oh, the flowers were beautiful.

I remember when we women got to vote, soon after Will died. I wondered how I would choose who to vote for without having Will to talk to about what to do. He seemed to always have an opinion but I know almost nothing about them things. Having the vote would be wasted on me

We heard that privies would be coming inside our houses and that paper came in rolls. We used to cut up newspaper you know. But I cannot imagine privies inside: they stink. Before the privy pans are emptied, the stench is pretty bad, like a barnyard, but worse. I would not call that progress! Me privy belongs at the bottom of the garden!

(Photographer: Unknown) I moved house into an end house at the top end of the village, near to Rosie and Alec. Yes, this is the back entrance to the house we called the "up the steps" house because it was built on a hill. To get to the back door, you would climb up the steps. Me up the steps house was at the top end of the village close to farmer's field and Stathern Woods. Here, Kathleen is having a party with her friends in my garden. Are they wearing crowns? It looks like a birthday party. She is on the right. Next to her is Lizzie's daughter, Nellie. Kathleen stayed with me from time to time in this house to keep me company.

Yes, here is Gidge with Jimmy's daughter May. It looks as though this picture was taken outside the school. Gidge worked at the garage on Main Street, just opposite The Plough where Jimmy and Will played their music. I was glad Gidge lived with me. He was company for me. I was glad he had somewhere to live

I remember me dad, George, he would come home from work in the fields, take off his boots and overalls and wash up before he came into the house. Even so, he smelled ever so slightly of manure. He and me mam loved having children around. We all could not make too much noise for him.

I have been a widow for many years, not living alone though because many of me family took turns living with me. Me granddaughter Dorothy lived with me as a young child after Beatie left that awful marriage and moved in with Alec and Rosie. That would be just after Kathleen was born. Rosie and Alec moved from that tiny place near the cheese factory to a new house on Main Street in the village. But still there was no room for five of them. So, I was glad when Dorothy came to stay with me not as a baby but as a little girl.

(Photographer: Unknown)
Elizabeth and George Slater.

Oh yes, I remember me mam and dad. Look how slender and posh me mam looks in this picture. That is the only one I have seen of them both. Me dad looks worn out. Me mam has a fancy bonnet with so many fancy bows. Yes. That is me mam alright! Just look at her tiny waist after so many children. Seven she had. She looks so spry but me da looks really old. He worked so hard in the fields. But she worked hard an all with all her children, the house, feeding us all, the washing and making cheese and our ale. She looks dainty and tough and she was!

I later moved to a row house very near me up the steps house. It was a small damp little place. It would be me last home. These houses were "herder's cottages." I lived in the end house nearest the street.

I watched Kathleen grow into a fine woman. She refused to go into service and found herself a job in Melton. She would have been about eighteen when she went to work. She would take her bike and off she went every day. The young people loved to dance. That was where she met her Reg.

The twenties were a settled, exciting but calm time: the thirties too until we heard rumblings again about a war. I remembered the dread of the last one and feared for the family once again. Kathleen's intended Reg would be called up to service. We were lucky the last time and might not be so again. The world had changed but the village was so much the same.

We were promised peace but instead, the war did start as we drew toward 1940. The war had started when Kathleen and Reg decided to marry. He would soon be off after that. We were worried for them all. We said goodbye to our lads: Reg as well as Reg's brother George and many village lads. We set in for a long time of fear, shortages and uncertainty. Then when Daphne was born, we had joy, a little person to take care of, a distraction as we faced rationing and despair.

Lizzie's Phil had somehow rigged up a wireless so sometimes we heard the BBC news. Four long years later, we heard on the wireless that the war will soon be over. We were hopeful. About that time, we knew Rosie was not well. She had a bad cough and looked pale. We had seen this before: Alec was worried. Then she was taken away from us to hospital, unexpectedly and quickly, no one was telling us anything. We were no longer hopeful. Alec had no way of getting in to see her in Leicester. I was afraid I would lose me girl before me. It is fortunate indeed that Kathleen was preoccupied with Daphne and was looking forward to Reg's return.

I am glad to tell you our family members did return. Shell shocked, sick, thin and angry they were: not the same men who left us. They smoked, refused to eat tinned corned beef and swore a lot. No doubt they had learned new words while they were away. But they were alive, ready to start their lives again.

That is about all I remember. I am glad of the photographs which helped me memory. My life was long and happy I think with all me family around me. I lost me Will too soon.

ENDNOTES

I hope I have been faithful to my great grannie Brown, expressing how I imagined she would have reflected on her life as her memory wandered through it. Your Nana and my great Auntie Beat talked of her extensively: I have used the information I gleaned from them: the rest is my imagination!

(Photographer: R. Heathcote)
Photograph from family records

Here are how the herders' cottages looked during my last visit to Stathern. Grannie Brown lived and died in the end cottage on the left. The gardens have been replaced with driveways; the privies did indeed move indoors. Garages took their place.

The musical talent of the Browns emerged into the next generation. Your Nana described her grandfather as a gentle fellow. Your Nana played the piano beautifully yet rarely. Jim's daughter, May, tried to teach me. Alas, I am not so musical.

Sadly, Gidge in his fifties, committed suicide by hanging himself while living with his brother James at the time in Stathern. I remember when that happened.

I have the Entry of Death for Grannie Brown. She died on February 6, 1945 at the age of 77. Cause of death was Cerebral Thrombosis and Arteriosclerosis. Her death was certified by Dr. Miles W. Atkinson, MRCS who coincidentally was the physician present when I was born: Small world in this community.

This photograph shows the front entrance to the up the steps house, rarely used. Renovated it looks very nice.

(Photographer: D. Field)

Dear friends, the Burgess's lived there in the 1970s and until Bob and then Win died sometime before your Nana.

I look at the photograph we have of Grannie Brown, a sprite, slender lady who lived a good life and left a legacy: no shrinking violet indeed, a hardworking woman who bore seven children because there were no choices. I can only imagine how difficult it was to do the laundry for her large family with no running water.

I don't remember her as she died too early for my memory. I have heard many stories about her. I know that had she lived a little longer, I would not only have appreciated her but would have been drawn to her. She was mystic and wise, a redhead like her father. Grannie Brown, the experienced midwife, would certainly have been helping your Nana when she gave birth to me. I wonder why your Nana never mentioned that piece of our history. Grannie and my Nana Rosie, played a huge role in the first three years of my life. Then within the next two years, they were both gone. The picture has emerged of a courageous, giving woman, one I am proud to have as an ancestor.

CHART 17. CAROLINE "KITTY" (SLATER) AND WILLIAM BROWN'S FAMILY

HUSBAND: WILLIAM BROWN

Birth:	1863 in Nether Broughton,
Marriage:	Jul 1887 in Bingham,
Death:	31 Dec 1927 in General Hospital Nottingham;
Father:	Elisha Brown
Mother:	Sarah (Elliott) Brown

WIFE: CAROLINE "KITTY" (SLATER) BROWN

Birth:	10 May 1868 in Granby, Nottinghamshire,
Death:	06 Feb 1945 in Stathern
Father:	George Slater
Mother:	Elizabeth (Gilding) Slater

CHILDREN:

1 M
Name:	Edgar Slater Brown
Birth:	08 Dec 1887 in Stathern,
Marriage:	Apr 1914 in Melton Mowbray,
Death:	21 Jul 1974 in Melton Mowbray, Leics
Spouse:	Alice M Bird

2 F
Name:	Sarah Elizabeth "Lizzie" (Brown) Jacques
Birth:	25 Mar 1889 in Stathern,
Marriage:	Jul 1910 in Stathern
Death:	26 Dec 1964 in Nottingham Hosp;
Spouse:	Felix Jacques

3 F
Name:	Beatrice C (Brown)(Hotchin) Green
Birth:	16 Feb 1891 in Main Street, Stathern,
Marriage:	Jan 1927 in Melton Mowbray,
Death:	27 Mar 1984 in Melton Mowbray,
Spouse:	Ernest (Ernie) Ezra Green

4 F
Name:	**Ethel Rose "Rosie" (Brown) Hubbard**
Birth:	21 Jun 1893 in Stathern
Death:	Jun 1947 in Blaby, Leicestershire,
Spouse:	**Wilfred Alec "Alec" Hubbard**

5 M
Name:	George William Brown
Birth:	Apr 1897 in Stathern,
Death:	Mar 1951 in Stathern,

6 M	Name:	Ernest James Brown
	Birth:	11 Sep 1902 in Stathern,
	Marriage:	Sep 1931 in Melton Mowbray,
	Death:	Jun 1969 in Melton Mowbray,
	Spouse:	Olive (Miller) Brown
7 M	Name:	Ellis Arthur Brown
	Birth:	01 Feb 1904 in Stathern,
	Marriage:	1925 in Nottingham, Doris May (Hall) Brown
	Death:	17 Sep 1992 in Basford, Age: 88 23 Sep 1992 in Nottinghamshire,

18.

THE SLATERS

Your Nana's maternal grandmother was a Slater. Firstly, the origin of the Slater name. The many generations and branches of the Slater family can all place the origins of their surname with the ancient Anglo-Saxon culture. Their name reveals a person who covered roofs with *slate*. Slater, an occupational surname, belongs to the category of hereditary surnames, surnames derived from the primary activity of the bearer. This medieval name originated in Derbyshire, close by where your ancestors lived on the North Leicestershire border with Nottinghamshire. But there were no roofers or builders of any kind, in the Slaters in your immediate past.

The Slaters lived in and around the small village of Granby on the Nottingham and North Leicestershire Border in the Vale of Belvoir. The village appears in the Domesday Book of 1086 with 99 households, a large number for the period. There was already a church and two mills. The village stands near the source of the River Devon, near the Grantham canal, and is situated about twenty-two kms from Nottingham. Census returns suggest a peak population of 439 in the 1891 census and a low point of 248 in 1951. The Marquis of Granby pub dating back to 1760 still serves a range of real ales and has won awards for the quality of its beer.

Much of Granby village and many of the farms were, until the 1920s, part of the Rutland Estate around Belvoir Castle[67] which is a prominent feature of the eastern skyline. The Castle, first built immediately after the Norman Conquest of 1066, according to the Domesday Book, has since been rebuilt at least three times. The name "Belvoir" is a Norman import by the French-speaking conquerors meaning beautiful view. The locals, however, had trouble pronouncing the foreign word, preferring to call it " Beaver Castle" and still do!

---

67 http://www.englishheritageartist.co.uk/historical-places/belvoir-castle-leicestershire/

Eventually, the castle passed to the Manners family. The title Earl of Rutland was created in 1525. General John Manners (1721-1770), 9th Earl of Rutland, was named Duke of Rutland. Belvoir Castle has been the home of the Manners family for five hundred years, and the seat of the Dukes of Rutland for over three centuries. The present castle was rebuilt after a disastrous fire in the 19th century, and was largely designed and rebuilt by James Wyatt, the great neo-gothic architect. During the filming of The Crown, scenes were filmed at the Castle posing as Windsor Castle! The 19th century's great landscape gardener, Capability Brown redesigned the gardens and parklands, one of his last and greatest creations.

The imposing castle and the Vale of Belvoir are seen here. While their physical environment was beautiful. I doubt our ancestors had either time or inclination to enjoy the lovely rolling hills, the woods with rhododendrons, bluebells, and songbirds. In my younger days the castle was just there, almost without notice.

(Photographer: R. Heathcote)

Apparently, Anna Russell, Duchess of Bedford, introduced the idea of afternoon tea while visiting Belvoir Castle in the 1840s. The back story is as follows: the normal time for dinner was between 7:00 and 8:30 p.m. An extra meal called luncheon had been created to fill the midday gap between breakfast and dinner, but as this new meal was very light, the long afternoon with no refreshment at all left people feeling hungry. She found a light meal of tea (usually Darjeeling) and cakes or sandwiches was the perfect balance. The Duchess asked that a tray of tea, bread and butter (some time earlier, the Earl of Sandwich had had the idea of putting a filling between two slices of bread) and cake be brought to her room during the late afternoon. The Duchess found taking an afternoon snack to be such perfect refreshment that she soon began inviting her friends to join her. Afternoon tea quickly became an established and convivial repast in many middle- and upper-class households, a fashionable social event. During the 1880's upper-class and society women would change into long gowns, gloves and hats for their afternoon tea which was usually served in the drawing room between four and five o'clock.

Returning to the Slaters: the earliest Slaters I could locate were William and Mary Gill Slater. We know little about them except that they married on February 1, 1799 in York. They were both 40 years of age. Mary was the daughter of Martha Gill. How they met and why William lived in York we do not know. There is no record of his occupation but we suspect he was a labourer. I could not determine how long they lived. For whatever reason, after William and Mary married, they set up home in the farming community of Granby close to where William was raised. Robert Slater was born in nearby Barkestone within the year. Robert was likely their only child.

Minimal records exist in the early part of the century but there is a record of Robert's marriage to a Mary Swain of Long Clawson on November 26, 1822. Mary was nine years his senior. A child, Rosa, had been born on March 9, 1822 in Granby, to Mary: parentage unknown. Rosa did not take Robert's name. Mary gave birth to Thomas in 1824, George in 1828, Obadiah in 1830, and James in 1832. At the age of 35, motivated by goodness knows what, Robert Slater committed a crime. On June 29, 1835, he was imprisoned for nine months for larceny according to the England and Wales Criminal Records. Mary would have been left to fend for herself with four sons, aged from 11 to 3, with 13-year-old Rosa. This is the only misdemeanour I have found in the family! This crime of theft resulted in his whole family paying the consequences for his deed by placing them in hardship. In the Grannie Brown story, you will hear how she remembers her Grandad Robert and Grannie Mary.

But the story gets worse! Son Thomas was accused of rape and charged in the Nottingham County Assizes on June 22, 1846 but was acquitted. He was 22. How much that accusation would have tarnished his reputation, we do not know. He disappeared from census records after that date.

Robert, an agricultural labourer all his life, lived with his son, our direct ancestor, George and his wife, Elizabeth from time to time. He died in 1881 at the age of 81. Mary had died six years earlier.

Our ancestor George Slater was born in Granby and his wife, Elizabeth in Orsten in 1823. They married in 1848. This is what a marriage certificate looked like in those days. Neither Elizabeth nor George were literate. Elizabeth's father is unknown.

The pair had four daughters and three sons over the next nineteen years. Your great, great Grandmother Kitty Brown was the last child to be born to Elizabeth at the age of 45.

The Slaters on our maternal side were essentially farmers, tied to the land by their physical location: land owned by the Duke of Rutland. At the start of the 19th Century, few alternative ways of livelihood were available. Some ventured into the new industries, such as the cement works and mining, activities that were as dangerous as they were physically demanding. They occupied dwellings that would have been either provided for them or rented. Ownership was not an option in their Victorian time.

Nevertheless, I believe they had an advantage over the Warburtons and Heathcotes. At least they were engaged in physical labour in the fresh air and endured a healthier lifestyle than the framework knitters.

The life of George and Elizabeth's eldest son, John Isaac was initially as a labourer but he soon ventured toward a new enterprise that was being built in nearby Barnstone in Nottinghamshire. He joined the industrial revolution – he worked at the cement works, like other members of the Slater family. He is shown in the 1881 census as a quarryman. His life, however, ended in tragedy. John's generation aspired to move away from farming toward participating in the new industrial age that had reached the East Midlands of England.

CHART 18
THE SLATERS

Caroline "Kitty" (Slater) Brown
b: 10 May 1868 in Granby, Nottinghamshire,
m: Jul 1887 in Bingham,
d: 06 Feb 1945 in Stathern

- **George Slater**
  b: 1828 in Granby,
  m: Oct 1848 in Bingham NOTTS
  d: Jun 1904 in Bingham, ;
  Died in Bingham Union Workhouse

  - **Robert Slater**
    b: 1800 in Barkstone, Leicestershire,
    m:
    d: Apr 1881 in Bingham, Nottinghamshire

    - **William Slater**
      b: 1759
      m: 01 Feb 1799 in York
      d:

    - **Mary (GILL) Slater**
      b: 1759
      d:

  - **Mary (Swain) Slater**
    b: 1791 in Long Clawson,
    d: Jan 1875 in Bingham,

    - **John Swaine**
      b: 1779
      m: 30 Sep 1802 in Stathern
      d:

    - **Name:**
      b:
      d:

- **Elizabeth (Gilding) Slater**
  b: 01 Feb 1824 in Elton, Nottinghamshire,
  d: Oct 1900 in Bingham NOTTS

  - **Simon Gilding**
    b:
    m:
    d:

    - **Name:**
      b:
      m:
      d:

    - **Name:**
      b:
      d:

  - **Mary Gilding**
    b: 24 Nov 1799 in Elton, Notts
    d:

    - **Thomas Gilding**
      b: 30 Nov 1771 in Eaton, Grantham, Leicestershire,
      m: 27 May 1793 in Croxton Kerrial,
      d: 07 Jun 1833 in Elton, Nottinghamshire,

    - **Mary (Burgin) Gilding**
      b: 1765 in Croxton, Norfolk,
      d: 15 Jun 1831 in Elton, Nottinghamshire,

19.

James Slater, the Entrepreneur and his legacy

Forgive me for not resisting this side story, one of intrigue that illustrates the times.

By the mid-1800s, the Industrial Revolution was underway. Railway tracks for steam engines were being laid so that cities could be connected. Reliance on canals for transport was being phased out. Steam power was replacing horsepower. Coal was the fuel, fuel that had to be mined and transported. There was less and less reliance on manual labour in the fields.

At that time, there were no stores in the villages. Everyone made their own clothing and entertainment and prepared their own food. Imagine, no take out! I discovered there was a pub in the village of Granby where these ancestors lived, in the heart of England. While there were no official communication mechanisms, the news would have travelled along with travellers and the mailman.

This interesting side story looks at the life of James Slater, the brother of your great, great grandmother Kitty Brown. In 1881 24-year-old James was living with his in-laws in Cropwell Butler, an agricultural worker. He had married Ruth Breedon, a lady with a past! I have the following story about Ruth gleaned from Ancestry:

> *Ruth was 19 years old when her first son, Thomas was born on March 17, 1878 (father unknown). Before she met James Slater, she worked as a servant in a big house. She would have been instantly dismissed when her employers were told of her predicament. Her parents supported her as Thomas was born at home in Cropwell Butler. Five months later she married James Slater, a labourer from Granby: they reared a large family.*

By 1891, James was a coal miner and had moved the family of seven children to Basford, Nottingham. By 1911 Robert had completely reinvented himself: he had become a general dealer and carter of fish, and eventually a hay dealer. He must have owned a horse and cart for the purpose. The story continues:

> *The Slaters later moved to the Manor House, Bullwell Lane, Old Basford: James became a hay dealer. James' two sons George and Henry helped him with the business, so it must have been thriving for 3 men to earn a living out of it.*

James died at aged 65: the only Slater with a legacy. He is my hero! Probate records state James Slater of Manor House, Bulwell Lane, Old Basford, a hay dealer, left his wife Ruth the sum of £60 13s 3d.

The above account tells of a cohesive family. Ruth must have been relieved to have married James who gave Thomas legitimacy, but he never did take the Slater name. Rather he was a Breedon all his life. Thomas became a railwayman, an engine stoker, and then an engine driver. He moved his family to Bletchley.

Kitty's brother James has my admiration by breaking the mould. Interestingly, it was this brother who met and married a young lady, Ruth, in trouble with a child conceived of wedlock, father unknown. Perhaps he was the father. Or the father was one of the household members where she worked. We will not know. We do know that James moved in with Ruth`s family, a supportive family with funds to spare. Thomas, the railwayman, moved his family to where the employment opportunities offered him a better life. Did I mention that both Thomas and James's father had red hair?

20.

AUNTIE BEAT TELLS HER STORY

Auntie Beat was our favourite aunt. This wonderful, kind lady was your Nana's auntie. After your great grandmother died, Auntie Beat became the go-to person for my Nana. So, in a way, she was my grandmother substitute. As I grew, she became so important in my life. As I have lamented before, I wish I had asked her questions, but I just didn't. So, here is how I think she might have told us her story………

You have asked me to talk about me life. I hardly know where to begin.

(Photographer: R. Heathcote)
Auntie Beat on the right with Grandma Heathcote, Auntie Olive Brown and Aunty Becky Heathcote

I look so serious in this picture. Perhaps I look thoughtful. I am opening me birthday card. Kathleen was giving me a party to remember me birthday. We are at her house.

I was born on 16th February 1891 so this celebration would have been in February although I don't remember the year. Perhaps it was my 80th, so it was probably 1971. This was quite the gathering with Grannie Heathcote, Olive Brown, and Becky Heathcote. They all look happy for me.

I remember Grannie Heathcote died not long after this photo was taken.

They all seem to have a drink in their hands, that is, except me!

You ask me to remember me life and what I first remember. Well, my brothers and sisters were all born in Stathern. I suppose I remember me mam, Kitty Brown, and me dad, Will. I would have been about ten when my memory starts. Me mam worked in the house when she had time. She was a lace worker. At home was Lizzie who was a couple of years older than me and Rosie who was a couple of years younger. Then a couple of years younger than Rosie was George William, named after our dad.

We girls went to Stathern School to learn to read, write, and do our sums. Mostly that was in the morning and then we helped our mam in the afternoon with cooking, gardening, the washing, and sometimes with her lace-making. We were always busy. But we had fun, we three girls. We had an elder brother, Edgar who had left home by then to work on a farm but he didn't leave the village. Then me mam had two more babies: Jimmy and Ellis. We were so busy looking after little ones with all that laundry. I remember that me mam's mam and dad both died during that time, early into the new century. So, there was joy and sadness all mixed up together. We didn't see much of our grannie and grandad Slater because they lived in Granby which wasn't far, just awkward to get to.

But me dad's mam and dad lived in Stathern and so we saw a lot of them. I remember that Grandma Brown died just before me little brothers were born. She was really missed. I remember Grandad Brown who was a maltster, y'know. But when I remember him, he worked on a farm. He lived with me dad's sister Aunt Lily with her family in the village. He died about 10 years after Grandma Brown. I don't recall exactly because I wasn't living at home then.

Our dad was a blacksmith. He walked to work up Tofts Hill every day to work at the Quarry with the other men who also worked at the Quarry. We all liked our dad. He made things for us like horseshoes so we could play the game "throw the horseshoe" and he made us a toasting fork, spades for the garden, and ornaments.

Stathern was a growing village with many families and many children. On our street were the Hubbards who had a big family. We all grew up together, playing around the streets and in and out of our houses. From the word go, our Rosie liked Alec Hubbard and he liked her. They had grown up together and seemed like the perfect pair. Our grandparents, the Browns, lived close by as well.

Me mam would tell us girls how she left her mam and dad, Grannie and Grandad Slater, to go into service when she was only 13. She left Granby to go to Langar which was close. She was preparing us for what was going to happen to us. Our Lizzie was the first to go. Sarah Elizabeth she was. I cannot recall where she went but I remember when she came home telling us she wanted to marry. She was more serious and quieter than I was and determined. She had met a man who was almost 15 years older than her and wanted to marry him. They married in July of 1910. She would have been 22 then and he was 35. Felix Jacques, he was. His name was pronounced as 'Jakes'. They had little Nellie right away, in the spring of the next year. They lived in Cropwell Bishop, a village Nottingham way. He worked as a groom/gardener. He was called Phil. Lizzie told us Phil was born in July 1875 but lost his mam. He grew up with his mam's folks. We thought him a little gruff: not easy to be with and get to know.

Then it was me turn to leave home. I was found a place as a servant to a Mrs. Sarah Rouse, a single lady who at 73 was a farmer in nearby Hose. I was on me own with Mrs. Rouse who seemed very old to me but then I was a teenager. The house was very big and I was all alone until I met Harold who suddenly appeared from nowhere and swept me off me feet. I was 21 and fell for his charms just a bit too much. I had to go home and tell me mam and dad I was in the family way. Harold and I did marry under a cloud and then he ran off to his family after me little daughter was born on September 14, 1912. Me dad did warn me that Harold would not treat me well. After I had Dorothy Caroline, Harold Hotchins disappeared from the area. We heard he moved back to Surrey where his folks lived. Sadly, I was left alone as he moved on. That is how it happens sometimes. I had to return to Stathern and moved around a bit with Dorothy. Those were unsettling times for us when she was a baby.

Oh, I forgot to tell you about Jimmy and Ellis being born after George. They were born around the time Lizzie and I were leaving home. We were all a bit crowded in the house after those babies arrived but me mam needed the help in the house.

But I really want to tell you about Rosie who came after me. Ethel Rose, the third daughter born on June 21, 1893. She was sweet and a little delicate. We looked after her. Lizzie and I were of stockier build like our dad, especially Lizzie. But Rosie was very slender like our mam. Lizzie and I had gone when it was her turn to leave. She wrote to us to tell us about her work for Mr. and Mrs. James at 10 Teversal Avenue in Lenton, near Nottingham, which Rosie said was a new terrace house. Mr. James was a grocer so I expect they had enough to eat! She was the only servant and so worked hard doing everything for the family. And there was a baby to take care of! But Rosie and Alec Hubbard were writing to one another and we knew they needed to be together. They married in January 1915 such a pretty little wedding. Rosie literally married the boy next door. They found a tiny house in the yard of the cheese factory further up Main Street in Stathern. A year later she had Kathleen. But Rosie had a gruelling time giving birth and vowed to have no more.

After about three years, Rosie, Alec, and Kathleen moved to a bigger house on Main Street and offered me a home with them. But there were only two bedrooms so I shared a room with little Kathleen. There was no room, sadly, for me Dorothy so she went to live with me mam and dad. Dorothy resented this, I am sad to say that was the reason Dorothy and young Kathleen never got along very well.

Kathleen was a baby during the Great War and we all suffered shortages. Housework was all I knew so that is what I did. I was glad to have a home with Rosie and Alec after the war ended. Dorothy really didn't thrive like I thought she should have. She seemed to mix with the rougher children in the village and speak as they did which was not like me at all. The way we talk makes all the difference, doesn't it? Dorothy seemed to get worse and put herself in a common class in the village by her behaviour. I tried to have a gentle manner, but Dorothy wasn't like me at all. As I look back, Dorothy was not a credit to me. I will always wonder what changed her nature and what I could have done differently.

All me brothers and sisters, except George, who we all called Gidge, eventually left home. I forgot to tell you that George did not grow properly. He was too short like a midget so he did not have a normal life. After me dad died, George went to live with me mam. I was so sorry when I heard what happened to Gidge.

After the Great War, we were seeing fewer horses in the village and the first motor cars appeared. This would have been sometime in the 1920s. So, then we saw a garage on Main Street in Stathern to look after engines and to serve petrol to fill tanks. Gidge was able to get work there. After me mam died, Gidge then went to live with Jimmy, Olive, and May just a little way from me on Penn Lane. This was in the 1940s. Oh, this is not a happy story. Gidge hung himself when he was in his 50s. Such a sad day, one I won't forget.

Ellis married Doris and moved Nottingham way but Jimmy stayed in the village to marry Olive whose family operated Miller's Dairy on Main Street in Stathern. Jimmy was the musical Brown who took after our dad.

Me dad worked hard as a blacksmith and was well thought of in the village. Me mam as well. I would say she was a pillar of the Stathern Community. A true giver, she who would put on her white overall to assist with birthing and also to "lay people out", that is wash bodies in preparation for burial: hatches and dispatches as I would later understand.

(Photographer: Unknown) Oh yes, here I am with Kathleen, Becky (she married into the Heathcote family), Ernie and our son, Reggie. I don't look happy but I was. This was in the 1930s, I think. This looks as though this was outside our cottage on Penn Lane in Stathern. Kathleen would tell me I had lovely thick curly hair. And I had.

While we suffered during the Great War, it was nothing like being there. I had many jobs during those awful war years and afterward, everything was so much better for us. I did house cleaning and also worked in a dairy making stilton cheese. Yes. I worked at Texford and Tebbitts making pork pies in nearby Long Clawson. I worked with Rebecca Fisher, who married Tom Heathcote. Those days were more settling times for me.

Sometime after the Great War ended, I met Ernie Green. I am not sure how we met. He was from the neighbouring Rutland County and was a little younger than me. But I was attracted to his gentle nature and he to mine. He was a decorated soldier from the Great War. I was proud of him. He told me a little about fighting over there. Ernie had been exposed to gas during the war which had damaged his lungs and often had a bad cough. We had to take care of him in the cold weather.

Ernie and I married in January 1927. I was glad to finally be able to offer Dorothy a stable home. But still, she didn't thrive. 1927 was a bittersweet year for us. Me dad took ill and died on December 31 that year. You can imagine me mam was distraught. They had been married for so long and relied on one another. We all took turns staying with her, including our Dorothy. I was almost beyond childbearing age when our son arrived. We called him Reginald.

In April 1934, against our advice, Dorothy chose to marry Bazil Bickerton whose mother I discovered was a Hubbard from Eaton and a relative to Alec. Bazil was a rough man, not the kind of man I wanted for her. I fear she chose as unwisely as I had. They had a son, Peter, and moved away from Stathern. Unfortunately, Bazil drank too much which caused Dorothy much distress. She eventually returned to Stathern on her own but really was not good.

Ernie and I found this cottage in Stathern. The centre cottage of a row of three cottages built at right angles to Penn Lane, a road on the way to Granby and Belvoir Castle. The tiny cottage had a living room and kitchen on the ground floor, two bedrooms upstairs, and the loo down the garden. The cottage had a vegetable garden which Ernie looked after. We were comfortable and happy there.

Rosie, Alec, and Kathleen had moved into a new house on the outskirts of the village: a semi-detached house. Lizzie and Phil lived in the attached house.

(Photographer: Unknown) Lizzie and Phil moved into the other half of the house with their children, Nellie and Thomas William. Both houses had large gardens to keep the menfolk busy. Lizzie seemed old and a little chubby in this photograph. I think the age difference between the two was a problem for Lizzie. Oh dear, neither look happy in this photo.

Oh, I remember, I would take Daphne and Maureen Nellie's daughter for an outing to Nottingham every year for a while until my age slowed me down and they were too old to want to go with me! We went on the bus and went shopping in Nottingham.

The thirties were peaceful but soon we were warned that another war was looming. Lizzie, Rosie and I talked a lot about it when we all visited me mam. She remembered the shortages and the fear for the menfolk during the Great War. I tried not to dwell on it too much for Ernie's sake. But then war became impossible to ignore as we became aware of the government making preparations. All Kathleen wanted to do was dance and she had a partner. I am glad me Reggie was too young to take notice. Kathleen decided to marry. So, Reginald Heathcote entered our family. And within the year, so did Daphne. Tom Jacques was in an essential service on the railway but when Reg, a bus driver, was shipped overseas in 1942, the whole family was fearful. I feel numb when I think of it. We kept singing and thinking: We'll Meet Again……..

We tried to carry on as normal, me mam, me sisters, Phil, Ernie, Alec….. I think Edgar's son Charlie was called up and returned alright and then married. Ellis and Jimmy had one daughter each. The little girls were a distraction for us all. We thought of the whole village as family so we worried about them all and ourselves as the planes flew over. But the village was spared this time. One cousin lost his life, the rest returned although Kathleen's Reg was much changed.

The Clamp family lived in the big house on the opposite side of the road from our house on Penn Lane. I would clean in that house sometimes, without realizing that the family had a connection to Alec's mam. In Stathern, it is a small world!

Our good neighbours, Lucy and Alfred Moulds lived in the end cottage near the road: a cheerful couple, such good neighbours. Daphne would sit on the wall that offered them privacy from the road. Alfred

This is one of me favourite photographs. Of course, I had been very close to Kathleen all her life. We became closer after we lost Rosie.

and she would sing together "If I were the Only Girl in the World and you were the Only Boy." Daphne would comb Alfred's hair to Lucy's amusement.

(Photographer: R. Heathcote) Oh yes, here we are outside our front door. As you see Ernie hasn't much hair. I remember Kathleen's son; Geoff made a classic comment about his Uncle Ernie when he was about two. On a particularly windy day when they were visiting us, Geoff said as he looked at Uncle Ernie, "Hair blowed away!"

(Photographer: R. Heathcote) Ernie Green was a good man. He took evening courses and became educated. I was so proud of him. He became a prominent member of the village council, a man we all looked up to.

Daphne suffered an ordeal with her health when she was very young. She could not talk to Kathleen about what happened in the hospital but I am glad she would talk to me. She did need to talk to someone. Without her Nana, I took over the Grannie role for her. We talked about lots of things she could not talk about at home. She would pick up our groceries from Goddard's shop using our ration books on a Saturday morning and then chat with me as she sat at our table. We would talk and talk.

Even before Reg returned, Rosie became ill. She was pale and had a cough. Suddenly, without fanfare, she was whisked away from us and placed in a hospital far away in Leicester. We were discouraged from seeing her. No one was talking. Kathleen and Alec were inconsolable. I was really happy to be there for Kathleen. We all loved Rosie.

(Photographer: Unknown) It was 1960. Oh yes, Lizzie and Phil celebrate 50 years of marriage. Neither one looks very happy in this photograph! Lizzie became a diabetic when she was 70. She needed to give herself injections of insulin. She didn't find those injections easy. But she practised on an orange and became very good at it.

Oh yes, I remember the Coronation of Queen Elizabeth II. It was a grand affair in 1954. We watched the event on the television. Reg had bought a television for the occasion. All the villages celebrated independently. We were given a mug with the Queen's head. We had races for the children and a meal for seniors. I was a senior at that time but Uncle Ernie was not. I am a few years older than he, you see, and so I enjoyed a communal meal in the village hall without him!

I would like to tell you about Lizzie and Phil.

Phil was first a groom but then he became a postmaster. And then he became a railwayman. But he was very technical and clever. He built a radio with huge valves. His ears would be glued to his radio, especially in the early 1940s during the war. Sometimes he seemed a grumpy old man who loved his radio. Perhaps the radio provided information for him which opened up the world beyond Stathern. Sometimes we would all stand around his radio listening to the news. He was better with girls than with boys.

(Photographer: R. Heathcote) Lizzie does not seem well in this photo even though both had a little smile. Both eventually could not live on their own and went to live with Nellie and Bill Doubleday in Granby. Lizzie died soon after that in 1964. Within a few weeks, Phil was also dead. The pair did not settle well with the Doubledays.

(Photographer: R. Heathcote) We had to move out of the cottage on Plungar Lane because the Council believed the cottages were unfit for habitation. Imagine! We moved to a cozy bricked over prefabricated house on Station Lane sometime later. I must say it was very nice to have indoor plumbing! I was glad that Lucy and Alfred Moulds moved with us into their own new home nearby. They were a little younger than we were so looked out for us a bit. Alfred was a bleeder though so had to be careful. Lucy was wonderful to us.

Oh, I remember, our Jimmy also developed diabetes. He died early in 1969. He was only 67.

There, you are up to date with me life. Looking back has been nostalgic for me. It is good to remember.

I will always remember Rosie. For Kathleen, Alec and me, living without her was so difficult. I don't think Daphne will ever remember her which is a great pity.

ENDNOTES

Uncle Ernie died first in March 1978 and left Auntie Beat in her cozy two bedroomed prefab home. The Clamp's house still remains in its grounds.

Former parish chairman's widow dies

The funeral service for Mrs. Beatrice Caroline Green, of 3 Birds-lane, Stathern, was held at Stathern Methodist chapel.

Mrs. Green, who was 93, was born in Stathern, and was a life-long member of the Methodist chapel. She was also a keen gardener.

Her late husband had been chairman of the parish council for many years.

Mrs. Green leaves one son and one daughter, and three grandsons — one of whom lives in Australia.

The funeral service was conducted by the Rev. Jessie Cobb, with Mr. Fred Singleton at the organ; interment followed in Stathern.

Mourners included Mr. and Mrs. R. Green, son and daughter-in-law; Mrs. D. Bickerton, daughter; Mr. Simon Green, grandson; Mr. and Mrs. E. Brown brother and sister-in-law and their family; Mrs. N. Doubleday, Mrs. K. Heathcote, Mrs. B. Jallands, Mrs. T. Draper, nieces;

(Photographer: D. Field) This is a clipping from the local newspaper. Note the level of detail.

As a little girl, I was led to believe that there was something sacred about the Clamps and that house. Auntie Beat worked there as a cleaner: So, the Clamps were "toffs," not of our class. Your Nana's came by her proficiency in social stratifications honestly! Auntie Beat took me inside the big house one day while the occupants were away. So, I saw the house was bigger than the houses in which we lived, the furniture was nicer and there was a lovely kitchen and an inside bathroom. Not magic, perhaps I felt a little let down. Little did I know they were our relatives!

I would walk to Auntie Beat's house on Saturdays when I was a little girl to tell her my secrets. Both she and Uncle Ernie were easy to be with and helpful. Your Nana would say I would talk to Beatie more openly than I would her, especially about what had happened at the hospital! She and I chatted about life, growing up and adolescence. Taboo topics at home.

I paint a picture of a wonderful woman, a firm favourite, who not only took over the grandmother role after Nana Rosie died but also a motherly role for your Nana. She was a woman with a beautiful kind nature with lovely curly hair. Understandably she became Geoff's Godmother.

I do regret that I didn't ask more questions of Auntie Beat. But I was too young to realize what a source of information she was. She would tell me about Nana Rosie, how sweet she was, how fragile too. I would later discover what happened to her, another taboo subject indeed. Auntie Beat became demented and sadly went into a nursing home. I recall your Nana saying that the nurses had permed her beautiful hair. We were shocked.

She died in March 1984 at the age of 93.

21.

CONVERSATIONS WITH MY FATHER

You three never met this grandad who died just before you were born. March 2, 1975, to be exact. It is a great pity you did not meet him. He would have been an incredibly positive influence in your lives. I did not have the opportunity to talk with him about his early days. Indeed, he wasn't talking and I wasn't listening. Such a pity. So, I have decided to ask him some questions and respond as I believe he would. I will encourage him to tell his story prompted by photographs and documents I found. And from my imagination of course.

I would like to have a conversation with you about your life. What you and I remember, if you like. Here are pictures to help your memory. Firstly, what can you tell me about your mother, my Grandma? What do you remember about her?

She was a loving mother to us all. I had an elder brother, Tom who I discovered was not her son. My father had been married before. After me came two brothers: George and Edwin. She made a happy home for all of us at 9 Springfield Street in Melton. The comfy house was just big enough for us all. She was much younger and more energetic than my father.

I didn't know her very well. She wasn't a Grandma to me in the sense that she was not part of my life as I grew up. She didn't influence my life as Grandmas sometimes do.

Distance was a factor. She lived in town and we lived in the village. She and your mother were never close which was a pity. I hoped your mother would visit her while I was away but that didn't happen. You need to talk with your mother about this. I don't recall that we went there for a meal. I would just pop in when I was passing. My mother always appreciated that. Later in her life, she would visit us in Stathern. She was gentle and quiet.

Your mother was very loving, I think, although I never felt that growing up. After I left England, we wrote to one another and she would always write: from your loving Grandma.

Yes, she would. I am sorry that you didn't know her better.

What was your earliest memory? Here are a couple of photographs.

Yes. Wasn't my mother an attractive woman? Of course, I don't remember this time!

Well yes, I was born a Beckwith. Beckwith was on me birth certificate so I was known as Reggie Beckwith at school. I was furious when I discovered I was born out of wedlock on November 20, 1915, in Melton Mowbray. I could not be mad at mam because she had treated me right. I knew that me Dad had a wife and they needed to wait a respectable time after her death before they could marry which they did in 1919.

(Photographer: Unknown)

(Photographer: Unknown) Oh, a school photo proved I went to school at some time! Unmistakeably me in the bottom row. I wasn't too good at school. Bookwork didn't suit me well. I left school at age 14. I got a job as a conductor on Barton's buses. And then I became a bus driver.

I remember growing up with Tom, George, and Edwin and then going out to work. Here I am.

What do you remember about your dad?

He was older as I said, an old man as it seemed to me. He was a railway wagon repairer. So, he could fix things. That was a useful thing to know. So, I tagged along beside him and learned to do that too. But when I was old enough to take notice, he seemed old. Then he found out he had a heart condition so after knowing that he sat in his chair all day. We were all mad at him for this.

Tell me about the thirties.

Also, soon after that, I knew I liked to dance, you know, ballroom dancing. We all liked dancing then. We had finished the Charleston days. Ballroom dancing was becoming more common. We danced every weekend. I became quite good at it! I was known as the dancing bus driver!

The thirties were happy days. I was in me early twenties having a great time dancing with the girls. That is until I met your mother who was light on her feet and could keep up with me!

I had seen a lot of your mother; we travelled around England on me motorbike over the next few years. That and dancing was our way of being together. She was working in Woolworths and I was driving for Barton's busses.

(Photographer: Unknown) Not yet 20 I would say. And smoking!

(Photographer: Unknown) Well, I had just left school about 1930 so I started working. And joined St John's Ambulance in the mid-1930s. I received a Certificate in Feb 1936. I am the second on the left. Standing in this photo.

(Photographer: Unknown) Here I am with me Bartons gang. Smoking and looking quite happy: Satisfied with my lot at that time! I am on the right. At that time, I was a bus conductor. I took the bus fares and gave riders a ticket. I had a machine to do that which was hung around my neck.

So, the thirties were really fun days until we heard that Hitler, who became Chancellor in 1933, was rearming the country, ready to take back territory lost after the Great War. But I was a young man and did not dwell on those things. I wanted to dance.

(Photographer: Unknown)

(Photographer: A. Thompson)

Here we are having fun together in the 1930s, at a fair with Kathleen's friends Valerie and Alvin.

But by 1938, we knew our Prime Minister, Neville Chamberlain, had negotiated an agreement with Germany, Italy, and France to achieve 'Peace for our time'. But no one trusted Hitler. Would war have been delayed, rather than prevented? We talked about it a lot. Chamberlain seemed to be preparing for war. We realized during the latter part of the 30s we all should, as a country, also be preparing for war. We couldn't believe it. We didn't want to believe it.

Then in March 1939, German troops seized Czechoslovakia. Poland seemed to be next. Chamberlain had agreed with the Poles to defend them if Germany invaded. So, when in September 1939, Hitler invaded, Britain declared war on Germany.

We were all terrified. I was 24 years old. That changed everything for us lads. After war was declared, we knew we would have to fight. George, Edwin, and I would be called up. We knew it. We heard the news that France had been occupied. We feared for our lives.

What skills did you have when your call up papers arrived in May 1940?

Well, I could drive a large vehicle and I had St John's Ambulance training. So, I was better off than some! But with three of us being called up, my folks were afraid and dismayed. They could lose us all. Tom was too old by then. Age 24; Height 5'5.5"; Eyes, Grey; Hair, Brown. That's me.

How did it feel when you received the letter?

I felt excited, scared. I didn't want to leave me way of life and your mother. But we were being talked into joining up. We had to defend our country. Yes, I wasn't surprised when call-up papers arrived in May 1940. I chose or was assigned to (I don't remember which!) The Royal Corps of Signals. The Royal Corps of Signals (often simply known as the Royal Signals - abbreviated to R SIGNALS) is one of the combat support arms of the British Army. That seemed the most interesting to me. I thought I could do that. I would be a driver.[68]

Then the Battle of Britain happened. London was severely bombed. We all heard about the terrible bombing of Coventry and its cathedral on November 14, 1940, which brought an even more terrifying twist to the campaign. Five hundred

The Corps motto is "certa cito", often translated from Latin as Swift and Sure. It is easily seen on any of the Corps Badges.

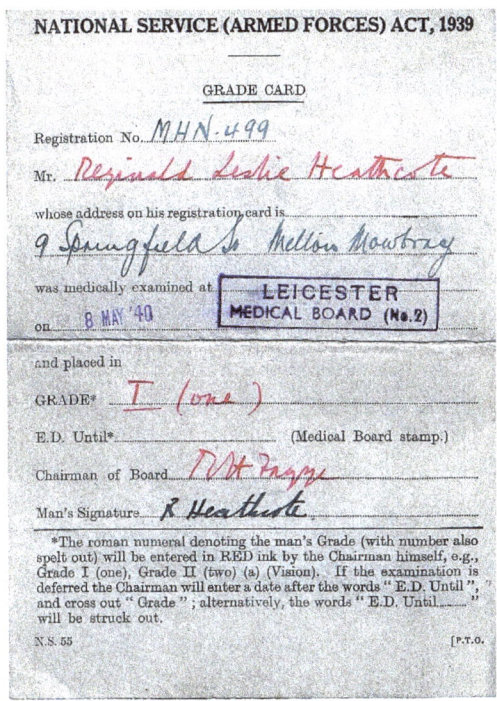

---

[68] Signals units are among the first into action, providing the battlefield communications and information systems essential to all operations. Royal Signals units provide the full telecommunications infrastructure for the Army wherever they operate in the world. The Corps has its own engineers, logistics experts and systems operators to run radio and area networks in the field. It is responsible for installing, maintaining and operating all types of telecommunications equipment and information systems, providing command support to commanders and their headquarters, and conducting electronic warfare against enemy communications. (https://en.wikipedia.org/wiki/Royal_Corps_of_Signals)

German bombers dropped 500 tonnes of high explosives and nearly 900 incendiary bombs on the city in ten hours of relentless bombardment. Hitler appeared to be trying to bomb us into submission but our new leader, Winston Churchill, said we should fight. Never Give Up was his motto. The Royal Airforce bombed right back and destroyed many German cities.

So, what happened next?

Basic training. I had to learn to become a soldier, learn to fight, to get fit, and learn how to use firearms. I also learned to swim. As a driver, I needed to know mechanics, how to take care of the vehicle if it broke down. I needed to learn navigation skills as well. And then we all needed to learn the work of the Royal Corps of Signals.

I was billeted in Taunton in Devon. We did a lot of training on sand which might have given us a clue where we were going! We knew we were training for a mission but no one was telling us what it was. None of us had been out of England; some, unlike me, had never left their home towns. I had travelled all over England on my motorbike. We trained for more than a year.

(Photographer: Unknown) Ok, I was to be a soldier in the 8th Corp Signals, a driver of motor cars, lorries, motorcycles, or any other propelled vehicle. That is what it says and I was available for service on September 13, 1940. The war was underway but we had much to learn. I felt proud when I wore the uniform.

(Photographer: Unknown) During this time, I persuaded your mother to marry me. She wasn't sure but I told her I had enough love for both of us. We had been seeing each other for a few years. I had a weekend pass so we married. By special license. January 1941 it was. You could say it was impulsive and I suppose it was. I cannot tell you more than that. At the time, it seemed like a good idea. I wanted your mother to be there when I returned. And if anything happened to me, I wanted her to have a Military pension, security for her.

Our marriage certificate.

We agreed your mother would stay at home. I was grateful her parents, Rosie and Alec, were there and willing. I was fortunate. I continued training for almost two years before me unit left England. Me unit started to think the war would be over before we got into it!

I had no opportunity to become a husband before I had to leave. But your mother and I had known one another for a while. So, it was when I returned I started to be a husband. We were different people in 1946 compared with 5 years earlier. We had so many different experiences, stresses, and fears. Your mother had a career I knew little about. And we had you! But we still loved to dance, we had a home in Stathern and we had a family. So, we just got on with it. For many years, life was not peaceful. Your mother was not easy to please!

OK before you tell me about returning, tell me about your war experience. You have never talked about the war. We were all afraid to ask about it. Perhaps not wanting to know the details. Can you give me some details now?

No one wanted to talk about it all because we wanted to forget. We were trained to kill, to save ourselves and our colleagues. We were deprived of our families and were deprived of good food and creature comforts. We never knew when we would get clean underwear and socks!

(Photographer: Unknown) Sometime in the autumn of 1942, we were given orders to prepare to be on the move. Here I am boarding the ship in Southampton. You can just see me!

So, after basic training and many months of training on the sand and the duties of a signalman, we knew something was brewing. We were being given mandatory inoculations and doses of pills. We all had more medical examinations. But this seemed to go on for months.

We were to be involved in Operation Torch and would be headed for Algiers in North Africa. We were told we would join up with the 8th Army and General Montgomery to get control of the Mediterranean. The 8th was on the march from Egypt. We travelled by boat, so cramped: nevertheless, we landed alongside our allies. We were not accustomed to the idea of allies. Americans and Canadians joined the attack, eventually helping force the surrender of all remaining enemy troops. We all spent a pleasant 1942 Christmas together before we got started.

It was hot and there was so much sand. The sand got everywhere. I had to make sure the sand didn't get into the petrol lines! We spent a lot of time cleaning our firearms! We slept in tents. Water was in short supply. We sometimes had to wait for supply lines to reach us before we could move on. The locals sometimes slit our tents and stole things but otherwise didn't give trouble. We were not fighting them after all. We were eager and young and ready. So not much

So, here I am in Tunis. Still looking and feeling well. So far so good. The locals were not as clean as they appeared and were not particularly friendly. But we did not fight with them so we didn't have to watch our backs! We preferred our food to theirs even though it all came in cans and was awful. I mentioned that already!

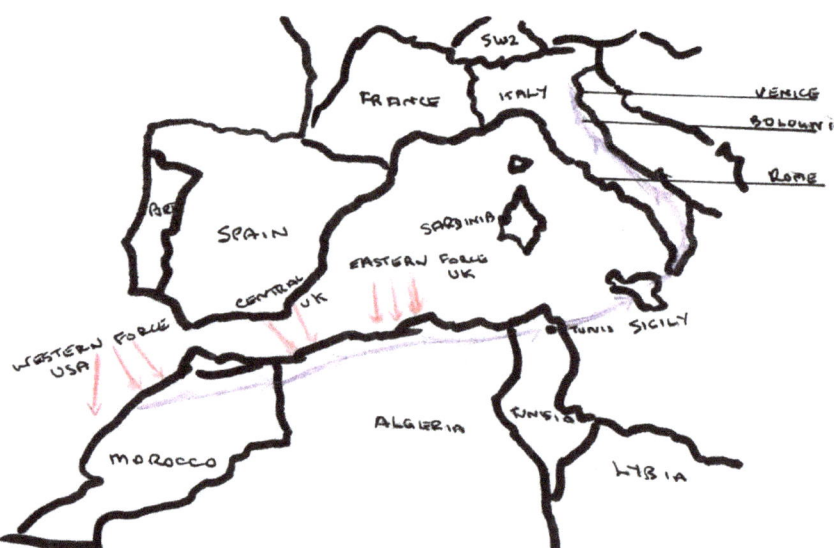

In this sketch you see the route we took: Eastwards across north Africa towards Tunisia and on to Italy, northwards along the east coast. After we landed in Algeria, we didn't experience too much resistance from the Germans. They seemed to have a weakened force. We installed signal equipment along the way. We reached Tunisia in May 1943 ending the Campaign for North Africa. We had achieved our objective to gain complete control of North Africa from French Morocco to Tunisia and joined up with our 8th Army as planned. The map here shows you where we were.

bothered us at that time at least. Except for the food they gave us. Canned everything. That put me off canned food forever. I am sure you remember that!

You went back to Tunis after the War on a holiday with Mother. So, you must have had pleasant memories.

Yes, it is an interesting place. Very well worth a peacetime visit. We were not disappointed. This place is so unlike England. I took your mother to Germany also. We went on a trip to Rhineland.

So, what happened next?

Well, there was a lot of waiting around but eventually, we were given orders to prepare to board boats with our equipment because we were to invade Sicily on our way to Italy. We started the invasion of Sicily, Operation Husky, on July 10, 1943. We began with airborne and amphibious landings on the island's southern shores. My unit joined up with other units for a time. We were then called the 10th Air Formation Signals, which was part of a force that sailed from Tunis and landed at Bizerta in Sicily on 1st October 1943, travelling through to Catania and Palermo. The volcano Mount Etna was showing signs of activity. Dealing with the smoke, the frightened Italians while watching our backs, added to the tension in the air. Soon, we arrived in Taranto, Italy. We were always on the move, it seemed. Did I mention war always involves some confusion, a familiar noise, and the smell of battle? The Italians eventually surrendered to the Allies but the German fighters in Italy would not give in. We were on the eastern side of Italy travelling North. We were pushing the German army northwards.

The Allies finally broke through and captured Rome on June 4, 1944. It took so long to capture Italy. That part was exhausting, stressful. We thought we would never make it. I remember the weather was awful. So

Yes, here are some members of me unit posing in Vatican City. I think that is me. Fourth from the right on the back row. We visited Vatican City to see all the wonderful sculptures. The Vatican had been declared an 'open city' and so escaped being destroyed as the German forces retreated further into northern Italy. We all walked up the steps of St. Peters and through the great doors, to look at the wonderful Michelangelo statue and other priceless works of art. The place was deserted and very quiet. I found this a moving and peaceful experience. After all, I had become accustomed to the noise of war and fighting. Quite spectacular although I have to tell you I was in no mood for being a tourist. My colleagues and I were all too exhausted and fed up with being away from home. I have blotted that part out of me memory. I chose not to return to Italy.

much rain. At that point, I had been away for nearly two years. We knew the German Army was weak but they refused to admit defeat. They were told never to surrender.

Hitler surrendered on May 8, 1945. Do you remember that day?

Well yes. From the map you can see where we had travelled: From Sicily up the east coast to Venice. It had been a long and difficult journey with lots of action as well as much waiting around for orders. The months just seemed to go by. The war was over but we were still away from home!

I was surprised by how long it took to return all the Forces personnel to the UK. I talked to my mother's friend Bill about this one day. He agreed that repositioning all the personnel did take time as all had to move in an orderly fashion with their units to ships via rail or road. Dismantling equipment and moving trucks, tanks and other equipment used in the initiative had to be coordinated.

Yes, we waited what seemed like a long time.

Postcard (Photographer: Unknown) This is Riccione on the east coast of Italy, close to Bologna.

(Photographer: Unknown)

We had four days rest in July 1945. Nice but we just wanted to go home!

You sent a copy of this photograph to your mother-from your loving son. It is dated October 13, 1945, and was taken in Venice. I see you have a triangle on our uniform. You all look relaxed and calm.

The triangles represent the Royal Corps of Signals. We may look relaxed but rest assured after being away for three years, we were anxious to return home. We had to wait for our units to come together and ready ourselves. We all needed to return home together with as much of our equipment as we could recover. We had to wait until transports i.e., a ship, became available. We had already waited for months and would have to be patient for a while longer. We were all wondering what life had in store for us. We had much thinking time, planning our lives. After all, we were all around 30. Very young really.

(Photographer: Unknown) *Oh, you look thin here.*

Yes, I think this is in Italy waiting to come home. We had been supplied with new uniforms and shoes! Even though the wait was awful, at least we were all safe. And your mother knew I would be home soon.

So, you were demobbed. Tell me about that. You seemed to have glowing testimonials but no promotion.

Yes, that reads well! I was released from service, "demobbed" on February 11, 1946, and was on leave until April 8, 1946, when I was transferred to the Reserves.

What skills did you have after the war was over? What had you learned?

I knew mechanics and was interested in electrical systems. I also knew a lot about practical radar that I learned on the job, not from textbooks. I had a plan. We had a long time to think and talk about this while we were waiting in Italy. So, I took the electricians course that was offered to me. That was something I enjoyed.

Tell me about returning from the war.

Oh, that was difficult because I had been through so much and so had you all. There were many things: we didn't know what each had suffered, the anxiety, the deprivation, the discomfort not to mention how we coped. I had you and your mother to think about and worry about. I was uneasy as I made the journey home by train. I felt I no longer knew either of you. We didn't have a home of our own. We were crowded. I had to move to Stathern, out of Melton into a

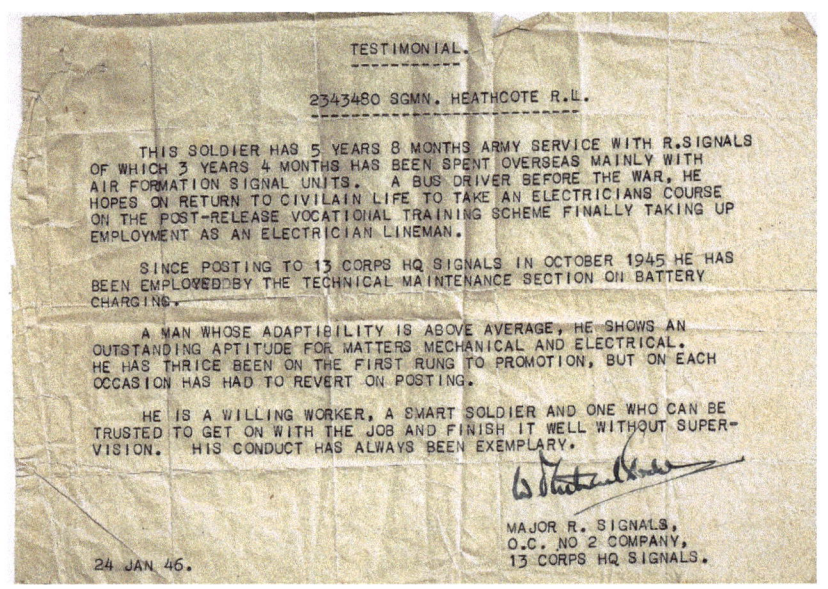

house with no running water and almost no electricity! I was grateful Alec and Rosie were there to look after you but when I returned, it was awkward for all of us. Another adult was entering the household, you know.

(Photographer: K. Heathcote) Here I am with me motorbike. I am in Stathern and looking very thin. So, I would say I have returned from service. I look happy enough to be at home. This is just outside Wood View in Stathern. I was glad to be back on me motorbike which I believe had been stored in Stathern. Your mother and I travelled all over England on that motorbike. But I was a family man and had to trade it in for a small used car! So, I did that.

Then Rosie got sick. That added to the stress we were all feeling. Then there was you! I discovered you already had a dad and were not keen to have me replace your grandad. After all, you did not know me. And I didn't know you. I had no experience with a four-year-old! I failed you miserably. You had been sleeping with your mother so when I pushed you out the resentment was there. I didn't know how to hook you in. I had not ever been around children. I didn't know what to do. And there were so many stresses to deal with at the same time.

You are allowing me to look back with an open mind. Believe me, at that time I was in a panic. I was not feeling or behaving as I should have!

Tell me about being a father.

You were a surprise. Your mother will say she was not pleased to have a child in wartime. But there you were! I had to leave you both. When I returned you were a little girl, set in your ways with your mother and grandparents. When I arrived in the family unit, everything all changed for everyone. It was not easy: More difficult than I thought it would be. I was not a father to you actually, not until you were almost 20. Before that I remember, we didn't have much to say to one another.

(Photographer: A. Thompson) The Heathcotes with Valerie, Vivienne and Grandad Hubbard. This photograph was probably taken in Skegness. Your mother liked the coast. She insisted her father come with us. You can see your grandad is really in distress. Rosie was in the hospital at this time. We are with the Thompsons. Here you see Valerie and daughter Vivienne. I look so thin! 1946 perhaps.

Being a father to Geoff was easier because I was there and could support him from the start. Then he and I had a great relationship because he was interested in all I was doing. You often seemed to be on the outside.

Tell me about being a husband.

While I visited your mother whenever I had some leave, I didn't see much of her until I left the service. And at that point, we had been married for more than 5 years. That was very awkward especially since we had changed so much in those 5 years because of our different experiences. We exchanged many letters but that is not the same, is it? We had no opportunity to become a unit, a couple. We could not start that until I returned. When I did, your mother had to give up her job and stay home. All the working women gave up jobs so there were jobs for returning service men. Your mother was worried about her mother who was in isolation in hospital. So, her life was upside down. Then she became pregnant. So, I would say, I had spent so much time with other men I found being with your mother was not easy. She was not happy with her circumstances and was difficult to please. She liked working at Woolworths and was not content being a housewife!

Rosie died just before Geoff was born in 1947. Alec was so unhappy. He took himself off to work and then spent time in the garden. Nothing could console him. Except perhaps you. He and you were pals and did many things together that I was not part of. After he retired, he drifted away from the family.

Sadly, there was often conflict within our household. All too often you were in the middle of it. I cannot blame any single thing. It was everything. The war, the time apart, unmet expectations, trying to restart our lives, our not being able to talk and express ourselves.

Tell me more about your father-in-law, Alec.

Well, I moved into their home, and soon after I arrived back, Rosie was taken away. So, it was awkward for him. He was a quiet man. He never criticized or complained. But I knew he was having a tough time. We included him in everything we did, outings and such. He was easy going. I was so grateful he took care of you and your mother during the time I was away. He loved his garden. I am glad he took care of it as I had no interest in gardening. Very sadly, Rosie died just before Geoff was born. There was so much to deal with, so many changes, in so little a time.

This picture was taken in 1949. I do not look well.

On an outing to the coast always with Grandad Hubbard. You had been ill with kidney problems and had your surgery. The doctors could not diagnose initially. We were terrified when you went into hospital and had to have an operation. You had been away from us for six weeks in hospital. You gave us quite a scare. We brought you to the coast because we thought it would be good for you.

(Photographer: Unknown)

(Photographer: Unknown) You do look as though you are struggling in the last picture. But you did recover I am happy to say. You look better in this picture.

(Photographer: Unknown) Yes. This was at Edwin's wedding, June 1950. You were a bridesmaid. There we are. Me mother is on the left and me dad is between George and Edwin. You are the smiling bridesmaid!

(Photographer: Unknown) (Photographer: Unknown

Do you remember dancing with me?

Well, now I remember. I think I mentioned later you were not light on your feet like your mother. But you were young in this photo!

I was really busy at that time putting in the water supply in the house, adding rooms, and generally modernizing the place. Edwin helped me with all that. You see, we were able to buy the house soon after I returned. Your mother was a good saver! And she point blank refused to leave Stathern. So, I didn't have much alternative!

So, after the electrician's course, you worked from May 1951 to November 1956 as a Charge Hand Mechanic at REME Old Dalby. You had a glowing reference.

Yes, I enjoyed working there, after I had completed the retraining after the war ended.

Do you remember the trip to the coast without me?

Yes, you point blank refused to be part of the family sometimes. I removed a valve from the television so you could not watch all day. It was mean but I was angry.

I wonder whether you realize I would always remember that gesture with immense resentment.

I am sorry you did. That was not one of my best efforts at parenting. I was angry with your behaviour.

Do you remember taking me to Nottingham to the cinema? Just the two of us?

Well yes. I was making an effort to connect with you. I think it worked! I took you to see Dam Busters, 39 Steps and Around the World in 80 days. And we went to the Pantomime, I think. There may have been more but those are the ones I remember. You didn't say much at the time but I think the Dam Busters made an impression.

I think you are right. I still remember that one and have thought a lot about it over the years. Each time I see spotlights in fact. I am still impressed by Derwent Water in Derbyshire. The idea was so clever. I cannot remember 39 Steps at all. Around the World in 80 was a fun film and made me realize there was a different world out there.

Do you remember giving me an orchid?

Yes. You were attending typing classes and had temporarily left home to live in Melton. You were working at the tax office. I thought you would like an orchid.

You left it with the teacher. I didn't know you had left it for me until much later! Do you remember driving me to work every day? We did not speak to one another.

Oh yes. I would eat my bowl of cornflakes for breakfast, drink my tea, and then we headed off. We just didn't have anything to say to one another. We could find no common ground. This would be the time I was working at Westmorelands. Most unhappily I must say. I had left The War Department at Old Dalby in 1956 because your mother thought it would be a good idea.[69] Alvin Thompson got me the job. But I was no good at selling electrical equipment. It wasn't my kind of work at all. It was a disappointing time for me. I wanted to repair it, not sell it!

Image from personal records

So, I returned to REME at Old Dalby and thrived. Unfortunately, although I had the practical experience, I had no education to match. I tried to pick up the courses required but found my limits. Nevertheless, I continued into the 1960s for as long as I was able.

Dancing was what you like to do.

Yes, your mother and I met dancing and danced all our lives. You came with us when you were old enough. This is us much older. Still dancing. In our thirties and into our fifties, I would say. When you were older, we took you dancing to Old Dalby. Do you remember that? Do you remember making all those cheese and onion sandwiches??

---

69 Geoff added:
   There was great resentment over dad being more or less forced by Mother to leave Old Dalby. She called it a place for 'old men'. This resentment continued, after he returned because those who stayed become qualified for promotion and also younger, less qualified folk were promoted ahead of him, due to his lack of education. He eventually tried to rectify this by home study. This was a very, very painful experience. It was exacerbated by the timing of my studies at Melton Grammar. It always seemed to work out that dad was studying topics that I took a year later. It was the more advanced math and science. So, we were both frustrated by the fact that I could not help him. Again, mother got the blame.

(Photographer: Unknown)

(Photographer: Unknown)

Here we are. We were out somewhere. I have no idea where! I think you can see we are both quite content. Dancing was what we liked to do. We did a lot of it. At least weekly. Do you remember the dances at Old Dalby? You would come with us when you were a teenager.
Tell me about the trip to Nottingham General with me.
I seemed to have heart troubles and since my dad did too, I was sent for tests to Nottingham General. Yes, You went with me. I am not sure why you did and not your mother. You were working in London and took

(Photographer: R. Heathcote)
And your mother fooling around!

time off during a visit home. After the tests, I was told I had angina. I was sometimes sort of breath. I took nitroglycerine as needed.

Do you remember teaching me to drive?

You were not a natural. You nearly ran over your mother when you tried to back up. We were down Blacksmiths End that day. Do you remember that? Then I took you into a field to try there. I agree that dealing with gears, clutch, and steering all at once was not easy. Then your brother got in the car and drove without a care in the world. You were furious. After all, he was only 12! Then you bought a scooter which gave you some independence. Your knowledge of the road was useful. I grilled you on the Highway Code. Remember be prepared to Stop, proceed with caution? We didn't have any traffic lights in Melton so you didn't get that you could not go on a RED even if there was no one around!

(Photographer: D. Field)
This picture is priceless! We all loved that dog our Suzie.

Yes, Suzie was special. I cannot even remember how or when she came into our lives. But after she did, she would go everywhere with us. Day outings, holidays: leaving her behind was out of the question. Our hearts were broken when she had to leave us.

Do you remember knocking the wall down between our two rooms?

Oh yes. Your mother went off to work. It was a Saturday, I think. I was fed up living in a cramped space. Not when we had an empty and unused front room. So, I got a sledgehammer and knocked down the joining wall. You and Geoff were amazed and so was I! I knew there would be trouble but the effects were remarkable. We had one large room to live in. Edwin came over to help with the bricklaying. Then we set about painting. I was able to put up wall lights that dimmed. Oh yes, there were fireworks when your mother returned from work that evening!

Tell me about constructing a television.

Yes, I did it. Was in the early 1950s I would say. I constructed the little television using a green cathode ray tube. We managed to see a little of the show "Robin Hood." Nothing much was televised in those days.[70] But you know I loved gadgets. We had dimmers on our lights long before anyone else did. I liked adding stuff to the car too.

---

[70] Geoff added: In the early TV days he built the antenna (aerial!) himself using chicken wire, wood and string. This contraption, under the roof, picked up TV from London! Of course, we had the first TV in the village. He loved gadgets. We had a magnifying lens filled with oil, in front of the 12" TV. This gave us an equivalent of a 14" TV!

Tell me about being Mr. Fixit

I found myself with a reputation! Everyone expected me to fix everything in the village and would bring me their small appliances or ask me to go around to their homes to fix anything electrical. Your mother would moan about this. But I wouldn't mind. It seems as though something was always being fixed on our dining room table. And then there was the annual fair. I was expected to fix their sound system![71]

(Photographer: Unknown)

And we socialized with the Doubledays!

Well yes, he was too much of a fast talker for me! I think we all enjoyed a Christmas visit to the Doubledays. That was our Christmas morning routine with sherry and mince pies!

You liked to travel around too and picnic.

We did. Firstly, on my motorbike and eventually in the car. Here we are in the Austin 1100. We would picnic all over England. I liked that car. I liked to add gadgets to the car. I designed intermittent window wipers which everyone thought a little funny but to me, they were very practical. I fixed up an electric razor which I used on my way to work. It was driven by the car battery.

(Photographer: Unknown)

(Photographer: Unknown)
With Anne and Roe, your friends, I think.

---

71 Geoff added: You are quite right about the sound. Ashley's Fair came to Stathern every year in May, and every year, Ashley arrived with a beat-up pile of old junk which was supposed to make the music for the merry-go-round. Every year dad fixed it up. Ashley insisted that the music (i.e., record player and amplifier) be located in the centre of the merry-go-round. Dad tried and tried to convince Ashley to locate the gear somewhere else near the merry-go-round so that it would not get shaken up by the ride. Ashley would have none of it!

In the band days, dad built us a PA system using a surplus amplifier and building a preamp/mixer from scratch; all valves of course. We did not have the cash to buy the professional gear. The boys continued the tradition by building loudspeakers. I am sure we sounded bad! (I was still building band amplifiers after university.)

Dad gave me a guitar for my 11th birthday. I plunked at it for years and still do! Every Remembrance Day, dad would provide a recording over a PA of 'The Last Post'.

(Photographer: R. Heathcote) Oh yes, this is Geoff's band. Terry and the Strangers. I had fun with them fixing up their sound system.

And you took up photography!

I did. As you can see, I had some fancy equipment. I also set up a developing and processing lab inside one of our closets! So, I had a dark room. Some of the photographs came out very well. I was able to enlarge photographs and generally play with the effects. I also had sound equipment so I could synchronize a slide show. I had fun putting it together but I am not sure I didn't bore everyone! [72]

(Photographer: Unknown)

---

72 Geoff added: Dad became interested in photography and built us a dark room for enlarging and developing prints. We also developed films: All black and white of course. He liked photography and used to bore everyone to tears showing colour slides at every opportunity. He developed from scratch a system of synchronizing sound from the tape recorder and the slide changer. This involved adding another tape head, recording and playback system, with separate tape head and track, along with the change slide interface. This was way ahead of its time.

(Photographer: K. Heathcote)

(Photographer: K. Heathcote)
I used to dress up in the village and parade around with an old cylinder phonograph belonging to Uncle Phil. Being the village clown was expected of me!

Do you remember dressing up?

I am not sure whose idea that was but when your mother's friend Valerie visited with Alvin, inevitably, after a few drinks, we would exchange clothes. Then we took photographs. I know that both you and Geoff were both embarrassed by this. But we were just having a bit of fun! This one was taken at Geoff's 21st!

So, then I moved to London.

You did. I was sorry to see you go. But I knew you would not be content in either Stathern or Melton. You came home a lot. I would pick you up at Grantham station. I knew Melton did not give you enough opportunities, even though you had a good job.

Yes, and you would slip me a 10-shilling note as I was leaving Grantham station to return to London. I know you were disappointed I left school too early. I soon realized that when I reached Canada. I was glad to pick up my education there.

I wasn't pleased when you left England. I felt I had just found you and we could talk to one another. I knew we wouldn't see much of you after that. I wasn't much of a writer but we tried. We did use the tape recorder sometimes too.

Tell me about your first trip to Canada. I realize now that your trip was soon after you had been given sad news from Old Dalby. You must have been feeling dreadful.

Well, you had left England to go to California to get married at the end of 1967. I remember the day we dropped you off at the airport. We were both so upset to see you go. When you were having difficulty and didn't marry, imagine how we felt? Next, we heard you had moved to Toronto to be near to Heather and had found a job. We wondered whether you would ever return. Then you told us you were ill and had lost a kidney. We were so worried about you. You told us very little. We decided to visit you in the summer. Yes, I was feeling very unhappy about my job situation.

It was a sad day indeed when this letter came.

Yes, it was. Although I did expect it. I had received several warnings. I tried to earn the academic qualifications but found school work was not for me. My time at the War Department was over because I did not have the academic qualifications they considered necessary to do the job: teaching principles of radar. I learned from experience in the field in North Africa. The spirit left me when I received the letter. Just as I was thinking about retirement.

It was in 1969. From the airport in Toronto, we watched the first man step onto the moon. We had an amazing trip. We stayed in your flat in downtown Toronto. You were recovering nicely from your surgery and were taking accounting courses at a Community College. I was pleased about that. We went north out of the city into the country. I was so impressed with the vastness of the country.

I recorded lots of information to replay later on my Marconi tape recorder. I took many pictures too. By that time, I was really into photography and bored many people with slide shows! Toronto was so imposing with its huge highways. I wanted to tell everybody!!

> 35 CENTRAL WORKSHOP R.E.M.E.
> Old Dalby, MELTON MOWBRAY, Leicestershire
> Telephone: Nether Broughton 351, ext. 27
>
> Our reference: Pers/7929
>
> 15 Apr 69
>
> Dear Mr. Heathcote,
>
> Further to my letter of 3 Apr 69 it is now confirmed that sufficient qualified applicants have been offered Technical Grade III appointments in this Workshop to cover all posts at present occupied on a temporary and geographical basis. You are therefore given this formal notice that you will resume your former duties in the grade of Electronic Mechanic Grade I from Monday, 19 May 69.
>
> I would like to express my appreciation of the satisfactory way in which you performed the duties of the higher grade during the past two years.
>
> Yours sincerely,
>
> (K. C. Smith) Lt.Colonel
> for Colonel
> Officer Commanding

(Photographer: K. Heathcote)

(Photographer: D. Field)

(Photographer: K. Heathcote)
Here we are enjoying the day.

We knew you had met a young man who was good to you when you were ill. You seemed to have started a career, one he did not share. We hoped you would outgrow him quickly.

(Photographer: R. Heathcote) Here we are meeting his family. His mother and sister are sitting next to your mother. We liked them all but felt that the young man, Hal, was not a good match for you. But you didn't outgrow him as we hoped. Your mother vehemently opposed your marrying and was not shy telling you her views.

(Photographer :R. Heathcote) Your mother's first trip to Niagara Falls. It wouldn't be her last! We are with your friend Sarah and her mother. And Hal.

You tried to persuade me to come to your wedding alone but your mother was offended and was having none of that. Remember? You looked lovely. Hal's family were so good to us. We stayed with Roz I think. But still, we were unsure about him.

(Photographer: Unknown

(Photographer: Unknown)

We met up with you in New England during your honeymoon. We toured around there a little. That was quite nice, I think. We drove around Vermont and went to Montreal.

You told me you had chosen a kind man like me. Sadly I thought that would not be enough. You thought and moved so much quicker than he. You, however, were unaware of the significance. We were concerned about you. But if you were happy so were we.

Soon you started university which pleased both of us. You seemed to find it all quite easy. That reminded me how difficult I found studying and school work about ten years earlier. We both knew you would do well. And as the years went by, you did.

Then Geoff left home and went to University. And we were alone.

When Geoff, having graduated, told us he was leaving for Toronto, we were devastated. Enough that you had left, but Geoff too was more than I could handle. I think you can see from the look on our faces. Tells you everything. My world came to an end. You had both left us.

I was struggling at work seeing the younger folk take over what used to be my job. I was relegated to mundane tasks.

About that time we became aware of good neighbours, Bob and Win, a young couple we befriended. They moved into and remodeled the house where your mother's Grannie Brown once lived! Bob liked to potter around the house and do jobs just like Geoff did! So we became mates. A void was filled.

(Photographer: Unknown) Yes, here we are with Roz, Hal's sister, and her husband Pat. We all had a lot of fun during your reception at The Embers. It was so hot, I recall. The air conditioning failed!

(Photographer: Unknown)

(Photographer: R. Heathcote)

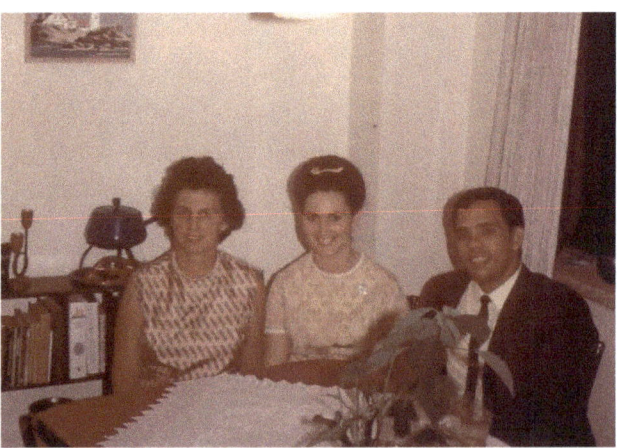

(Photographer: R. Heathcote)

Soon we visited you both and enjoyed a stay with you. You gave us a nice time. We met Geoff's young lady, Sue. We both were concerned about your relationship. You didn't seem to be particularly happy together.

And then I brought Hal over to England in April 1973.

You did. Everyone made him very welcome. We went on a road trip to Wales and Coventry which we all enjoyed. You noticed, I think I had difficulty keeping pace with you and needed nitro glycerine. That was also the time when Heather returned to England unexpectedly because her mother had suddenly passed away. You rushed over to Saxby to be with her.

Yes, I did. I had only recently visited her parents in Saxby and was very concerned. Just a few days before actually. I was distressed for Heather. Her mother took her life which was devastating for all of us.

And then Geoff and Sue had news of their own. Yes. August 21, 1973, was the date Geoff and Sue decided to marry. They married quickly without much fanfare or preparation. We had no time to organize a trip over. Geoff and Sue's wedding with Daphne and Hal on either side of Geoff and Sue.

(Photographer: R. Heathcote)

So, in 1974 you are thinking about retirement and thinking also about us in Canada.

Yes, you had been working so hard and had completed your courses. You seemed satisfied that you had passed your final exams and would qualify as a CA. We were delighted for you. You never mentioned Hal.

Then first Geoff told us that Sue was expecting a baby and then a few months later you told us you were too. Imagine, we were to be grandparents twice over. Everything was going so well for you and Geoff. We were talking about a trip over to see you.......

(Photographer: Unknown)

(Photographer: Unknown) The pair seemed very happy together. They visited us that year for Christmas.

(Photographer: Unknown)

(Photographer: Unknown)

And we continued to dance together.

(Photographer: Unknown)
My dad and his favourite flower, a cornflower.

(Photographer: D. Field))

I am so sad I missed all those years.

ENDNOTES

And that is where our story ends on March 2, 1975.

Your grandfather took your Nana dancing for their final dance while visiting with friends in Woodville.

He drove them all home, said he didn't feel well, got into bed, and left us……Massive heart attack.

He was a man so far ahead of his time, taken from us far, far too soon. He never had a chance to grow old.

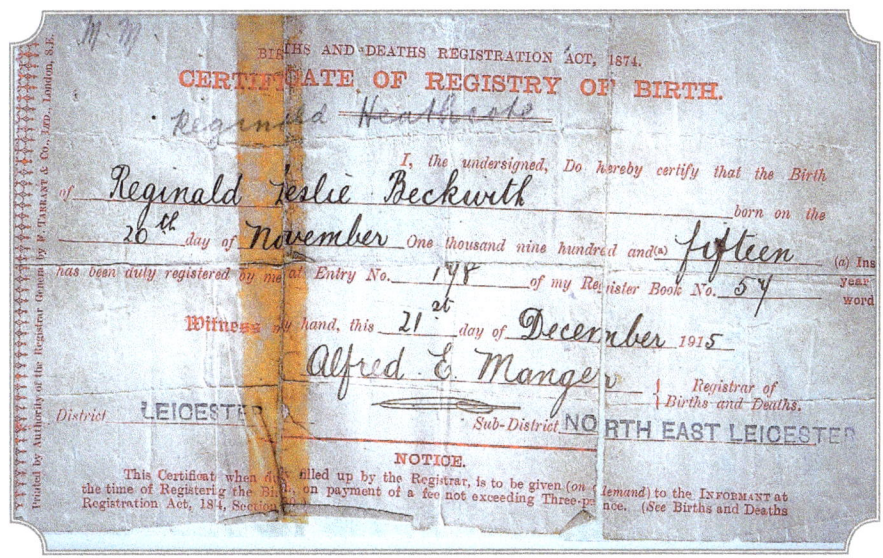

His birth and Baptism certificates.

22.

CONVERSATIONS WITH MY MOTHER

Your Nanna lived to a ripe old age. You all came to know her very well as you grew. When she became too old to travel, you wrote letters to her and spoke on the phone until she couldn't hear too well. I want you to know her better and will ask her to tell us her story, by responding to the questions I pose to her. Her response will be from my imagination, her letters, and my recollection of her words. Today a woman died who was significant in her life: Vera Lynn. She was a war-time singer who entertained the troops. She was 103 years old. Your Nana will tell us her story assisted by my questions.
My questions and comments are in italics.

I would like to tell the tale of our life mainly for your grandchildren, who would like to know who you were. I will help you recall your life by asking you questions and showing you photographs, my father may chip in too. Let's begin at the beginning, even before your memory. On November 28, 1916, a brown-eyed baby girl was born in the tiny cottage, which no longer stands: torn down and given way to the patio in the yard of Mrs. Jean Steward next to her outbuildings. And you were baptized on New Year's Eve! You said you had a happy childhood.

Yes, I didn't expect much and didn't get much either. But we were happy, contented.

Houses had rain barrels in those days for our water supply because none of the houses had running water into our homes. So, water was precious and was used for household and personal purposes as well as watering the garden. Little girls wore overalls to keep our dresses clean. This habit stayed with me, didn't it as I would always wear a blue check overall when at home! Girls didn't wear slacks or pants in those days.

Tell me about Christmas.

For Christmas, there would be a stocking with an orange in it. No gift was expected. Christmas was the only time we had stuffed chicken. We made puddings and mincemeat.

Tell me about your school days.

This is a school picture. I went to the local two-roomed school, located in a narrow lane near the church. The school was old with outside toilets. Yes, here I am at Stathern School-seven years old. Right in the middle of the bottom row with a bow. So many children in 1923!

(Photographer: Unknown)
Here you are with a cat outside your house in Main Street, Stathern.

(Photographer: Unknown)

(Photographer: Unknown) I am older, about nine, in this photograph which was taken outside the school. I am seated, the first girl on the left in the bottom row. I am again wearing an overall and have on my boots! You are watching me grow up in these school photographs.

(Photographer: Unknown) Stathern School, 1928. So, I am 12. Front row fourth pupil from the left. I am standing on the front row with very white socks, wearing a very smart outfit.

You told me Miss Goodson was the schoolmistress in the class with younger children at Stathern School while Mr. Leveritt, considered a good teacher, was in the elder class. He had the task of identifying those pupils who would benefit from an academic education. Both your best friend Mary and you earned the right to receive a scholarly education but both of you declined. Why?

Yes, Mary and I were offered these positions. But we had already decided that we would refuse because the Grammar school was for clever people and we were not Grammar Gogs. Mr. Leveritt was extremely disappointed that we refused the opportunity. I look back with regret.

Why did you refuse?

Because I was stupid! We thought we would not fit in: so, we declined: "like fools." Mary and I didn't like change and unfamiliarity: we placed limits on ourselves. Mary and I both remained at Stathern school until we had to leave at age 14. I was able to perfect my handwriting!

So you went to work in Woolworths.

Not right away. After leaving school at 14, I went into service, for Mrs. Moore who lived at the top of Stathern Hill. I didn't like that at all. My dad came and fetched me home.

Mary and I eventually got jobs in the newly opened Woolworths Store in Melton[73]. Imagine the only department store in Melton! Mary was a supervisor and I a cashier in the office, managing the invoices and the tills and calculating the wages with no calculator: pounds, shillings, and pence whizzed around my head until I balanced. Wages were £1 a week.

(Photographer: Unknown) Here we are, aged 14, ready to leave school. Don't we look older than 14? I am on the back row, the second girl on the left. With teacher Mr. Leveritt, the teacher I admired. Best friend Mary is second from the right on the first row, with the smart jacket.

Two country bumpkins with high-level jobs! In the thirties, life was isolated in the village. "All we did was work" Monday and Wednesday until 6 pm; Tuesday until 7 pm; Thursday until 1 pm; Friday until 8 pm and Saturday until 9 pm. On Sundays, I visited Auntie Beat, went to chapel or church, or went for a walk Later, during the war, I became part of the emergency workforce and was promoted to a management position.

Tell me about living in the village.[74]

It was a quiet little village but I had many friends there and all the Brown and Hubbard families.

There was an association "Girl's Friendly Society" in the rectory near the school. Missionaries ran the society. Grace was a missionary-she went abroad. The missionary girls played games and amused the Stathern girls. There was a magic lantern that gave pictures on a screen of places they had visited and worked in. They wanted to show the girls who were the beneficiaries of the pennies, given to the Missionaries.

Young people would congregate outside Buxton's Fish and Chips where one could buy a bag of chips for 1 penny (there was no money for fish). It was a safe environment. They would also practice dance steps that they were being taught at school.

---

73 Woolworths opened in Melton in 1933. Your Nana started working there in 1934 (aged 18). Woolworths recently went bankrupt.

74 Life in the village was isolated, so isolated that the world flu epidemic that occurred at the end of the Great War was unknown in the village. The only transportation available was one's bike, by horse and cart or by train. So, no one went very far. Melton was the place to go for work. Your Nanna told me she recalls going to the seaside once as a child with her Auntie Liz and Uncle Phil, by train.

Best friend in the early teen years was, as you know, Mary Shipman whose family had a farm in the village quite near to us. There were six of them and I became part of the family around the corner. I helped Mrs. Shipman in the farmhouse, pegged rugs, washed milk buckets.

When a circus came into the village, Mr. Shipman made rope and rings; "To be a swallow" was named by the circus. We all played on the rings. Carpenter "Spud" Murphy made coffins. Mary and I played hide and seek in his workshop.

Mary and I had our differences. While Mary went to the Anglican Church, I went to the Methodist chapel. There were tennis courts at the back of the village institute: Mary could play but I could not. These things eventually seemed to cause a rift between us later in our relationship which ended abruptly. I cannot remember the reason exactly.

I took piano lessons from when I was 8 to 12: I was good at it and liked to play "In a Monastery Garden." I loved to play on the lovely rosewood piano my parents bought for me. But then other things got in the way. We had no radio. There was a Parish magazine to read, the Daily Herald and the Sunday Observer.

We moved into the Wood View house in 1934, one of two semi-detached houses built in the 1920s, by Mr. Rowbottom. The Jacques's, Auntie Liz and Uncle Phil, lived in the other half. Auntie Liz was Nana Rosie's sister. At that time, there was an outside toilet and no running water.

(Photographer: Unknown) The train from Stathern to Melton Mowbray cost a shilling a day. So, I rode my bike until I left home to stay briefly in Melton Mowbray with a Mrs. Clamp. Yes, here you see both houses: we lived in the one the left and connected to it was where Auntie Liz lived.

(Photographer: R. Heathcote) Here is Mary with me on your dad's motorbike.

You told me you made some foolish mistakes in your life. Refusing to attend the grammar school was your first. I wonder why you placed limits on yourself? Why didn't you make the most of the opportunities presented to you? You regarded yourself as somewhere between a country bumpkin and a "toff." You could stratify people into a myriad of levels of social structure evident in the village. How were people so stratified? What was the criterion? Could one move up and down? Why did the Titcombs, he a vacuum cleaner salesman, achieve so much status in your mind? Why did you invent this?

How can I answer all that? That is how my mind works! Yes, I made many mistakes. I wasn't very good at making good decisions. Not going to the Grammar School was indeed a foolish decision.

You really liked the seaside.

We did. I like the feel of the sea on my feet. I know the sea is cold but I love a dip in it.

You met Valerie Sykes at Woolworths when you both were 20. Here you are with your boyfriends in the late 1930s, at the seaside. Valerie and you look slender and attractive. I wonder if you knew then you would go through your lives together.

We never thought about that! Your dad danced like a dream and was known as the dancing bus conductor. We loved to dance together.

He was a mild-mannered kind man whereas I would describe you as tough with passive-aggressive tendencies. He would say that he had enough love for both of you and he would need it. So, dancing appeared to be the main attraction for the two of you and the main activity during the 1930s and beyond. Dancing was a passion for you both throughout your lives. I have heard it said that if two people danced well together, they were in sync for their lives. Well, you two loved to dance together. But in sync? Not so much particularly in the early days. Later in your lives I would say so.

(Photographer: A. Thompson)

Well, you seem to have that figured out. I am sure Valerie and I didn't look that far ahead of our lives.

(Photographer: R. Heathcote) Here I am with Auntie Beat and Uncle Ernie with their son, Reg. This would be mid-1930s. The photo was taken outside their house on Penn Lane. Beckie is there too, standing next to me. She was married to Reg's brother Tom.

(Photographer: Unknown)

This is cousin Nellie's wedding. She married Bill Doubleday. I was the bridesmaid on her left. That was quite the extravagant wedding. Look at those huge bouquets. Bill was a butcher, a businessman. So Nellie did well. This is in the 1930s before the war. He was a bit of a letch, even made a pass at me on his wedding day!!

Soon after this, you had to prepare for war.

Well yes. We weren't worldly enough to know what the war was about, although we knew it was about territory. We knew the Germans attacked shipping bound for Britain, trying to starve us into submission. This would lead to shortages of food supplies so the government decided to introduce food rationing, which made sure everyone received an equal amount of food every week. The government was concerned as food became scarcer, prices would rise and the poor might be unable to afford to eat. There was also a danger some people might hoard food, leaving none for others.

Every man, woman, and child were given a ration book with coupons. We needed coupons to buy rationed goods. Each person registered at the grocery store, which was provided with sufficient food for registered customers. We took ration books with us when shopping, so coupons could be cancelled.

At first bacon, butter, and sugar were rationed: tea, cheese, sweets, and meat soon followed. One egg a week was the ration in 1941. Not all foods, however, were rationed. Fruit and vegetables were never rationed but were often in short supply, especially tomatoes, onions, and fruit shipped from overseas. There were no bananas, so younger children, including you, did not see their first banana until the war ended. But we managed! In our part of the country, there were plenty of vegetables, especially potatoes and carrots. Everyone was encouraged to eat more of them.

There were no supermarkets, so people visited several different shops: For fruit and vegetables, the greengrocer: for meat, to the butcher, for fish, to the fishmonger, for bread and cakes, to the baker and for groceries such as jam, tea, biscuits and cheese to the grocer. Other shops sold clothes, shoes, medicines, newspapers.

I remember the 'Dig for Victory' campaign started in October 1939 and called for every man and woman to keep an allotment. Lawns and flower-beds were turned into vegetable gardens. Chickens, rabbits, goats, and pigs were reared in town parks and gardens. We villagers were encouraged to grow fruit and vegetables in our gardens and allotments. Of course, my dad was already doing that and continued with enthusiasm. He had learned to garden from his dad. And then we had the hedgerows to gather berries and fields to catch rabbits. So we weren't short of food in the village.

So you were all preparing for war and dad had been called to serve.

Yes, it was a terrifying time. We tried to forget for a while and keep on dancing. We had no idea what to expect. We knew life would not be the same.

The romance between the two of you flourished through the late 1930s and you danced. I think we can say my father won your heart on the dance floor! So why would anyone marry during wartime, amid terror and uncertainty?

Because I was stupid. I was 24 and your dad was 25. Auntie Becky went with me to Leicester to buy a wedding suit, which was brown. We got a special license and were married in St. Guthlac's Church in Stathern on January 22, 1941, during a 48-hour leave with a week to plan the wedding. Yes, that was the size of it. Here we are on the street outside our house. With snow on the ground, no one seemed to have a warm coat!

(Photographer: Unknown)

Oh yes, there is Grandad and Grannie Heathcote on the left and a friend of your dads at the back. Next to me is my mum and dad. I don't know who the lady is. Your dad returned to his training in Taunton, Somerset, with no time to become a husband in my family home. We had no opportunity to be newlyweds together. For me, there was little change. I continued my job at the Woolworth's store in Melton. But I was a war bride!

But first, you had to modify dad's name, I understand.

Well yes. They pronounced the name like Hethcutt which I didn't like at all. So, we changed to "Heathcoat" which sounded better.

Another 48-hour leave in March had major consequences. Despite precautions, a baby was conceived, not a welcome addition to the family. There were attempts to abort apparently which did not succeed. Imagine the dismay when a pregnancy was confirmed: the unthinkable, a baby was to be born in wartime. In December, just two weeks before Christmas, the unplanned war baby arrived, a Thursday's child with far to go. A 6 3/4lb baby with dark blue eyes and measuring 19 inches arrived at 7 am on December 11.

Yes, you kept me awake all night! You were delivered at home by a local doctor, Dr. Atkinson. We were very lucky to have a crib, clothing, and pram, passed down from villagers. I recorded the following gifts in your Baby Book: Silver egg cup, pram covers, a bonnet, a dress, two shawls, two dolls, a brush and comb set, and a total of twelve shillings and sixpence in cash. You were wanted after you arrived.

That Christmas was a time of optimism; Britain was no longer alone in the fight against Hitler. Earlier that month, the USA had entered the war, after the Japanese attack on Pearl Harbour. In the public view, there was now no doubt that the Allied forces would eventually win, despite the undoubted prospect of set-backs - and indeed, on Christmas Day, Hong Kong surrendered to the advancing Japanese, although we didn't hear about that at the time.

I remember, during this time there were shortages of many items: manpower, food, and clothing. Rationing was in effect of course. We had become used to that. Jam, cheese, eggs, petrol (gasoline), and coal were all rationed during the year. Clothing and textiles were rationed from June 1941 as production focussed on uniforms. Although there was less meat, locally grown food was readily available in the village. There were coupons for clothing, so we made items last. Sheets were sewed sides to middle, socks were darned and we became an expert at making something new out of something old: Make do and mend mode.

And soon after that, in the autumn of 1942, your dad left for service overseas without really getting to know you. I was glad to be home with my mum and dad who became major caregivers to you when I returned to work as Manager at Woolworths in Melton.

(Photographer: R. Heathcote) I didn't want a baby in wartime. Who would? But once you arrived, we all felt different. You were a little rosebud.

(Photographer: R. Heathcote) Here you are with my mum and dad. My cousin, May Brown is there too. You are wearing your new white coat which was a birthday present. So, you are 1 in this photograph. My mother took very good care of you while I was working. She was very gentle and kind. You became close to my mum and dad. You called my dad "Daddad" and would forget he was my dad and not yours!

My mum and dad looked after us well all during the war. Oh, they encouraged me to socialize. I ambivalently resumed dancing and otherwise lived as best we could. We tried to forget the war for a short time. Dancing helped. You and I slept together in the front room for our comfort.
Tell me about Wartime.

Wartime was very scary because planes overhead dropped bombs. While your dad was overseas, I would find a dance. Anywhere. Often it was on a service man's base, such as at the Langar Air Base with Canadians. One never knew whether the crew we met one weekend would be there again. Sometimes the whole crew would be gone. We would say, when the drone of the planes stops, we will never complain about anything again. But one does! Nothing was permanent in those difficult times. Vera Lynn would assure us, "We'll meet again. Don't know where, Don't know when." There was so much uncertainty. Your dad was trying to keep safe but we never knew when or if he would return. The war seemed to go on and on. Then we realized Hitler was attacking on too many fronts at the same time and was in trouble. Apart from that, we were being led by Winston Churchill who urged us never to give up.

(Photographer: R. Heathcote)
Oh this is a photograph of me.

We communicated as much as we could during wartime. Letters, cards, and the like.

(Photographer: D. Field))

(Photographer: D. Field)

And then it did end and it seemed like ages for your dad to return. We were almost unprepared for his return. We were so accustomed to his being away. I couldn't imagine what our lives would be like with him.

So then my dad returned and you continued to dance. Reconnecting with the family and to civilian life must have been an ordeal for him after the stress, loneliness, and suffering of the prior four years.

Having him back was a challenge for the rest of us as well because a different man returned from the one that left. He felt like a stranger. The existing family unit, my mum and dad, you and I, were thrown into disarray when he appeared around the corner even though we were so pleased to see him. Your dad needed to insert himself into our family unit. Yes, he had difficulty, especially with you. You did not understand you could no longer sleep with me which caused a big rift. He was a new arrival, an unknown, someone with authority. And he did not know how to be a father to his four-year-old daughter. You were a baby when he left: he did not watch you grow. We failed to prepare you for his arrival.

Post-traumatic stress syndrome was unheard of at the time. Dad did not talk about his experiences. I recall Dad smoked and brought back colourful adjectives: You disapproved.

I recall, after the war, it took time for the rationing to come off food items. There were limits to the cheese and other staples that one could buy. I remember buying small quantities of sweets. We were fortunate in the village that eggs, milk, and even meat were available because we resided in a farming community. There was a slaughterhouse in which local animals were killed that fed the village for a while. Meat was sold in the butcher's shop then located in Red Lion Street: For us, a half-pound of meat fed the whole family.

Yes, well there wasn't much money around then.

But your dad set about running the water lines to the house so we would have water with the support of Stathern Council. There was an initiative after the war to modernize the villages. Then we were able to buy the house. After that, your dad added a bathroom and another bedroom upstairs for my dad. He added a downstairs toilet and some outbuildings. He also upgraded the kitchen. Later the old fireplace was replaced with a modern coal burning fireplace. Space heaters were added. [75] It seems he was always adding something.

It was a total surprise, no, shock, to me when your dad knocked through the living room to the unused front sitting room! I was angry at first but had to admit it gave us welcome living space and so much more light.

You have told me you had a happy childhood. Would you say I did?

Well, it was a different time. Even though we lived under the threat of the war, you were well taken care of by my mum and dad while I worked at Woollies. You had a very close relationship with them.

After your dad returned, everything was different. The relationships changed, my mother was gone, Geoff was here, we all tried to figure out how to live together. I would say you and Geoff lived through these struggles and you got the short end of the stick. Life was not easy for you. So, I would have to say your childhood was unsettled and not so happy. My dad was still a constant in your life. I am sure you felt you didn't need two dads. But your dad was home, trying to fit in and assert himself. Sadly, you were often caught in the middle.

I missed my mother dreadfully and so did my dad. The mid-1940s were not happy times.

The Thompsons lived in council property near your dad`s mother in town and later moved into a new bungalow on the way out of Melton Mowbray towards Grantham. The pair never owned their own home which was a sore point between us as they compared their financial circumstances with ours. Indeed, we became homeowners by good fortune: we were able to buy my parent's old rented house which we then renovated. They, on the other hand, seemed to spend their money. On reflection, Valerie and Alvin were not a good match and stayed together because of Vivienne. Alvin had an abrupt manner, a salesman which indeed he was. He was brash and overpowering: a red-faced, jovial sort, constantly making silly jokes: little wonder with a January 23 birthday.

So, on reflection, 1947 was a bittersweet year for you.

Yes, it was. I was expecting Geoff but my mother had to be taken away from us and was in hospital. She was in isolation in a hospital near Leicester. We could not see her easily and visits were not welcomed. She died in June and Geoff was born in July that year. He took the pain away a little, you know. Your dad wanted a son and here he was.

(Photographer: R. Heathcote) We had a dreadful winter that year, I remember. There was so much snow. That was an unforgettable winter. Here I am with a snowman they built up Tofts Hill.

---

75 After that no further work was done to modernize the house which became drafty, damp and inhospitable in the winter. She could have added gas central heating but did not. Another poor decision made. The house was so cold.

Along the side of the roads up Stathern hill were Nissan huts used to store ammunition. In 1947 they were still there. That year, there were huge snowfalls that covered the huts. One could walk on top of them. I recall walking up the hill toward Eaton with Geoff in tow in a pram.

I recall spending time with Geoff as a baby with you, doing the laundry, ironing, and eating Cadbury's chocolate. I clearly remember wash day was frustrating for you.

Do you remember all that? Do you also remember we played Snakes and Ladders? And you played snobs with a neighbour.

I was seven when I became seriously ill. I remember so well. I am sure you do too. I was able to eat only tomatoes with a large quantity of Heinz salad cream. Anything else would make me nauseous. I lost a tremendous amount of weight. A trip to the doctor's office entailed walking from Harby to Long Clawson-a couple of miles. I recall the walk back with you armed with new tablets, M & B to be exact, a new antibiotic, a huge pill quite unsuitable for a small child.

Yes, I remember that. We crushed the pill and put it in a strawberry! I know how awful they tasted. Sadly, the wonder drug, penicillin, was unsuccessful. Mrs. Belt, the cook at the Stathern school, would give you your pills and ensure that you had your allotment of milk, milk in small bottles was provided to school children at the time by the government. Mrs. Belt cooked the school lunches.

Next came a trip to the Children's Hospital in Nottingham by Barton's bus. On arrival in Nottingham, we transferred to a city bus. Remember the very large green City buses that ran frequently without a schedule which completed the trip? Once at the hospital, you were whisked off, alone. Parents were not allowed into consulting rooms! You refused to tell me anything about your examination.

On the second visit there, a Mr. Sheahan, nephrologist and surgeon, told me – "I'll have to keep her in" the hospital. I couldn't believe that until he said: "Do you want her to die?" I went home alone with your clothes in a plastic bag in tears. Auntie Beat had been able to glean out of you what had happened at the hospital whereas I had not. We nearly went mad when we thought we might lose you.

(Photographer: Unknown)
Oh yes, another trip to the coast. You don't look very well here.

So, there I was, lonely and abandoned, in the Duchess of Portland Ward, Children's Hospital, Nottingham where I was not allowed out of bed. I wonder if you can imagine that. I was so young.

We could not visit because the hospital didn't want to disrupt routines. But we did visit and brought gifts. We waved to you once as we walked from the hospital. Imagine how we felt when we were told you were to have surgery? There was no explanation-just that exploratory surgery was conducted on your left kidney. What did they do? No one knew! You had a scar that extended all around your waist on the left side. After you were discharged, you had been in bed for about six weeks and had to learn to walk all over again. You were dreadfully weak. Friends came to call. I was worried about your schoolwork.

I did recover from the ordeal but was not the same little girl. I was more self-sufficient, self-reliant, and aloof, I expect, and accustomed to managing without parents. Innocence was lost. Six weeks was a long time to be away from home for a young child who had been secluded in village life without exposure to strangers. Even though I had reached the age of reason, I could not understand what was happening. I now had secrets from you: I know another way of living without you. This seemed to set the scene for me to be apart from you: excluded by my choice and uninvolved. I would be an outsider. This was a pivotal year that set the way for my future.

Yes, your illness and your absence from home, made you different, distant. But I was preoccupied with your education. You needed to earn a place at the Grammar School. A sensitive issue for me. Here we are on holiday in Skegness in 1950. You look better, quite recovered.

I decided I might like to become a nurse during that time. There were no female doctors and so becoming one did not enter my head. I wasn't sure I liked the nurses' uniforms. You commented that I would not like to wear black stockings. This gave some indication of the depth of analysis I was likely to encounter in future decision making.

(Photographer: Unknown)

I don't know what you mean!

I think as I look back with many years under the bridge, the trauma of that time, the surgery by myself, the aloneness, the feeling of being cut off and abandoned, affected me more than I originally thought. At seven, I became accustomed to being alone, to surviving alone which resulted in my not needing anyone for survival. So now I am older, I don't want anyone around. Does that sound possible?

Oh, that's too much for me to take in. We were all just surviving ourselves at that time, you know.

Looking back over the 40s, that was an awful decade for you after the relative peace of the 30s. You had real turmoil to deal with.

Yes, I did. I married, had two children, lost my mother, suffered through the uncertainty of war, and all this while your dad was away. There was even more turmoil after he returned home and we had to deal with your being ill and missing school. I was glad when the 50s started! Also, after the war ended, I lost my job and had to stay home and be a housewife. I was not at all happy with that situation.

(Photographer: R. Heathcote) *New bicycles were not available in 1948 when I was ready to be mobile. I recall this three-wheeler, unexpectedly for sale by a family in the village. How lucky was I? Somehow you also managed to find Geoff a bike too. I see you have a stick in your hand ready to push Geoff should the need arise*

Here we are walking *around the lanes* just outside Stathern. We are on our way to the Station, Harby, and Nottingham. After about half a mile, we would turn right, by a farm along the long lane toward Bottesford before turning right again back to the village by where Auntie Beat lived. This walk was a couple of miles. We walked this route often. Here I am being a mother but, as you know, that was not enough for me. I was not the mother who enjoyed cooking and baked cakes. I was not the best mother to you both.

Yes, I remember there was much conflict in our house. It was not a happy place to be for any of us. You and dad did not seem happy together in the early days. My education was always on your mind!

Yes, it was. You had missed so much schooling. You needed to pass the 11+ examination to make you eligible for the Grammar School. You were unconcerned and more interested in catching tadpoles and watching them develop in a bucket in the garden. I didn't think you would be well prepared for the exam in Stathern School. So, I investigated the Melton Mowbray Convent School and managed to secure you a place in the fall. The fees were six guineas which was a lot of money. Then there would be a uniform to buy and bus fares. Do you remember committing some indiscretion over the summer? I cancelled your spot in the school. You were unconcerned. I relented: you did attend the Convent school for two years and passed the 11+ exam easily. At least you were going to the Grammar School which neither your dad nor I managed. You did very well at Melton Mowbray Grammar School. You wouldn't listen to anyone and left school at 16. I feared you would regret that decision and you did! You read a lot and were a good student, unlike your brother who could not read nearly as well. Both your dad and I wondered what would become of him.

I believe you made unkind comments about Geoff at the time and were very critical. You were wrong about him, weren't you?

I am glad I was! As he grew older, he went around doing jobs with your dad and became a chip off the old block. I was impressed when he built a radio in his room with wires attached to the water pipes.

I would read all the Fab Five books that Enid Blyton wrote but was otherwise starved of literature. There were few books in our house. I never recall being read to. There were no reference materials except for one Volume of "Everything Within" that I had to use for research at school – even the Grammar School! I simply didn't know what was out there and what I was missing. An enquiring mind was not being fostered. There was no interesting conversation around our dinner table. I was never taken to the library.

How could I teach you or tell you what I didn't know myself?

I recall I started to menstruate in the middle of Miss Topliss's French class. I felt as though I was leaking. I was shocked to see blood all over my underwear. I had no idea what was happening believing I was ill. I took the school bus home as usual, concerned that I would leak all over the seats. I chose not to tell you. How could I explain the embarrassing event to you? I convinced myself I would deal with the problem on my own as I had no idea how to describe what was happening.

But you spotted blood in the bathroom later and confronted me. You responded on cue by explaining to me this leakage was quite normal and was a signal that I was now a woman and could now have a child. Since I was but a child myself, I found that explanation both unsatisfactory and frightening. I had no intention of having a child but was it inevitable? You offered no other assurances or explanations. I would have "a visitor" every month: my peers and I would refer to this as the "curse." I wondered whether everyone would know when I had my period and was greatly concerned.

You did not possess the courage to explain what was happening before the event. I had earlier allowed you to explain when I asked you what was in the blue box you had recently purchased. Sugar you said which I knew was untrue as the box was too light. You had missed your cue! Did you feel ill-prepared for your smart daughter? I don't recall you took any interest in my scholastic life. Was I raised by neglect?

No one told me anything. I didn't know what you already knew. We didn't talk about those things in my day. How could I help you if I didn't know anything about what you were learning?

Do you remember telling me to have "the talk" with Geoff when he was about 15? Did you think I knew what to say?

Your dad and I believed you could broach the subject easier than we could!

Do you remember in my final report card I earned two As, five Bs, and two Cs. While the headmaster wrote: "We wish her well for the future" and gave me a final *.

I will always blame Miss Chamberlain for your leaving school too early. The two of you didn't get along.

During this time, you and dad continued to dance.

Well yes, we always had dancing to fall back on. The Quickstep, was a favourite, with a faster tempo. The experts would say it was a fast-moving dance based on 200 beats per minute. "Mr. Sandman" was the correct beat for the Quickstep. Victor Sylvester was the one to watch. Remember: "slow, slow, quick-quick-slow?" We all watched the dancing shows on television in the 1950s. We went dancing I would say every weekend somewhere: Barnston, Burton Lazars, Old Dalby. There would be a dance somewhere every Saturday in the village halls.

(Photographer unknown) Oh yes, here we are with our friends.

Do you remember picking blackberries in season? A group of neighbours would pick many berries.

We did and then we made blackberry vinegar, syrupy red that we would pour over Yorkshire pudding when eaten as a dessert. We also made jam and blackberry and apple pies. Very good!

Do you remember which words of wisdom you gave to me as a teenager?

I certainly told you how to look after your teeth. I massaged my gums with salt. But I suppose that is not what you mean! I think I told you to listen to the little voice inside which is what my mother told me.

You did. I had no idea what you meant but I did grow up with a strong sense of conscience. You also told me not to come home pregnant without telling me either how I could get pregnant or how to avoid it.

(Photographer: Unknown)

(Photographer: Unknown)

These photographs were taken at Uncle Edwin's wedding. I was a bridesmaid. My dad said he was more comfortable dancing with you than me. He would say I was not as light on my feet as you. I would interpret that as saying I was like a cart-horse. Uncle Edwin married Betty; I was invited to be a bridesmaid. Geoff reminded me that Edwin was a bricklayer and helped our father with the renovations. Sadly, Edwin passed away from cancer in 1955. I recall seeing him just before he died. He looked like a skeleton; his skin yellow. He passed away soon after that but the image of him remained with me.

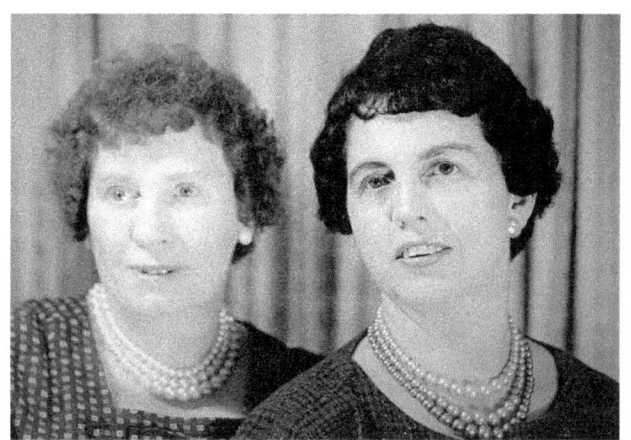

(Photographer: R. Heathcote) *The date on this photograph of you and Valerie is 1964! Both wearing fake pearls! Must have been the in thing!*

Yes, I am sure it did. Perhaps I should not have taken you to see him. You would have been about 13 then.

We spent a lot of time with Valerie and Alvin over the years. We were always together for Christmas, well Boxing Day. Sometimes I drank too Much!!! We all liked to dress up which was a bit of fun. Yes, you and Geoff were embarrassed by all these antics.

Here you are socializing with Auntie Nellie and Uncle Bill. I notice Uncle Bill is holding Auntie Nellie's hand as well as having an arm around you!

You had him sized up by then. Remember we all liked to go over to the Doubledays on Christmas morning? You would enjoy the mince pies and the usual chatter. With their four children, there was quite a house full.

I remember being with you at home when the doctor called. They made house calls in those days. I think you had started Menopause. You described symptoms I now recall and understand. He prescribed Valium and suggested you go out and buy yourself a new hat. Amazing what we remember.

Yes. I had an uncomfortable time. And Valium was the drug they prescribed at the time!!

Here you are with Auntie Beat. You had a special relationship with her, didn't you?

(Photographer: Unknown)

(Photographer: Unknown)

Oh yes, she was special. She moved in with us when we lived in the house on Main Street. She had her Dorothy and was on her own. So, she came to live with us. I shared a room with her from an early age. Then she met and married Uncle Ernie. After my mother died, we became even more close. She helped me a lot. Then you became close to her too. You would tell her your secrets. Do you remember that?

Yes, I do!

With Auntie Beat
(Photographer: R. Heathcote)

(Photographer: Unknown) Then a special animal came into our lives, Suzie. She literally went everywhere with us. She was a wonderful Corgi dog. Here we are in the sea somewhere. As long as we were there, she would go anywhere.

(Photographer: Unknown)

(Photographer: R. Heathcote)

This is a seaside trip with Auntie Annie, Grandma Heathcote's sister. I have no idea how we happened to be with her here at the coast. She was a favourite. We had no idea Grandma Heathcote had other sisters! Why didn't I talk more to them both?

I can't answer that one. We just didn't ask questions in those days.
True but I now wish I had a more enquiring mind about my dad's family.
Dad wanted to relocate us to Melton, a move he considered would be good for all of us. I recall visiting a potential house on Brightside Avenue. You refused to leave Stathern and your dad. But your dad seemed to drift away from us during that time, a man so important to me. Probably my Granddad felt he no longer had a home and was not part of the expanded family.

Another of my numerous mistakes! Yes, my dad did visit family in Nottingham frequently until he retired in 1950. Then he seemed to be gone most of the time. The house was small. He had a hard time fitting in after your Nana died. It was not a good time for us all. Not peaceful enough for him or any of us.
You told me you took two aspirins every night.

I did. I am not sure of the reason. I slept better. I used to think two aspirins cured all my ills!
I wonder whose wedding this was! You look smart and slender. I would be about 20 and not very stylish!

Yes, I do look good. I believe this was Sandra's wedding. I expect Geoff took the picture. We are on

(Photographer: G. Heathcote*)*

the road outside the house, I think. I remember making the boutonnieres with flowers from the garden! We used the silver paper from chocolate bars. Very professional!

You left England in 1967 to join Dave in California. He had cancelled wedding plans twice so we were concerned. But you seemed so sure. We were anxious. You told us nothing. Geoff wanted to visit California but your plans were uncertain. He had to call off the trip.

I had nothing to tell you. Dave was dithering around. I finally gave up on him. I decided to move on. I was sorry Geoff's plan did not work out. I offered him Toronto but he had settled his heart on California. To think I was in Mountain View before it became Silicon Valley!

Suddenly, you had moved to Canada, found a job and a place to live, and were studying. We sent you a sheepskin coat to keep you warm! But then in the early part of 1969 you became ill, kidney again! We were again upset and worried especially when you told us the left kidney was not working and would be removed.

1969. It wasn't a good time but I was young and strong. I gave up on Dave and decided to try Canada. Heather urged me to join her in Toronto. Everything seemed to fit into place so it was meant to be.

(Photographer: B. Hopper)

I soon recovered after the kidney was removed. Here I was though with a pre-existing condition that would go with me for the rest of my life! The right kidney has kept me going very well.

Oh, that picture is much later, I think. Heather with baby John with her mum and dad in their garden in Saxby. Heather must have been over for a visit. About 1970 perhaps?

I had met Hal who was very helpful and kind, particularly when I was ill and vulnerable.

Oh yes, this was my first trip to Niagara Falls! Your friend Sarah is here with her mother. We are with Hal. That is a good picture because I am at one of my favourite places! We liked Hal and his family and were not surprised when we received a letter from Hal asking permission to marry you. Nevertheless, we thought he was not right for you. You moved so much quicker than did he. We thought you would leave him behind. And you eventually did.

Pity you and dad were not around and I could have discussed this with you and eventually seen this. He seemed like a kind man, one I needed right then. On the other hand, I really didn't want you to be around then voicing your opinion. I thought you might upset everything on my wedding day. So, I asked dad to come alone.

(Photographer: R. Heathcote)

Yes, you tried to encourage your dad to come alone but you might know I would not accept that. So, we decided to return to Toronto and have a little holiday too in Vermont and Montreal. You had a lovely wedding but that didn't stop us from thinking you had not met your match. We just had to hope all would be well and that you would be very happy. That's what we wished for you.

We were sad to know that the likelihood of your moving back to England was slim. I wanted you to be around the corner like my friend's daughters. And then Geoff told us he was moving to Canada too. Your dad and I were devastated. Your dad kept bursting into tears. We decided then we would widen our circle and go out more. And we would travel a little.

We went to Tunis, to Spain and Germany as well as trips around England and Wales. That took our minds off your absence. I think this photograph was taken in Heather's parent's garden in Saxby. Well yes. This looks as though we had just returned from Tunis. Your dad insisted on bring you a three-legged chair. Do you still have it?
I do!
Remember this one?

Yes. This was taken at Rita's wedding. Rita's parents, Dorothy and Chris, lived in Wembley. We stayed with them sometimes to and from our trips to Canada. They were good to you also, I think. You would break your journey too.
They were. I remember staying with them too.

In a letter to me dated February 23, 1975, was a note from dad. "Mum and I are busy just now making up a film show which we are showing to the chapel people next month. And we are still getting around quite a lot. Next weekend we are going with Betty & Ernie to Burton Town Hall to dance to the organ which has just been installed. Will tell you about it later."
He didn't of course because we lost him during that weekend.

(Photographer: Unknown)

(Photographer: Unknown)

23.

MORE CONVERSATIONS WITH MY MOTHER

Life cruelly changed for your Nana on March 2, 1975, when she became a widow and was forced to reinvent herself. She even gave herself a new name: she became not Kath but Kathy. Our conversations continue as your Nana had another life to live alone, alone for the first time….

My words are in italics…

Are you able to tell me about that day?

We were with friends, Betty and Ernie, in Woodville for the weekend. We went dancing and had a lovely evening. Your Dad drove us all to their home and said he wasn't feeling well. I suggested he slip into bed while I made a cup of tea. When I went back upstairs, he had gone. We tried to revive him and so did the doctor when he arrived. But it was no use. His last words to me were: "What have you done to me?" I don't even want to think about it.

You decided that you didn't want either Geoff or me to come over to you.

Yes. I had enough support here at the time and felt I would need you both later. In any case, you were expecting a baby and would need me and Sue was also expecting a baby. Of course, I was delighted when Darien arrived and decided I would come to Canada for a few weeks to help you both. Being there with you and my new grandchildren would be something to look forward to. I didn't have to think about things in Stathern and being alone.

Then what happened?

Everyone was so good to me. I had about 100 cards and letters. You know, when Geoff and you left, we decided to widen our circle of friends. First, I went to stay with Val and Alvin. I didn't want to go into an empty

(Photographer unknown) I stayed with Val and Alvin for over six weeks: they were indescribable angels to me. Here we are looking so sad.

house. But then I had to go to find certain documents. Alvin did jobs for me and so did Bob and Win, who took care of the house and garden. My future seemed a blank space as your dad and I had looked forward to an early retirement. I felt strong then but didn't want to return to Stathern. There I would find many transparencies which we had left in disarray. We were preparing for a presentation, intended for a Chapel Get Together for the ladies.

I felt sick at heart, having to do things alone, and was not brave deep inside as I realize what had happened to me. I made plans for my flight to Canada: June 20 to September 7, 1975. Then I returned to work! Work was a welcome distraction. Everyone was so kind at Woolworths. Little did I know I would soon be turfed out.

I had to decide what to do with the car. I was encouraged to learn to drive it. And so, I applied for a learner's permit. I took lessons with Jim Titcomb and went driving with whoever would sit with me. It was a mighty struggle but I did it.

For many, many years you wrote the following in your diary on March 2:
    Like falling leaves, the years roll by but my thoughts of you will never die.
    Memories are like stars that shine: they last until the end of time. To Reg from Brown Eyes.

(Photographer: D. Field)

(Photographer: D. Field)

You do look in your element here with the babies. I think Geoff, Sue, and I appreciated your being here. I, in particular, was glad you bathed Stuart. I had no idea how to take care of him!

You know I had lost my dance partner and life partner. All my life I had loved to dance. Now that had been taken away from me. No one danced like your dad.

(Photographer: H. Field)
Here I am with Geoff and you.

(Photographer :D. Field)

You and Geoff took me to Ed's Warehouse which was a favourite. I liked the food. I had been there before. I didn't have to think too much. I was painfully thin in these pictures! And sad too.

I visited Ann and Art Teskey in Orillia. I had met them before. They made me so welcome.

I don't remember how or when you met Ann and Art Teskey. Certainly with Dad. Here you are helping them sell corn by the roadside. But I do remember driving you to Orillia when I was very pregnant. I left you there, I recall.

Yes, you had Stuart while I was in Orillia. I liked Ann and Art very much. They had children who were so good to me. In the photograph, there is Ann and Art with one of their sons. That corn was so good. I had never eaten corn like that before.

(Photographer: Unknown)

And you stayed until Sept 7. Saying goodbye to you was difficult. You had been very helpful.

Yes you four, plus the babies, helped me to forget I was alone for a while.

Do you remember returning to Canada the next year all by yourself? I graduated from university that year, 1976. You came to the ceremony with me. Remember? Here is a photograph of us. You are wearing one of your signature shirts waisters!

I do. Of course, I had made the trip alone before so nothing was new. I was so proud that you had graduated from university. It was so hot that day! I stayed most of the time with Geoff that summer because you were working. In the heat, those dresses are the best and they are my favourites!

Both Alvin and Valerie were incredibly supportive of us all. I recall that when I visited you, with Stuart in December 1975, Alvin sent one of his men to meet me at Heathrow. He brought us to Alvin's home in Melton where the car was waiting. I was overwhelmed by his kindness to me. Stepping into my dad's car was quite something. I will not forget the feeling. On my return trip, Alvin drove me to Leicester and helped me onto the bus destined for London.

Yes, he was a good chap. He liked riding horses in his younger days. With Gladys, Valerie`s sister, we had an opportunity to drink sherry with Prince Charles in 1979.

Tell me more about Alvin.

We had known one another for years. After your dad died, he would come over to Stathern to help me with household chores. He gave me courage as I learned to drive the car. I was surprised about the attraction but he was a good friend. Valerie either did not know of our close relationship or chose not to acknowledge it. Val and I continued to be great friends. Alv and I vehemently denied any relationship. But we would go on trips together, particularly to the coast, even staying a week. He visited me every Wednesday, bringing food for our meals. On other occasions, I would drive to his office in Leicester and stay until he was ready to drive home.

(Photographer: Unknown)

I recall on one of your visits to Canada in the late 1970s he phoned and sang: I just called to say I love you, a song of the era. On a visit to the UK one year, Alvin took me aside and assured me of his sincere intentions. He told me he loved you but you would not allow him to move in. Apparently, you valued Valerie`s friendship. Neither of you would hurt Valerie for the world. Nevertheless, you both rationalized you were not taking anything away from her. Alvin would say that his relationship with you made it possible for him to stay with Valerie. We visited you in 1978 when Stu was 3. Remember? I came with Neil.

(Photographer: Unknown)

(Photographer: D. Field)

Oh yes. I didn't like Neil much. I hoped he wouldn't stay around. I didn't like the way he treated Stuart. Look, we went to Skegness with Alv. This is a nice picture with the horse at Skegness on the beach.

Alvin was a diabetic who did not control his condition well. He did not look healthy in this photograph. Indeed, he developed Hepatitis C or cirrhosis, I am not sure which. I suspected he reused insulin needles and caught the disease himself. His decline happened in the early 1980s. He dyed his hair red which looked quite striking!

And then you lost Alvin. I was so sad to read your diary.

Yes, his health was failing in August 1986. I moved in with the Thompsons to Valerie`s relief as she was not strong enough to deal with his end of life. I felt awkward but was doing for Alvin what was necessary. I gave him his morphine,

(Photographer: D. Field)

dealt with the feeding and bathing. He preferred my comfort to Valerie's and was not shy in expressing his feelings in that regard. Valerie acquiesced. We watched as his condition worsened.

On Aug 21 you wrote: A dark day. Poor Alv left us at 9 pm. My God how I shall miss him. That cheery smile and helping hand always ready. The little gifts that meant so much. He was a wonderful chap. To know him was to love him. Night. Night, Dear.

Did I write that? I was stronger then! When Alvin died, I had a warning, whereas I had none with your dad. Alvin's death knocked the stuffing out of both Valerie and I but me in particular. I had relied on him so much: he was my rock. On the other hand, Valerie had been living a life without his emotional support: she missed him less. We never discussed Alvin in the context of my relationship with him.

(Photographer: Unknown)

(Photographer: B. Hopper) Here I am at home. Comfortable but alone. I hated being alone in that house. I would take off up to the Titcombs every evening and play games with them. Scrabble mostly. They were very good to me. And I used to think they were so posh. It was all pretend. But I loved going to the Lake District with them for Christmas. They made me so welcome.

This 1980s photograph is the last one I have of you three trio possibly taken in the Thompson's back yard. Valerie celebrated her 70th. Do you remember writing in your diary; Look back with Gratitude; Look forward with Hope; and look onward with Confidence?

Did I write that? Somehow, I bounced back from all this. I had the car insured and tested and drove all over the local area visiting friends and family. I even managed car troubles in my stride!

Valerie and I remained friends although we saw one another less frequently. She was, shall we say, delicate. She was sweet and gentle and required attention! She became worse as she aged. She fell one day and broke her hip and died after she had a hip operation-April 20, 1999. I missed her dreadfully.

I would spend summers with you and spend winters at home alone. I enjoyed being with my favourite grandchildren. I just loved Niagara Falls. I insisted on a visit each year. Do you remember?

You lost Jim Titcomb in 1986, remember? He was a good friend to you. Then you continued your friendship with Alice and the rest of the family.

I would go out a lot. Bingo, swim, out to lunch at senior's centres all around, visiting friends and family. I was able to get around in the car!

In later years I would visit Jean Steward every afternoon! I was glad of her company. Remember, I was born in a little cottage in her yard! Her daughter Susan would visit sometimes. I liked her.

(Photographer: G. Heathcote)

(Photographer: G. Heathcote) Here I am with my grandchildren. 1980 perhaps? One of my many visits to Canada. I know you both encouraged me to emigrate but I couldn't bring myself to leave Stathern. One of my regrets!

I think this is 1982. You went on a camping trip. Everyone looks happy except Lesley. I am not sure I liked being in a tent! But I was willing to give it a try.

Do you remember in 1983 I was ill and called you from the hospital? I asked you to come right away to take care of Stu?

I certainly do. We were all worried about you. You had surgery again and were just released from the hospital when I arrived. You took it easy for a few weeks but then insisted we went on a road trip to Manitoulin Island. You packed everything in the car and we set off. We loved the ferry and the Island. You purchased a picture, I think.

(Photographer: D. Field

(Photographer: D. Field)

Then we came home via Sudbury and you started to get tired. The whole trip was nice but too much for you after your ordeal.
Yes, it was. I thought just driving would not be too much but it turned out it was a long way! But we did enjoy ourselves and we stayed in some interesting and primitive places!

(Photographer: D. Field) Stuart's birthday with his grandmothers. We both look a little thoughtful. I think we were both widows then. Hal's mother was such a lovely lady.

(Photographer: D. Field) *Wow, that Lavatera has grown. Almost shadowing your roses!* Yes, it has. I have to cut the damn thing down!

(Photographer: D. Field) *This was taken when I lived on Bingham Avenue! You were so flexible. I wish I could do that!* Oh, I have always been flexible. Look at my skinny legs!

(Photographer: Unknown) *I think this is one of your favourite spots.* Oh yes, it was. I loved the Boardwalk and would be there all the time. I met so many nice people and talked with everyone.

Yes, you did seem to talk with everyone easily whereas I never could. I could spend the whole day in my little bubble and not talk with anyone. I wonder why that is?

(Photographer: Unknown)

Do you remember this occasion? Yes. Let me see. It was Stu's birthday! He wanted to go to a Greek Restaurant on the Danforth!

Oh yes. This is Jean Steward's house. I was born in a little cottage on her property. *Jean would welcome you every afternoon for tea and a chat. Indeed, a visit was expected. I was also welcomed when I visited. That is where I hooked up with Susan again.*

(Photographer: D. Field)

Yes. Jean didn't visit me. I was expected to visit her, rain or shine, in her house on the main street, an old dairy with a lot of land with fruit trees. In a state of disrepair now. I like her daughters Susan and Alison. Sue would make a point of visiting me when she could. She lived in Brighton; I think. We both worried about her and her love life!

As a teenager, Jean went to college to learn to type. During the war, she and three girlfriends investigated joining the forces. They were all signed up on the spot but when the recruiters realized that Jean could type, she was placed in a communications area and took messages from a teleprinter, thus dealing with confidential information.

(Photographer: D. Field) Goodness yes. This is the spot where I was born! In the yard of Jean's house! Her daughter, Sue had to have the old houses removed because they were dangerous!

We visited Jean in Egerton Lodge where she lived in care in her declining years. You were shocked by her condition, her behaviour, her agitated condition, her distress. We did not realize this was in store for us as I aged and my health declined. We didn't want to think about it!

Jean died in January 2008. Coincidentally she died at the same time as Mary Parrott another friend of yours. I remember you would enjoy Sunday Lunch with her at the Church Restaurant in Eaton until she couldn't go anymore. I would drive us there when I visited although Mary, a former nurse, was profoundly deaf and became difficult to be with!

(Photographer: G. Heathcote)

(Photographer: G. Heathcote)

Here we all are at 24 Hazel Avenue. Friend Aideen Brown was visiting from Ottawa.

Oh yes. I decided to stay longer because I hated going home and being alone in the dark days of winter in Stathern. I hated it. But then it was getting cold in Toronto in October so I felt it was time to go back. My grandchildren are growing up fast! I am glad to be here to see them grow.

That year, I have a letter from you dated October 13, 1985. You told an amusing story. You wrote:

> "After my lovely time with you dears, I had just one week at home when Valerie's daughter Viv's mother-in-law of 83 years, Mrs. Truman, who I understood to be an ogre, fell in her concrete yard and broke her wrist. So, they called me to ask for my help. How could I refuse when I had no home ties? Poor old girl, could not manage in her farmhouse in Old Dalby. I thought I would be helping out but soon realized I would be taking full charge. Tea in bed at 6.30 was expected. Then the poor girl asked me to wash her all over. I told her I had never done this kind of thing before. She assured me if I didn't mind, she didn't either. So, it is powder puff in delicate parts. With an arm in plaster, it was tricky dressing, thank goodness for her front fastening bra, we fix the first three hooks and heave her floppy bust individually into the harness. Then it is plain sailing with her slip and dress. Pulling on passion knickers and her stockings and garters was a struggle. Now, out of the container, I fish the false teeth, having the previous evening soaked them in Strident, under the tap and brush with minty toothpaste. My charge tells me they taste lovely and clean. Next, I comb her hair, she has lots of hair. Then I wash her specks under the tap and polish them on a clean piece of nylon material which she says makes them shine. I now slip on my clothes, a quick wash for me, no messing. My ward sits down at the table saying she is ready and looking forward to her brown bread, marmalade, and more tea.
>
> I cooked each day, something different, including dessert. I was cooking for 5 or 6 each day: Paddy the odd job man and Vic's son Mark, sometimes Vic and the cleaning lady! I cooked a joint of meat, a ham or a chicken every day with all the trimmings. I also looked after 3 dogs and a large ginger tomcat!
>
> Then a small milk churn arrived. I had to fill 6 extra clean bottles. As I undressed her for bed each day, made her pillows comfy, she thanked me for the day. I am whacked out but am happy to help this lady."

This is such a story. I wonder where Valerie was during this time!

Oh, she had some good reason why she could not help.

(Photographer: D. Field)

(Photographer: D. Field)

I didn't believe I could still ride a bike. But one never forgets that, I think. So here I am riding your bike down Hazel Avenue. Your house is in the background.

Your cousin May was important to you. I liked to visit her when I was in the UK. She had a soothing effect on you, I recall.

She did. I particularly liked her and enjoyed being around her and her children and grandchildren.

She was good to me and would take me dancing with her when I was a teenager. She also tried to teach me to play the piano with minimal success! She was one of the musical Browns!

(Photographer: D. Field)

Talking of the piano and the musical Browns, you played the piano beautifully but rarely. I wonder why that was! You didn't encourage my efforts to play. I wish you had.

I worked at it. I played on the lovely rosewood piano my mum and dad had bought for me. I loved that piano. It seems I was doing other things and never had the chance to play. When we had a sing-song around the piano I played. I never knew you were that interested.

Stu and I visited you in May 1986. Stu could not be without his skateboard. The first activity upon arrival was always to walk around the village. Here you both are looking at the house where great-granddad Hubbard lived on Main Street in Stathern.

Yes, I was glad to see you both. I don't remember it well and am glad for the photograph. Looks like a chilly day. You always liked to walk around the village when you arrived to see what had changed and what was the same.

(Photographer: Unknown)

(Photographer: G. Heathcote)

Back in Canada, Geoff took me somewhere on a road trip. On a trip to the Niagara region. 1988, I think.

Then in 1994 Stu graduated from Malvern Colliegate and entered University. Do you remember we dropped him off at the University in Guelph for his orientation?

Yes, I do. You were anxious about him but he seemed to meet a young lady quite quickly! He made it clear we should not stay around! But you were an anxious mother!

In 1995, I went on a trip of a lifetime.

Yes, you went to Australia and New Zealand, Fuji and Hawaii. I came over as usual for my annual summer visit. You left me with Stu, who had a job in a park, and a young man who was studying at University was living with you. Nice young man. You were gone for a long time. Many weeks. But we managed!

(Photographer: Unknown) I liked going to the Caribbean Festival in Toronto. It was exciting, musical and there was lots of dancing which you know I liked. I would go alone. I loved it. So lively, and noisy.

(Photographer: Unknown)

I helped a friend with her gardening! Violet perhaps? But I particularly liked being with Edna.

You made a life for yourself in Toronto every summer and would rekindle your friendships every year.

Oh yes. I did. I liked line dancing and particularly going to the Beach. There was a programme for oldies put on by the city and run by youngsters. It was marvellous. They made us burgers! Stu came sometimes too. I met so many wonderful people.

(Photographer: Unknown)

(Photographer: Unknown)

(Photographer: Unknown)

I know you were very close. Nick became ill with Alzheimer's I recall and died.

Yes, he did. Edna and I would write to one another when I returned home to Stathern and then rekindle our friendship again the next year. Here she is again. She was special.

I wonder whether you remember, you were living at Scalford Court. I was visiting. You said you had not heard from Edna lately. I picked up the phone and called her number. We were told she had died. You were deflated but accepting. Her sister called us back to explain what happened.

I had no choice but to accept. All my friends were going but not me. Why not me?

Stu and I visited you in 1996. Heather's John was married then. We both wanted to go to the wedding. It was a quick visit I think.

It was, but enjoyable, I had a good time. You had decided to sell your lovely house and to get a teaching job. You didn't know where you would be but since you were completing your doctorate, you needed a new job. And I didn't visit you that year either. But then I was quite busy. In my diary you see I swam a lot, I went to Bingo and visited friends: Jean, the Titcombs, Marie, Daisy, Emily, Marianne, Kay, Sheila, Mary, Janice, May, and Win. And I was busy in the garden as well as painting and doing things in the house. Those were good days when I could go out and be with people. I went around to the Titcombs most evenings. I liked their banter. We played scrabble. Did I mention, for many years I was invited to spend Christmas with them in the Lake District? They treated me so well. I loved my Christmasses there.

(Photographer: D. Field) *These are my special friends, Edna and Nick. Edna is sitting next to Nick. Edna and I considered ourselves sisters. She was certainly the sister never had.*

(Photographer: Unknown) *Heather visited us. Here we are outside my house on Hazel Avenue, Toronto.*

(Photographer: R. Heathcote)

After you and Geoff left, a young couple came into the area and lived in the Up the steps house I knew so well. Bob and Win became good friends and help me so much. Bob took care of the vegetable garden and did many jobs for me. I am sorry that I led him a bit of a dance with the kitchen fan. Of course, It needed to be there but was a bit draughty. Win did my cleaning when I could not. She took care of me and then I took care of her. Bob suddenly died in his 60s which was a shock to us all. He took care of many village activities as your dad had done and so was sorely missed. I was so, so sad when Win became ill. She recovered once from cancer but when it recurred, she could not recover. You got along well with her, didn't you? Walks, visits to the pub, and later you liked to prowl around the local stores.

Yes, I did. She represented the Stathern way of life. She made me a lemon cake when I visited. I was so sad for her that Bob left her and then sad again when she became ill and eventually died. She was so brave. She was concerned about how you would react when she died.

I was in Scalford Court by then. I remember the day you took me to see her in her home in Stathern. She reluctantly told me the cancer had come back. She wanted to explain why she had not been visiting me at Scalford Court. I was devastated for her. I couldn't believe it. But she said she was going to be with Bob.

Oh yes. You married again in 1997. I did not especially like John, mainly because I didn't understand him very well.

You didn't keep your opinions to yourself at all! Recall I had been alone for 20 years. I thought I might like a companion.

With my favourite grandson! Dari and Les were your bridesmaids. Nice pictures. I am glad Heather came over for the occasion.

(Photographer :G. Heathcote)

(Photographer: S. Field)

(Photographer: S. Field)

(Photographer: G. Heathcote)

(Photographer: Unknown)

(Photographer: G. Heathcote)

There you are dancing! Just like old times! You looked nice. Then you told me your dress had been purchased in a jumble sale!

(Photographer: Unknown)

You had left the beach area so my lovely summers by the beach were over. But I did return a few times to visit my old friends. But it wasn't the same. Perhaps I was older and so were they.

Your marriage was over very quickly. I was not at all surprised. But sad for you as you had been alone for so long and now you were to be alone again. I didn't take to him as you very well know.

I think you were not shy about expressing your displeasure. Just one look at your face told me everything. You were perhaps overly critical of your only daughter. In fact, you were particularly judgemental, I recall. Not just of me, but everyone! Much of the time I was with you I needed to have distance from you to protect myself. Did you realize that? Do you remember when John and I visited you in Stathern? We stayed at the Redmile Inn.

(Photographer: B. Hopper)

(Photographer: B. Hopper)

(Photographer: B. Hopper) At home during one of Heather's visits.

I was right about him, was I not? And then you came again the next year on your way to France. That was the year Hal died, I think. I was with you when Stu called to say Hal had had a heart attack and had died. That was a shock for us all.

Heather and Brian visited you often.

Yes, they did. I was so glad. Heather would bring something nice to eat. She would usually find me sitting in my chair where I could see the garden.

In early 1999, I went to Barbados to take care of Hal's mother who was in trouble. I was there for two weeks helping my sister-in-law Roz find her mother a nursing home. Then you had your hip replaced. And so I came to visit you to take care of you. That would have been in May. You were waiting for me at your door wearing the blue and white gingham overall you always wore around the house.

Yes. You did. I had just been delivered home when you arrived. I was pleased to see you as I could not have managed on my own. You were a great help. With encouragement, I did my exercises faithfully. You borrowed a wheelchair and so we were mobile. You had rented a good size car and so we were able to get around with the wheelchair. Remember I had moved my bed downstairs into the living room which worked for me. It was much warmer!

In your diary on May 2 you wrote "Daph proves to be a Godsend and we are much closer and understanding of each other." And later, "Daph good and kind."

Well, you were. I would have been in trouble without your help. There seemed to be friction in the past. I seemed to say the wrong thing.

Yes, you were very critical of me. When you were displeased, there would be a look of thunder on your face. I often needed to keep my distance from you to avoid being hurt.

Remember I visited you again that year in October. You were much better. You wanted to go to the coast so off we went. Hunstanton, I recall. We had a lovley walk on the promenade. But: You had a TIA while we were eating lunch and scared me to death. You fell face-first into your fish and chips!

Yes, I remember not feeling good which upset you. You drove us home quickly and put me to bed!

Do you remember the year I came over and we went to Countesthorpe where Grandad Heathcote was born? We visited a historian who told us there were no Heathcotes left in the village. She also told me Grandad's first wife, Ann, had no children. I discovered that wasn't true! You told me I was more interested in dead people than alive!

One year, perhaps 2002, Stu visited both of us from Muenster, Germany. Then to our surprise, Jennifer, alone in Muenster, said she was coming too. I was amazed that she navigated her way through France, on the train under the channel, around London, and all the way to Grantham where we met her.

Yes, it was great to meet Stu's lady friend. We took her all around and introduced her to Stathern and Melton.

This is 2005. Stu has earned his PhD and was preparing for his next move. He visited you and here we are in Eyam, Derbyshire where they fought the Plague. Then you wanted to go to the coast.

My goodness, he had grown up! I was so glad to put my feet into the water again. That brought back old memories. I didn't think I would ever do that again! The coast is one of my favourite places.

(Photographer: D. Field)

(Photographer: D. Field)

Do you remember your 88th birthday? November 30, 2004.

Well yes. It was a Sunday. You called and sang Happy Birthday. You were forgiven for being out of tune! I had been to lunch at The Church in Eaton with Anne Titcomb. We had lamb which was very nice. Win brought over a lemon cake and Janice a plant. I received umpteen cards and one from you that made me cry. I don't think I deserved the kind words and thoughts of my friends. I had a card from my grandson with photographs. Geoff also called.

(Photographer: B. Hopper)

I had had a wonderful birthday weekend, the highlight of which a visit with Heather and Brian. [76]

I called around to see if there was a hunt gathering nearby. I was given the name and address near Bottesford by a friend in the village. So off we went. We walked across the field to where the horses and hounds were gathering. We petted the dogs and chatted with the folks around. Soon afterward, along came the sausage rolls and the port. I had managed to name drop in the meantime and so it was assumed we were part of the group.

(Photographer :D. Field)

It is 2006, I was visiting. I remember thinking: you are 90 and are shrinking: your body shape is changing-wide in the hips, narrower around the chest. I hadn't seen you in six months: you were diminished. You looked at me with not your big brown eyes but the rheumy eyes of an old woman. How quickly the roles reverse. I am the carer now. Often you say: "Oh God, Daph" and "You aren't going to leave me, are you?" So, I would visit you hoping to give you company and solve some of your problems but….

No! You would tell me I wasn't eating properly-too few fruits and vegetables. But you didn't know your bodies change as you grow older. I couldn't digest them. Oh yes, I used to eat lots of fruit but now cannot. I like my weekly fruit cake made especially for me by Jean in the butcher's shop in Stathern. That same shop is the focus of village gossip and sells the best ham off the bone.

Do you remember trying to buy shoes for you?

Oh yes. That was a real treat for you. Not so much for me. My misshaped feet, with a bunion on the right one, would not squeeze into most shoes. They have to be so soft and flexible to accommodate. But when we saw a pair of German-made leather shoes on the market in

---

76 Heather's recollection is as follows:
  Yes, she did enjoy herself yesterday and so did we. She walked all the way across a field to see the hounds and join in the Meet and enjoyed the glass of port and sausage rolls which were on offer! I just thought of it last week as of course hunting with dogs is to be banned from next February so I asked her if there was a local meet we could go and see while we were visiting her. She tucked into her lunch as usual and we had a really happy time together. She is an amazing lady and we are both very fond of her.

Melton Market, I was surprised by the quality. I tried them on, by the roadside. I agreed the soft leather was good, so I bought two pairs: one beige to replace a 20-year-old pair and one red pair for the winter.

Do you remember when we tried to buy a bra for you?

That was very funny. I tried on bra after bra –in the store-sitting in the cubicle. We laughed together as I popped out underneath of my usual size. We did not realize I was no longer size 36C until the patient store clerk gave us the right size - 34C! You asked me later: how is the bra? I said "fine-good bra." I assured you I was wearing it! But then laughed: it was still in its packet!

So, when I would visit you, you liked to go to the grocery store.

Yes, because I had to rely on others to buy my food. I often had a half chicken which Win would buy for me and which I would eat for several days. So, when you came home, I relished the trip to the supermarket. Food shopping was a real treat. I loved to be pushed around Morrison's in a wheelchair, selecting my purchases, particularly attracted to the 2 for 1 deal. I was like a kid in a candy store. I remember buying salmon and embarrassing you somewhat by insisting on buying two pieces from the centre of a salmon. Of course, an old lady's demand was not refused!

So, what did you eat?

I cook in the microwave. I love a baked potato with baked beans as well as Cornish pasty. I will eat anything someone else has cooked for me. I seem to be given lots of cooked food-kindly neighbours. For breakfast, I have 2 cups of tea followed by 2 pieces of toast. And cooked chicken of course. You know I still have my own teeth but they don't work as well as they used to. Actually, nothing does!

You would like a bath when I visited.

I kept myself very clean with a wash down every day in the kitchen sink even though there is a bathroom upstairs. One plastic bowl exclusively for washing myself not to be confused with the one used to wash dishes. But when you visit, I can use the bathroom upstairs. I sit on the bench propped up on the sides of the bath while you pour water over me. That feels so good. I love having my back washed.

And then I would try to update your wardrobe. Auntie Nellie always looked so smart in comparison with you! After Bill died, Nellie lived in a lovely bungalow overlooking the fields and woods in Granby (Grannie Brown's birthplace). She always kept her home neat, tidy, and spotless: she would be well dressed, making you look shabby by comparison.

I looked forward to visiting Auntie Nellie, on my visits to Stathern. As visitors, we would always be welcomed with cake and tarts and given some to take home. Eunice who lived opposite took great care of her mother in between other cleaning jobs. Was she back into service? Nellie passed away in 2002 at age 91. Do you remember?

I have a lot of dresses that have been around for 50 years. I see them in photographs-less faded then than now. But I wear the same clothes day after day, especially a favourite yellow cardigan.

I like poking around the Charity shops to see what I can find. I look at the clothes but am not tempted to buy them. My closets are full of lovely clothes I don't

(Photographer: D. Field)

(Photographer: D. Field) *Here you are with Aunty Nellie*

wear-perhaps now too big. My friends give me things, thinking I have none! I just prefer my old clothes! I feel most comfortable in them.

You know I would tell you a podiatrist cuts my nails and I would also have a pedicure frequently.

Yes, I don't do that even though there is a chiropodist who could cut my nails. My toenails are discoloured and tough to deal with. But I do it anyway. I like my feet dried well and moisturizer applied.

I think I have mellowed in temperament as I have aged. I used to be critical of my gardener, my cleaner, and of my daughter (but not my son!). But I have become more appreciative.

Well yes. Do you remember when I came to visit for a couple of weeks, I would escape to Heather's because you and I were at loggerheads? I needed to distance myself from you to avoid being hurt by your comments?

So, you love your television, especially the dancing and want to dance like I do! As I look at you, I realize this will be me one day as I have your genes!

Next is the story of a friendship: a special one, a final one.

Every Sunday, you enjoyed Sunday lunch at The Church restaurant up the hill in Eaton with one of your lady friends.

Yes, there was the usual fare with lots of vegetables. I would bring home leftovers in a plastic container brought for that purpose.

On one particular Sunday, while I was visiting, I spotted a gentleman eating alone. I suggested we ask him to join us for dessert, which he gladly did. And so, a ten-year relationship started.

(Photographer: D. Field)

This is a very nice photo of you and Bill. He was good to me. He would pick me up to go to lunch on a Monday to the Plungar Institute and then we would see one another on Sundays. Usually, lunch then we would go back to his lovely bungalow in Bottesford for tea. Having a companion was very pleasant for him and nice for me. He had lots of fine tales to tell. We did Sudoku together! I knew Bill and his wife, Dorothy who had recently passed away. Dorothy was a Stathern girl having spent a lifetime in the area as Bill's wife and mother to a son and a daughter. Dorothy died of cancer and was buried in the Stathern cemetery where my mum and dad are buried.

Plungar lunch was a spot on a Monday, hosted by a community centre. Another was The Gap in Mussonbelow with friend Win.

I liked The Gap until it deteriorated in later years. It comprised a buffet carvery with beef, ham and turkey and lots of vegetables. Win would come with us sometimes. Bill was a diabetic who managed the disease well. He would surprise me by giving himself an injection through his shirt, as we sat in his car, just before we entered the restaurant!

Bill would take me, and sometimes you, for a drive around telling us all about the area and spinning his yarns. Afterward was tea or coffee in the bungalow followed by a nap for us as we sat contentedly together on his sofa.

On one of my visits, I happened to mention that I like black currents but couldn't find any to pick. Bill showed me his garden at the farm and told me to help myself to the produce in the garden which was plentiful.

Bill was charming and entertaining. He would take us to local events like the photography show in Plungar. To my surprise you bought a picture, I think. He had told us about his daughter, Valerie, and her struggle with breast cancer. During your visit one year, Valerie lost her struggle: Bill was devastated. She had no wish to leave two young children behind. I never invited Bill into my house in Stathern and he never seemed presumptuous. My home was inferior to the lovely bungalow.

(Photographer: D. Field)

Bill would not have been concerned about that. He thought you were a "fine old lady."

You tended to feel insecure on your feet, so we went to Grantham to purchase a walker. You called it your bike. You liked the security it gave you and used it constantly for your walks around the village. Do you remember we went to Lincoln Cathedral? You were secure with your `bike.'

Photographer: D. Field)

Photographer: D. Field)

Yes, we did. That was a nice day when we went to Lincoln and looked around the Cathedral.

When I returned to Canada, I would leave you with Bill which was easier than leaving you alone. You two seemed to enjoy an easy relationship.

After a couple of falls in your kitchen, Geoff and I decided you could not live alone. I had already decided the Scalford Court Care Home was the place for you. The home is situated between Melton and Stathern and is very pleasant. You seemed to settle easily in your little room. I then attempted to clear out Wood View a sell the property which took over a year.

After you moved into Scalford Court, Bill would collect you in his Ford Focus to take you for your usual drives, particularly back to his bungalow. On one particular visit, I recall he asked me if I thought he could afford Scalford Court. I told him the costs and surmised a move was on his mind.[77]

In 2010 you had a stroke and we quite thought we would lose you. But you rallied after rehab and returned to Scalford Court. I visited you in September of 2011. I wondered whether you would recognize me but you did. You said, "I do love you; you know." I was so surprised. All I could manage was: I know you do. You have never ever said that to me before. I would hear you tell Stu you loved him but never me. Usually, you would say: you are not going to leave me, are you? Which made me feel so guilty.

Well, we never said those words in England, did we?

NO. I never felt affection as a child. That was sorely missing in my life and made quite a difference in how I managed my life and how I relate to others. I spent that Christmas with Stu and Jen and dropped in to see you on the way to Germany. We called you but you didn't feel well and didn't want to get out of bed. I felt sad about that.

Yes, Bill did move into the Scalford Court Care Home in the autumn of 2010 about two years after I did. I didn't spend much time with him then. I couldn't be bothered with him. I sat with my women friends and ignored him. He seemed content with the company of the four other men at the Home.

I think that was unkind. When I visited, I spent as much time with him as I could, making a point of tucking him into bed each night. Bill loved the attention.

In February 2012 you called me. You sang to me:

> *You are my sunshine, my only sunshine:*
> *You make me happy when skies are grey.*
> *You'll never know dear how much I love you.*
> *Please don't take my sunshine away.*

I was completely blown away. That you would remember all the words and that you would sing to me. Mind you, we were 3,000 miles away! But you never did express yourself like that to me.

You were always my sunshine. I just didn't know how to tell you.

In 2012 I had to have a shoulder replaced because I slipped, fell, and broke my arm. I didn't tell you until I visited you. Heather, Brian, and I went on a Rhine Cruise in Germany. You had been there and to my surprise knew the area. Then you noticed I was wearing a sling!

Rhudesheim. I remember being there. I didn't see your sling at first. Then was concerned for you! I was Scalford Court where I was looked after very well.

Sadly, Win was in a bad way and died soon after I saw her in hospital.

---

[77] My notes from my May 2010 visit: *Off to Scalford Court. Picked up mother who was ready with a walker. Much better than I expected. Met Bill at the Gap. He is not as good as expected. Tea at Bill's and then to Stathern. Mother insisted on going upstairs! To my amazement she did and then said: there is nothing here I want.*

(Photographer: S. Steward)

(Photographer: D. Field)

Here is Bill with a Stathern friend, Sue Steward. Sue was the daughter of one of Nana's friends. Jean. Sue was very fond of you and made the trip to see you whenever she could.

Yes, I liked Sue. She was lively and entertaining. She and I missed her mother. We both worried about Sue. She seemed so far away in Brighton. Oh, I remember Jean and all those afternoons in her house. Sue would visit her as well.

I look like a real old lady in this picture. But then I am, aren't I?

I hope I have portrayed who you were. Very friendly, cheerful, helpful, and liked by many. You seemed to attract people and befriend. Unlike me, you never seemed to be without a male partner or friend. You and I had our moments. We were better friends when apart I fear. On one card you sent, after your hip surgery, you wrote, "Your kindness and understanding are much appreciated. I am a grumpy old so and so at times. Shall we put it down to AGE?" On another occasion with my Birthday Card, you wrote you realized I was special. "I feel so badly at the way I behaved when you were over. What is the matter with me?" You called me the sweetest girl. You said you remembered the details of when I come into the world. I was a sweet little rosebud!

But I remember on the last occasion I saw you in Scalford Court, you told me I wasn't fat!

(Photographer: D. Field) With Bill at Scalford Court

Then when I tried to organize your pillows for you for sleep, you became frustrated because I couldn't get them right. I was upset too and had to ask the staff for help! You left me feeling I couldn't do anything quite right!

EPILOGUE

Four years after moving into The Scalford Court Care Home your Nana completed her life on May 16th, 2013 in her 97th year. This was a week before Geoff and I planned a visit with her: she had been told of my planned visit: Geoff decided to join me when we were advised that her condition had deteriorated. With her timing perhaps she wished to spare us further anguish.

When I arrived at the Scalford Court Care Home, I rushed to Bill who seemed to have good and bad days. Again, he loved the attention. Sue Steward arrived to spend time with us too. She liked Melton and Stathern. We three enjoyed pottering around together. She and your Nana enjoyed a particularly good relationship.

Geoff and I took Bill out whenever we could for the week we were there. He pointed out interesting railway related spots, entertained us with stories, and was generally very connected to his environment. We took him for a walk around the Care Home in a wheelchair. He loved the sight of the green fields. I was sad to say goodbye to Bill who had been a great companion to your Nana in the last 10 years of her life.

To give closure to your Nana's friends and family and in place of a funeral, I hosted an Ashes Scattering Ceremony at the Loughborough Crematorium. Heather came with me, along with some of Geoff's friends. Cousin Sandra, Cousin Sally and your Nana's cousin May were there too.

Jade from the Scalford Court Care Home was there also: Jade had been with your Nana during the night she passed. Jade explained that Bill had also recently passed away. He had a heart attack. Jade told us that the attention we paid to him in his final days had been tremendously beneficial in the absence of Valerie and his son who lived in Scotland. I have enjoyed Bill`s company over the years: a cheerful, gentle soul I will miss. I would never have guessed that the two friends would pass within two weeks of one another.

Heather added: *Enjoyed reading the revised document. So many more photos and it has taken us right to the end of her life. Had forgotten she made it to 97. Loved her dearly. Think of her every day though whenever I have a drink from her mugs bless her! a life well lived, I think.*

I would like to thank everyone who participated in this journey of mine into the stories of our ancestors and hope too that everyone who reads them enjoys the read.

I now must leave the distant past, honoured and not forgotten, to focus on the present with gratitude and the future with optimism!

CPSIA information can be obtained
at www.ICGtesting.com
Printed in the USA
BVHW010101110323
659876BV00006B/1